"Today we have the choice of living in an insanely busy and frequently meaningless world, or we can live in the midst of the "great mysterion." In ancient times, it was not uncommon for people to take time out of their busy lives and immerse themselves in the vast unknown through the mystery schools. After experiencing the vitality and richness of several days spent saturated in the mythology of their dominant culture through ritual and symbol, they came back with a deeper sense of how to integrate the sacred and numinous in their lives. *This is the experience that Qabalistic pathworking offers us today.*

"By mapping archetypes on the mystic diagram of the Tree of Life, we trace mythological themes and numinous symbols that stir the psyche on deep inner levels. Through this process, we inevitably stumble on images that resonate on a rich and very personal level unique to the individual. The Qabalistic Tarot is an important tool because it affords the opportunity to bridge our conscious learning mind and our subconscious mind, which is the reservoir for the collective soul. Qabalah teaches that this treasure-house of myths and symbols is the medium understood by the subconsciousness of all races and peoples and the means by which an undifferentiated consciousness can project itself into the tabernacle of the mind. Universal truths are frequently imparted in this way through symbolic language—thus bypassing the conscious mind, which tends to dissect and analyze.

"This book balances both sides of the brain because it is written in two sections: (1) a scholarly approach to deciphering the archetypal symbols behind the etymology of the Hebrew letters, names, and numbers and (2) an experiential approach in utilizing Qabalistic techniques to bring this material alive in the reader's subconscious mind."

—*Hans Nintzel*

About the Author

Madonna Compton has degrees in Psychology and Criminal Justice and an M.A. in Religious Studies. She is a symbolic artist, poet, and teacher in the San Francisco Bay area. She has also worked with prisoners, halfway-house clients, and as a drug counselor. Her bliss, however, is writing, although a close competitor is watching seeds grow into plants which then metamorphose into herb and incense compounds.

She has done numerological pathworking analyses for clients for several years and helps individuals chart their own unique pathworking journeys. She is a long-time student of the goddess cultures, as well as the Golden Dawn, Rosicrucian, and similar traditions, and is presently a member of Builders of the Adytum (B.O.T.A.). She is co-founder of Hermetica West, an East Bay organization which studies Qabalah and other hermetic texts as well as sponsoring workshops and films, and she has recently founded a school called Western Tradition Studies, which offers classes in western mythology and philosophy.

Madonna is a member of the ACLU, Amnesty International, Unity of the Spirit, and the Newman community in Berkeley. She loves to dance, hates dogs, and has one son, who is brilliant.

How to Write to the Author

We cannot guarantee that every letter written to the author can be answered, but all will be forwarded. Both the author and the publisher appreciate hearing from readers, learning of your response to this book. Llewellyn also publishes a bi-monthly news magazine with news and reviews of practical esoteric studies and articles helpful to the student, and some readers' questions and comments to the author may be answered through this magazine's columns if permission to do so is included in the original letter. The author sometimes participates in seminars and workshops, and dates and places are announced in the *Llewellyn New Times*. To contact the author, write to:

Madonna Compton
c/o THE LLEWELLYN NEW TIMES
P.O. Box 64383-104, St. Paul, MN 55164-0383, U.S.A.

Please enclose a self-addressed, stamped envelope for reply,
or $1.00 to cover costs.

Llewellyn's Spiritual Perspectives Series

ARCHETYPES ON THE TREE OF LIFE

The Tarot as Pathwork

Madonna Compton

1991
Llewellyn Publications
St. Paul, Minnesota, 55164-0383, U.S.A.

FIRST EDITION

Cover Painting © 1991 Charles B. Hanna
  in cooperation with Spirit Art, Minneapolis, MN
Tarot card illustrations by Pamela Colman Smith

Library of Congress Cataloging-in-Publication Data
  Compton, Madonna, 1947-
  Archetypes on the tree of life: the tarot as pathwork / Madonna
Compton. — 1st ed.
        p. cm. — (Llewellyn's spiritual perspective series)
  Includes bibliographical references.
    ISBN 0-87542-104-0 : $12.95
    1. Hermetics. 2. Tree of life—Miscellanea. 3. Archetype
(Psychology)—Miscellanea. 4. Tarot. 5. Cabala. I. Title
II. Series: Llewellyn's spiritual perspectives series.
BF1611.C723 1991
133.3′2424-dc20   91-27605
                                                              CIP

Llewellyn Publications
A Division of Llewellyn Worldwide Ltd.
P.O. Box 64383, St. Paul, MN 55164-0383

About Llewellyn's Spiritual Perspective Series

SIMPLE, PRACTICAL, EFFECTIVE, COMPREHENSIVE, AU-THORITATIVE, INDIGENOUS TO OUR CULTURE

In a world and time that is becoming more complex, challenging and stressful, filled with "over choice" and "cognitive confusion," we are making available to you a unique series of books for self-exploration and growth that have the following distinctive features:

They are designed to be simple, cutting through abstraction, complexities and nuances that confuse and diffuse rather than enlighten and focus your understanding of your life's purpose.

They are practical; theory always leading to practice to be crowned by devotion when followed through by you as the experimenter. You are the ultimate "laboratory" and "judge."

They are effective, for if you do the work, you will obtain results of psychospiritual transformation and expansion of consciousness.

They are comprehensive because they integrate the exoteric with the esoteric, the sacred traditions of the past with the best insights of modern science.

They are authoritative because they are all written by persons who have actually lived and experienced what they tell you about.

They are part of our Western Culture and philosophical and Mystery Traditions, which must be understood if the synthesis of the Eastern and Western spiritual traditions and Universal Brotherhood is to be realized.

This series will reconcile the fragmented aspirations of ourselves, synthesize religion and science to bring about that psychosynthesis which is the greatest need of our age and its highest aspirations.

*This book is dedicated to all my beloved teachers, with special
reverence to the memory of Ann Davies*

Special thanks to:

Vernice Solimar, for her advice and encouragement; Lloyd
Nygaard, for his infinite patience in teaching me the computer; Scott
Weitz, for his brilliant proofreading and insightful comments; Hans
Nintzel, dear friend and mentor; Paul, Dennis and everyone in
Hermetica West

"This is the key to the mystery of the sacred letters. Fix thy mind on the object set before thee by any letter, and hold thy thought to meditate thereon. Then shall the inner nature of that object be made known to thee, and by this means shalt thou draw nigh to some aspect of my being."

—*Book of Tokens*

"In 32 mysterious paths of wisdom did Jah, the Jehovah of Hosts, the Living Elohim...engrave his Name by the 3 Sepharim: Numbers, Letters, and Sounds."

—*Sepher Yetzirah* 1:1

"As a result of the activity and your concentration on the letters, your mind will become bound to them. The hairs on your head will stand on end and tremble...the blood within you will begin to vibrate because of the living permutations that loosen it...you will experience ecstasy and trembling, ecstasy for the soul and trembling for the body."

—**Abraham Abulafia**
Treasury of the Hidden Eden

Contents

Introduction
by Hans W. Nintzel

"The Times They Are A-Changin'." So sang Bob Dylan in the '60s. These are prophetic words that hold true for almost any and every era. However, they are most true now in these most extraordinary times in which we live. Until now, there just hasn't been anything to compare with current events. Five years ago, what do you think would have happened if Czechoslovakia had told the Soviet Union, "you have to get your troops out of Czechoslovakia"? Or if the East Germans were to have said, "We are going to tear down the Berlin Wall"? No doubt there would have been some "heavy" action on the part of the Soviets. But today? They all but gave hammers to the folk dismantling the Berlin Wall. And seem eager to pull troops out. Astonishing, isn't it?

There is even more to make one sit up and take notice. Never before have we seen such outright greed, self-aggrandizement, dishonesty, lack of truth and other emerging distasteful human attributes. We are witness to presidents of the United States appearing on public television and lying to the audience. We find the government giving out misinformation of various sorts. We notice the hypocrisy that is prevalent and even the bankruptcy of certain religious organizations. Headlines in a March 1990 newspaper declare that "Americans are seeking spirituality...but not particularly in the pews." A priest is quoted as saying "The people are spiritually starved." In the same newspaper an article discusses college students (in particular) and how materialism is creating cheaters. Clearly the world needs something, is looking for something.

The greed and corruption is so powerful and so pervasive that public figures and even officers of our country have been enmeshed to such an extent that they are forced to resign in disgrace. Heads of countries are obliged to flee and frequently face summary execution. Bribery among governmental and business officials is widespread, to such an extent that individuals are willing to sell the birthright of their children and grandchildren for the sake of profit. This gives rise to corporate takeovers, pollution and other environmental hazards. The "hole-in-the-sky," strip-mining, clear cutting of forests, dumping toxins into the waterways and into the ground are almost total assurance that the planet will be uninhabitable 50 years from now. As evidence, the Wilderness Society has recorded some 10,000 fuel spills in the past year. Our planet is being despoiled for material gain.

Indeed, Rudolph Steiner's prediction seems to be coming true. He indicated that at about this time, the decade prior to the turn of the century, the forces of greed, represented by Ahriman, and the lust for material things will become *so* powerful that Ahriman will be able to incarnate on this planet in a human body. As we look around and see such evils as toxic waste dumping, corporate takeovers, junk bonds, drug sales, defrauding of the government and the like, it is clear materialism is on the rise. It could well be that Steiner was right on

The very foundation for many of us, the "anchor," has started to become very insecure. I speak of various religions, systems and philosophies that have consistently hidden the total truth from the "unwashed" and are now seen to be as greedy as anyone! We find their teachings vague, unsatisfying, hollow and filled with hypocrisy. I realize this paints a rather gloomy picture; however, there *is* good news. There is a place for us. A system, actually, whereby the truth may be gleaned. A set of teachings that have withstood the test of time. A set of principles to guide us in everyday living. A method for complete development of our latent faculties. In fact, information that is buried in the tenets of several religions and systems, but never brought to light. This book incorporates these very disciplines and shines some light on them.

How often have we heard the phrase: "He just never realized his full potential"? There is much to this statement. Most people, in living ordinary ("normal") lives do *not* develop to their fullest. This is partly because they have no idea of what they can achieve nor do they have a clue as how to do this. The way to achievement is via the "system" referred to. Oh yes, we have hundreds of so-called systems. We have even dabbled with a few. And some of them will indeed provide some results. However, there is one that has been tried and proven. This is the Hermetic Path.

The Hermetic Path encompasses, in the main, the disciplines of Qabala and of Alchemy. The two are actually inextricably intertwined, and a knowledge of Qabala is essential for being a good Alchemist. Well, what now? How does one acquire this knowledge, learn this system? It is usually a matter of finding the right teacher. The old saying "When the student is ready, the teacher will appear" is not a very satisfying idea for those of us who want some action right now! However, we can take comfort in the fact that the teacher often is right under our noses, teaching away, and we know it not. These "teachers" may not take the form we often expect of a "guru." And there are more of them than we think. Each teacher, as he or she impinges on our lives, may have a singular purpose. Once that lesson is learned, or shown it will never be learned, the teacher moves on or is replaced.

The teacher is almost always another human being. Sometimes they operate from what is called "the inner planes" and remain invisible. The techniques of teaching are quite varied. It can be word-of-mouth, a flash of intuition, a dream, a school, even a book. Yes, books have a definite place in our lives and in the environment of our being taught. We are often simply led to a book. Someone gives us one, we are attracted by an ad, we see something in a used bookstall or we have just gone ahead and bought one such as this. And this *is* one of those books that you have been led to!

Dr. Israel Regardie, the late writer on Hermeticism, lived on the same street as I did. Naturally, I sought him out for advice and for counsel, which he graciously gave. He strongly advocated a study of the Qabala and then, when well grounded, becoming involved with Alchemy. These two disciplines are the major aspects of the Hermetic Path. Fortunately, there were and are a great number of books that the student can acquire. Some date back to the 1200s and more modern ones are being printed even as I write. This is also slightly *un*fortunate, as most of these books are rehashes of what has been said before. Very few present new ideas and very few new techniques are coming forth. In your hand, however, is one of the rare exceptions.

Regardie always advised me, among other things, to "Work

with the Tree." He did not dilate on this to my satisfaction. However, I *took* this to mean to memorize the Sephiroth and their correspondences. This was, partially, correct. But there was more and it took a long while for me to discover what this was. In a word: *pathworking.* I immediately set out to gain new knowledge of the Tree by using pathworking. Whatever *that* was! I was dismayed to find that very few seemed to have written much, if anything, on one of the most important aspects of the Tree of Life. The Tree, of course, is the mighty diagram that epitomizes the Qabala and Alchemy. In this one superb diagram, we have a representation of the macrocosm and the microcosm. Moreover, we are afforded an opportunity to see the relationships between the two. Between God and Man. This diagram, with its 10 circular "paths" and its 22 linear ones, can supply the answers to life's most recondite questions. It can explain where we came from and where we are going. It can help us to develop those latent powers we spoke of previously, to fully develop our potential. These "promises" have not been found to be wanting. Hermeticism is neither "airy-fairy" nor riddled with hypocrisy. Does this not sound like the kind of study *you* would like to get involved in?

The marvelous thing about the Hermetic Path is one can try it, test it and, if found wanting, discard it. Most likely, anyone setting foot on this path will become very excited and be permanently drawn to it and thus be able to extract the great benefit that can be derived therefrom. In ancient times, it was not uncommon for people to take time out of their busy lives and immerse themselves in the vast unknown through the "mystery schools." After experiencing the vitality and richness of several days spent saturated in the mythology and symbolism of their dominant culture, they were empowered with a deeper knowledge of how to integrate the sacred and numinous in their everyday lives. This is the experience that the Hermetic Path offers, and one technique for this is the process of "Pathworking."

By mapping archetypes on the Tree of Life, one can trace mythological and religious themes as well as those particular symbols that stir the psyche on deep, inner levels. Through this process one can uncover images that resonate on a rich and very personal level, unique to the individual. An integral set of symbols to this process is the Tarot. These images provide an important tool to permit the bridging of the left and right brains, our conscious learning mind and our subconscious. The latter has long been considered as the reservoir of the "collective soul" for racial archetypes.

This treasure house of myths and symbols is the medium understood by the subconscious of all races and peoples and is the means by which an undifferentiated consciousness can project itself into the sanctuary of the mind. Universal truths, such as found in dreams, are frequently imparted through symbolic language and thus bypass the conscious mind's penchant for dissection, judgment and analysis. The Tree of Life represents this type of symbolism extant in the Hermetic wisdom. The Tree has the Tarot Triumphs (commonly called "Trumps" in modern parlance) affixed to its linear paths.

The origin of these cards is shrouded in obscurity. The main point is that, whatever their origin, they do indeed provide a useful tool. A tool that has been put to the test often and found to be quite effective. Questions often arise about the Tarot, such as is it really the work of the "White Brotherhood" or is it a fortune-telling device stemming from the gypsies? Is it Egyptian, Hebraic or even Christian (since at least one Triumph, the Empress, is depicted in "The Revelation" of the Christian Bible)? Metaphysicians have pondered this for some time and have not, as far as it is known, come to a rational conclusion. To my mind, it is a tempest in a teapot. It is always good to know the epistemology of something but, in the long run, if it "does the trick," if it is "tried and true," that is the main thing.

In truth, the Tarot transcends, as it should, all religions. We can indeed find its influence in a variety of races practicing a variety of spiritual disciplines. Of some interest is the publication of a book entitled *Meditations on the Tarot*. This is a book dealing with the Tarot from a very Christian viewpoint. In fact, the anonymous author calls for a reconciliation between Christianity and Hermeticism. This author believed he was under karmic impulse to write the book and that one of the major religions of the world had a karmic responsibility to publish it. The book was indeed produced by the publishing arm of one of the largest Christian denominations. Mute testimony to the fact that the times are indeed changing.

The Tarot and the Tree of Life and Qabala are all part of Hermeticism. Incidentally, this word derives from the Greek God Hermes and is used in alchemy to mean "sealed," literaly,

xviii   ARCHETYPES ON THE TREE OF LIFE

"airtight."

The connection between these disciplines and Alchemy is too vast and too encompassing to describe in a brief introduction, but be assured, as you look into these matters, you will see the connection. Alchemy is also a spiritual growth system. While visions of turning lead into gold immediately come to mind, the truth is that Alchemy is primarily a tool for spiritual growth. It accomplishes this, in part, by revealing to the practitioner the secrets of matter and the secrets of creation. The Qabala provides a theoretical foundation for this as well as its own set of techniques for clearing the mind of dross and enabling the seeker to come to grips with himself and ultimately know the truth.

All this seems quite "heavy," and indeed it is. Nonetheless, it does work. This material is well explained in this book by Madonna Compton. Madonna, whom I have known for a long time and who has dedicated herself to exploring, utilizing and teaching Hermetic truths, has also been a self-supporting artist for many years and has published a variety of poems and articles dealing with the Tree of Life, the Goddess and other esoteric subjects. As a student of mine in Alchemy, I know her love of Gaia to include working with the earth in clay as well as growing plants and herbs which she uses to make incense. She studies rebirthing and other practices utilizing breathing techniques. She presently holds an M.A. degree in Religious Studies. In short, her wide knowledge of esoterica enables her to do excellent research and to write lucidly on arcane subjects. This book is the result of her vast and painstaking efforts.

But why should one read this book? First of all, it does plow new ground and is not a mere rehash of previous efforts. It offers the opportunity to bridge the known and the unknown using both critical thinking and intuitive analysis, through the exploration of symbolic language. All students of the "Mysteries" quickly come to the understanding that canonical texts, writings on esoteric subjects and the like, are written either in symbols or in code. The Christian Bible is a prime example of the utilization of both techniques, which I dilate upon in my classes. A knowledge of such coding techniques as "Gematria" and Hermetic symbols will enable the reader to penetrate to the vital core of what is being written. Texts hitherto obscure, such as the *Sepher Yetzirah*, and veiled, such as the Bible, now become intelligible.

Secondly, while not all-inclusive, this book provides a lot of data on some of the coding techniques referred to so one can gain some insight into these. Gematria is a letter/number coding technique that can be applied to Greek and Latin text but is primarily associated with the Hebrew language. Hebrew is an incredible set of symbols that contain more wisdom than can be fathomed. In fact, the "Meru Foundation" of San Anselmo, California, is dedicated to exploring all the mysteries of this "Alphabet of Fire." Madonna, in the present text, presents the etiology and etymology of Hebrew letters and words and the significance of number. The first part of each chapter focuses principally on the interface between Qabala and Christian Hermeticism, Alchemy, Greek myths and the Rosicrucian tradition. She displays the common thread linking all these disciplines.

The second part will enhance creativity and intuition through the meditative and process work. The pathworking sections and exercises will enable the student to contact inner psychic states which correspond to energy points on the Tree that the student would like to access or learn to balance. The student will be able to investigate the mystical and allegorical interpretations of not only the Old and New Testaments but find greater insight into canonical texts from almost any system of spiritual growth. For the Qabala is the great filing cabinet that encompasses every system and religion, and all can be found on the Tree of Life! The end result of following the material presented here will empower the student to mobilize powerful inner resources of psyche and soul to realize goals, needs and dreams. More germane, the continued study of Hermetic Wisdom will lead to a clearing of the misinformation and confusion about what life is really about. One will be able to discern the truth, to find an internal peace and to be, at last, free.

—Hans W. Nintzel
Richardson, Texas
March 21, 1990

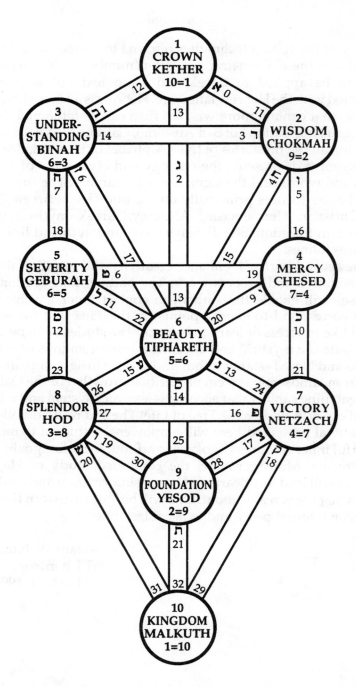

The Tree of Life

CHAPTER ONE

History, Myth, and Meaning

There is a Jewish legend that all souls existed with God before the creation of the universe, carefully stored beneath the Divine Throne until the time of birth. When a child is conceived, God removes the soul from the divine realm and plants it in the mother's womb. On the journey to earth, an angel accompanies the soul and during its gestation instructs it in all the mysteries of the universe. At the time the baby is born, however, the angel taps it lightly and it promptly forgets everything it has learned. Therefore, it bursts into tears. Life is the journey of the soul back to God, attempting to recapture forgotten wisdom on the way.

In order to find one's way anywhere, it is useful to have a map. Although acknowledging the truth and beauty of all religious paths, Qabalists believe that the ageless glyph of the Tree of Life is a map which not only leads us back to the throne of God, but also restores all our forgotten knowledge as we go.

What are the basic historical roots of this strange map and the philosophical meanings hidden behind its mysteries and mythologies? The origins of Qabalah are difficult to track down; for every erudite scholar's definitive assumption, there is a myth or legend that points to something different. Since the archetypal symbolism of myths speaks a universal language, and it is this very symbolism that is the heart and soul of Qabalah, it is generally the myths and symbols that most deeply impress the student of esoteric knowledge.

But let us attempt a brief review of history. A mystical system generally sprouts from a historical religion and therefore reflects the rites, symbols, and principles of the tradition that nurtured it. Frequently, however, the distinctions separating such traditions are much more ambiguous when reflected through their mystical disciplines because the esoteric themes of any mystical tradition often include elements common to other religions. Broad lines can be drawn, of course, such as those associating Sufism with the Islamic tradition, Gnosticism with Christianity, and Qabalah with Judaism.

We know, however, that since at least the medieval period, there have been Christian Qabalists as well as Jewish ones. The distinction which has generally been recognized as identifying them in their respective "camps" is that a Christian adhering to this mystical tradition generally spelled it with a C (Cabalah) and the Jewish branch with a K (Kabbalah). Most modern Qabalists use a Q. The mystic philosopher Dion Fortune said that the Qabalah is the Yoga of the West (1935). If we examine the root of the word "yoga," which means "union," we recognize that anyone therefore who seeks union with God (or whatever other name one chooses to call this Great Mystery, the universal nature of Being Itself) through this Western esoteric path is welcome to utilize it, much like people of any religion can practice the yogic disciplines of the East.

Many historians believe that the origins of Qabalah are rooted in 11th or 12th century France or Spain—the same time and era, in fact, to which the origins of the Tarot can be traced. How far back either of these systems go has been hotly debated for at least a hundred years and is really a matter of conjecture. Qabalah means simply "to receive" and implies an oral tradition rather than a written one. In the Jewish Talmud, oral traditions designate the non-Pentateuch parts of the Bible. Interestingly, the authorship of the three main texts which comprise the basic structure out of which the entire Qabalah has evolved—the *Zohar*, the *Bahir*, and the *Sepher Yetzirah*—has remained a mystery. Like many ancient sacred texts, they are said to be divinely inspired. Jewish Qabalists believe they illuminate the great secrets hidden in the Torah. Christian Qabalists see in them prophetic revelations hidden in the mysteries of the Christ. Students of mythical traditions recognize in them the ancient mysteries of Greece, Egypt, and Rome.

The *Zohar* (or *Book of Splendor)* was published by Moses de Leon (1250-1305) but bears the name of second century Rabbi Simeon bar Yochai and is written in Aramaic. The *Bahir* (Book of Illumination) also was thought by medieval Qabalists to have originated in Talmudic times or before and to have been simply transmitted orally from generation to generation, adhering strictly to the rule of preserving this hidden knowledge by keeping it contained within a master-student relationship. It seems to reflect the period, however, because it undoubtedly draws on unknown sources that include Gnostic terminology and attitudes. Both the *Zohar* and the *Bahir* attempt to explain and explore what was insufficiently explained by a literal interpretation of the Bible, thus elucidating its mystical symbolism. In all the Qabalistic texts, for example, the feminine as well as the masculine aspects of God are given attention.

It is important to note, as we make our way through Qabalistic "history," that Ancient Wisdom will always be shrouded somewhat in mystery and ancient religious texts will always be interpreted in a variety of ways. From a Jungian point of view—and many modern Qabalists examine the archetypes of the Qabalah and Tarot with a critical Jungian eye as well as an esoteric one—what is most important is the *meaning* and relationship that Qabalah has *to human consciousness* rather than "proof" that some particular text has its origins in this or that author. This is the phenomenological point of view.

If we look to myth and legend, we inevitably discover that Qabalah is as old as history itself. One legend tells us that this hidden knowledge was revealed by God to Abraham, another that it goes back as far as Adam. Still another would have us believe that Moses received the secrets of these primordial archetypes hidden in Qabalah and Tarot from the Egyptian priests when he was an initiate in the ancient Hermetic mystery school there. (Contrary to what most people believe, ancient Egyptian religion was a monotheistic one.) Esoteric thinkers of the Renaissance were undoubtedly fascinated by the mystical continuity of Hebraic and Egyptian wisdom; i.e., of the confluence of Moses and Hermes Trismegistus.

Sometime during the 12th century, a book appeared called *The Book of Ratziel* (the Archangel who resides in the sphere of Chokmah), which is attributed to the Qabalist Eleazar ben Judah of Worms. The legend is that the original *Book of Ratziel,* however, belonged to Solomon and was engraved in sapphire. *The Book of Enoch,* part of the apocrypha of the Old Testament, also contained Qabalistic secrets said to be dictated to Enoch by God. Myth tells us

Enoch later ascended to heaven, where he became the angel Metatron (who resides in Kether on the Tree of Life). It is said that God placed a crown on his head and gave him 72 wings as well as thousands of eyes.

Such myths have always moved the psyche on deep levels, giving birth to bursts of imaginative archetypal stirrings. One of the ways of working with Qabalah delineated in this text is called *pathworking* and includes intimate involvement with visionary and mythical imaginings. As Qabalah evolved, it was discovered that, using this glyph or map called the Tree of Life, one could move around the geography of consciousness, so to speak, contacting or balancing various personal energies by contemplating various aspects of the God-energy using myths, legends, visions, and dreams, represented by the archetypes of the Tarot.

The main text for exploring this system, which is therefore used as the principle focus of this book, is called the *Sepher Yetzirah*, or *Book of Creation*.* This is a tiny but classic Qabalistic work, the composition of which probably dates somewhere between the second and sixth centuries, around the same time the Talmud was being finally molded. It is possibly of Hellenistic origin; some have recognized in it many similarities to the Coptic *Pistis Sophia*, a fairly recently discovered Gnostic text. The Jewish scholar Gershom Scholem has noted (1962) that there is a parallel through the Divine Name "Yaho" or "Yah"—the Jewish attribution of the Godhead which "writes" creation into being in the *Sepher Yetzirah*—with Valentinian Gnosis and the secret name of God, IAO (equivalent to the same Hebrew "vowels"). Many Jewish scholars tend to regard the *Sepher Yetzirah* as somehow suspended in a vacuum in the midst of evolving religious traditions. The prophet Elijah, who is considered to be the guardian of rabbinic tradition, is said to have appeared to Jewish mystics throughout the ages to reveal its hidden Qabalistic secrets.

However, the essential Gnostic character of this ancient text is generally attested to by most historians and scholars. As Qabalah developed into such a magnificent and flourishing movement in the 12th-14th centuries, it is difficult to believe that it did not transcend

---

*The translation of the *Sepher Yetzirah* used in this book is that of William Wynn Westcott. Note that his numbering of the verses differs from that of the Isidor Kalisch translation.

the boundaries separating Judaism from Christianity, and in fact Spanish Qabalists who are thought to have been the instigators of the present day Tarot probably included both Christian Gnostic and Jewish ascetics.

Although the first painted images of the Tarot are recorded in the 14th century, it is believed that the Hermetic wisdom which encompasses it (and includes Qabalah, alchemy, and astrology) probably flourished in Alexandria around the second century, when Gnostic learning had its first flowering. The next recorded Qabalistic Renaissance began in legend (again, perhaps the most reliable carrier of ancient knowledge). It is rumored that, beginning around 1200 AD, a group of adepts from all over the civilized world met at various designated intervals in Fez, Morocco, just separated from Spain by the Strait of Gibraltar. After Alexandria was destroyed, Fez became one of the most prominent scientific and literary centers of the world. Together, these masters of esoteric wisdom pooled the ancient teachings and characterized them by the archetypes hidden in the major arcana of the Tarot. They did this knowing that images are the only universal language. The skeleton of these 22 images was the system of numbers and letter archetypes in the 22 Hebrew consonants.

These hidden teachings spread into southern Europe, retaining their purity by still adhering to the tradition of being passed from master to student, even though the cards themselves fell into use among the common people, who sought in them a means of fortunetelling and card games. Then followed the Inquisition when any form of esotericism was frequently viewed as heresy or witchcraft. In 1492, tens of thousands of Jews were shipped *en masse* out of Spain if they did not convert to Christianity. Many ended up in Safed, high in the hills of Galilee, where Jewish Qabalism continued to flourish, drawing an extraordinary community of scholars, rabbis, and mystics. Famous Qabalists of the Safed school are Moses Cordovero and Isaac Luria, who exerted a tremendous impact for centuries.

Meanwhile, Qabalistic and Hermetic teachings became an important factor in shaping the Renaissance that had exploded in Western Europe. In the early Renaissance, Hermetic and Qabalistic studies were not discouraged by the Roman Catholic Church unless they bordered on magic or witchcraft. One of the greatest of the early Christian Qabalists, Egidius of Vilerbo, was a cardinal. Other distinguished Qabalists included Roger Bacon, Raymond Lully, Albertus Magnus, and Thomas Aquinas. Carl Jung and his foremost disciple, Marie-Louise von Franz, wrote extensive commentaries on the alchemical works attributed to Aquinas.

Pico della Mirandola was a Christian theologian who wrote at least 130 theses on Qabalah, claiming, like the Jewish schools, that Qabalah had been orally transmitted since Moses. However, he discovered in it also pre-rabbinic truths which he felt were developed fully only through Christian theology. For example, the name Jeheshua (IHShVH), or Jesus, is the full development of the secret name of God (IHVH), claimed to be unknowable and unpronounceable by the rabbinic Qabalists.

Many great doctors, scientists and philosophers of the period——Paracelsus, Robert Fludd, Johann Wolfgang von Goethe, Sir Isaac Newton, John Donne, Jacob Boehme, Francis Bacon, Santa Theresa de Jesus (and probably many more women unrecorded by history)—who shaped the evolving world at that time, were in turn shaped by Qabalistic thought, albeit their involvement with the Hermetic tradition was rather discreet. Too much brashness could get one burned at the stake. Frequently, therefore, thought was censored only if it was published; e.g., Goethe was thrown into prison when his writings got too much out of hand; no one ever knew Isaac Newton was an alchemist and Qabalist till his unpublished papers were discovered after his death; and the Dominican Giordano Bruno was burned in Rome for his major work, *The Art of Memory,* which taught that by means of an ancient magical art of memory, one can tap the powers of the cosmos.

As the witchcraft hysteria was mounting throughout Europe, however, certain works were released and widely distributed which either had no author (such as the "Rosicrucian manifestos") or were entirely clothed in allegory. Finally the French monk, Marin Mersenne, through his massive attack on the entire Renaissance tradition, particularly Hermetic, Rosicrucian, and Qabalistic ideas, cleared the way for the rise of Cartesian philosophy (René Descartes was his close friend). This, of course, ushered in the scientific age but dealt a death blow to the imagination which lasted for several centuries.

The Invisible Rosicrucians (or order of the "Rosy Cross") was mainly instrumental in carrying Qabalah and alchemy into England, where it again experienced a revival in the 1800s. This

Fraternity was supposedly started by a monk named Christian Rosencreutz, who wrote about a magical language and writing which his order used daily to give praise and glory to God. This "invisible" order observed several rules, the first of which was to attend to the sick without any monetary reward. Another was to travel, presumably for the purpose of spreading and absorbing knowledge. They were instructed not to wear any habit and to follow the custom and dress of the country wherein they found themselves. They were to meet once a year at their center—the House of the Holy Spirit.

Although the Rosicrucian manifestos were published at least as early as 1614, the order was able to maintain such "invisibility" that much speculation exists concerning whether they were purely imaginary. A humorous story is told by Frances Yates (1972) concerning the period in Descartes life when he withdrew into solitude to think his heavy thoughts. After his return to Paris, it was rumored that he had enrolled in the company of the Brothers of the Rosy Cross. To prove he hadn't, he argued that he was obviously *visible* and therefore could not belong to the Invisible Order. Somehow, this proof was accepted, demonstrating again the logic of this great philosopher!

At any rate, Qabalism experienced its next great revival when several influential (and very visible) figures banded together to form the Hermetic Order of the Golden Dawn in England. Among the members was the famed mystical poet W. B. Yeats, and MacGregor Mathers, who translated the ancient texts and explained their relationship to other mythical and mystical systems, was one of the founders. Mathers, in turn, was influenced by a French Catholic occultist named Eliphas Levi, who wrote numerous books on magic, Qabalah, and Alchemy, focusing on magical symbolism in a way that was basically archetypal.

Others from that tradition included Dion Fortune, herself a great mystic and psychic; Aleister Crowley; and A. E. Waite, whose version of the Tarot appears in this book. Among the occultists writing in that period, Waite was probably the best scholar, albeit he is, at times, somewhat dry. He gave us valuable insights into the secret traditions of the Rosicrucians, Freemasonary, and the Grail mysteries, as well as Qabalah and Tarot. Waite did not "preach" Hermeticism, although he personally took the mysteries very seriously. When writing, he attempted to be painstakingly correct in his scholarship, always going directly to the original sources.

Following on the heels of the "great revivalists" of the late 1800s was the Liberal Catholic priest, Dr. Paul Foster Case, who eventually began an offshoot order in the United States called the Builders of the Adytum (B.O.T.A.). Dr. Case wrote extensively on the Qabalah, Hebrew number mysticism, and the ancient images of the Tarot. He has been called by many the master of gematria in our age.

A Jewish Qabalist by the name of Israel Regardie, now quite famous in the United States, was also very instrumental in introducing this esoteric system to the West, writing particularly on Qabalah and its interface with archetypal symbolism and Jungian thought. In terms of the "practical work," a close friend and former student of both Dr. Regardie and the alchemist Frater Albertus, Hans Nintzel, continues to explore and elucidate the mysterious secrets of that part of the alchemical work which can only be fully discovered in one place: the laboratory. Nintzel has translated and made available many of the ancient cryptic texts on alchemy. He networks with many other alchemists around the globe and works ardently to keep the alchemical fires burning to keep this rich tradition from evaporating from view. Nintzel is also a Liberal Catholic priest, another Christian Hermeticist who seeks to bridge the gap between the ancient "heresies" and modern understanding of how the Mysteries relate to evolving consciousness.

Jung was well aware of how invaluable Alchemy and Qabalah were in describing various levels of consciousness or psychic states. A third of his writings, in fact, focused on the alchemical processes of transformation alone, and this idea was perhaps the single most important metaphor for Jung in understanding human consciousness.

How are the archetypes of the Tarot linked to the Hebrew letters and what is their relationship to the magical little "Book of Creation"? It is believed by Qabalistic mystics that by means of the 22 Hebrew consonants heaven and earth were created. This may seem a bit difficult for today's rationalist to swallow; nonetheless, an investigation into the mystical or mythical systems of any religion, from primitive times to our own "sophisticated" era, shows that an uncanny relationship exists in the human unconscious between speech and creation, or manifestation. Early proponents of this idea, such as the great rabbinic figure Isaac the Blind (1160-1235), were doubtless influenced by the philosophical tradition known as neo-Platonism, according to which reality results through a process of divine unfolding or *emanation.* In the famous Qabalistic glyph called the Tree of Life, the 10 primordial emanations are called *Sephiroth*—a Hebrew word which means "number" or "to count." The Sephiroth are the metaphysical principles of the universe, or stages in the creation of the world. The building blocks, so to speak, of the Sephiroth are the 22 Hebrew letters.

In the writings of Isaac the Blind, there is a systematic description of the Sephiroth, which are said to emanate from the realm of God's "thought." This bears close examination. Various modern interpretations claim to see beauty in the Qabalistic system because it appears "polytheistic" instead of dogmatically monotheistic (i.e., as will be seen, each Sephera appears to be a separate manifestation or "god" and includes worldwide mythologies by virtue of its system of correspondences, to be examined shortly). But ancient Qabalistic theory reminds us repeatedly that God is a unity that is simultaneously transcendent and immanent. In Judaism, of course, the question is not so much *"Where is God?"* as it is "What is God's relationship to *us?"*

God is perceived as transcendent, or the *Creator* of all nature, and therefore apart, and an awe-inspiring mystery. But God is also perceived as immanent, involved with humankind and history. In an esoteric system, however, transcendence does not mean deism, nor does immanence mean pantheism. Transcendence implies the unknowable, and immanence implies an "abiding within." God has many various Names in the Bible to identify the particular function or role which God is playing at the time. As transcendent Creator, God is called Almighty One, or El Shaddai, for example. In a closer relationship to nature and humankind, God is known as the Divine Presence, or the Shekinah, who is regarded as feminine. In examining the Divine Names, we will note that Qabalah is definitely not a patriarchal system in the sense that the exoteric Judeo-Christian tradition is—some of these names of God are male and others are female.

In the 10 Sephiroth or emanations are revealed the manifest parts of an infinite and unknowable God, called in Qabalah the *Ein-Sop* (or Ain-Soph), which means "without end." Ein-Sop is concealed and unreachable because thought cannot conceive of it. From this Ain-Soph, however, flow divine radiances (the Sephiroth), which in Qabalistic literature are called the "garments," "faces," "limbs," or "names" of God, and they have highly distinctive characteristics. They are as indistinguishable from the transcendent God, however, as rays are from the sun. The first "ray" is called *Kether* (the Hebrew word which means "crown") and is represented by a point, beyond which imagination cannot penetrate. The second is called *Chokmah*, or "beginning wisdom," also identified as the masculine principle within God. The third is called Binah ("understanding") and represents the Divine Mother principle or womb from which the remaining Sephiroth unfold. The 10 Sephiroth and some of their characteristics are listed in a table at the end of this chapter.

We can see therefore that *numbers are ideas* and ideas are the Powers of the God-energy (or Elohim) of creation. Ain-Soph, which could be represented as 0, represents that which lies behind and beyond all thought. In mathematics, we see it is an appropriate symbol of Infinite Space and Time because anything multiplied by it vanishes into its ocean of eternity.

The Tree of Life is a schematic representation of these number-archetypes, showing us the development of not only the Sephiroth themselves but also the 22 connecting Paths between them which are the 22 Hebrew letters, represented archetypally by the 22 major arcana of the Tarot. Each Hebrew letter is *also a number* (B, for example, in Hebrew would be Beth and is the same as the number 2) as well as a word that *means something* and therefore reminds us of its underlying image or archetype (e.g., Beth means "house," "enclosure" or "in.") Together the 10 Sephiroth and the 22 Hebrew letters constitute the "32 Paths" of the *Sepher Yetzirah*. It is through these 32 Paths of wisdom that God "engraved and created" the world.

The 22 letters are divided into three groups, the first of which are called the "mother letters": Aleph, Mem, and Shin. They *correspond* to the three elements of Air, Water, and Fire. Here we see the first stirrings of what is to become a very elaborate system of *correspondences*. The second group consists of the seven "double consonants," so called because they have both hard and soft consonant sounds. They correspond to the seven planets of the ancients: Mercury, Mars, Venus, Jupiter, Saturn, the Sun, and the

Moon. They relate to the seven days of the week and the seven orifices of the body. They also characterize the seven fundamental opposites in human life: life and death, peace and war, charm and ugliness, wisdom and folly, fruitfulness and sterility, domination and servitude, and wealth and poverty. Finally, they correspond to the six directions of space and the temple at the center of the world.

The simple consonants correspond to the 12 months and the 12 signs of the zodiac, the 12 principle activities of humans (such as touch, smell, and so on) and the 12 limbs of the human body. Each of the Tarot archetypes, of course, corresponds to a planet or a zodiacal sign as well as many other correspondences which fit precisely with those delineated in the *Sepher Yetzirah*. Therefore, an easy way to work with the energies of any particular Qabalistic "Path" is to access it through its system of correspondences.

We must keep in mind that, although many modern Qabalists include in the Tree gods and goddesses from a variety of cultural pantheons, the system arose because the *attributes* of such deities matched the attributes of the Sephiroth. We know that there are many correspondences between the Greek and the Hebrew myths—the *Aeneid* is very similar to Exodus, for example— probably because they both stem from the same Palestinian source. The earliest Hebrew myth which recounts the creation story in Genesis is thought by the majority of both Jewish and Christian scholars to have been influenced by the earlier Babylonian and Assyrian creation epics. The seven planetary deities were combined into a single transcendental deity at Jerusalem, but they are still commemorated in the seven branches of the Menorah candlestick as well as in the creation story in Genesis 1, where each day the order of creation corresponds precisely to the planetary gods in the Babylonian week. The first account of the creation story in Genesis, in fact, uses the plural for God in Hebrew—Elohim—which really means "the gods," and was composed sometime soon after the Babylonian Exile. The second creation story (Genesis 2), although purportedly written prior to the first account,* uses the name of "Yahweh" (IHVH) to designate the God-energy, a name which was probably changed during later editing. The reason "Yahweh" is used is because it shows the presence of the monotheistic ideal

---

* Merely dating the writing does not necessarily resolve the problem of dating the individual documents or traditions contained in that writing.

which replaced polytheism as human consciousness developed. In Ex. 3:14 and 6:3, we are told that God did *not* reveal the name of IHVH (which means I AM) to the patriarchs. God was still known as Elohim (the Gods) or El Shaddai (the Almighty).

So we see that the ancient texts, both Biblical and Qabalistic, reflect the attributes personified by the earliest mythological archetypes while developing over time the concept of Unity or, as we see in the later neo-Platonic schools, *emanations* from that Unity. It is these emanations which come to be characterized by an elaborate set of correspondences.

The *Sepher Yetzirah,* which delineates these correspondences, is a very compact discourse (approximately 2000 words), and Hebrew scholars note that, although it is the oldest of all the known Qabalistic texts, it undoubtedly reflects Greek as well as early Talmudic speculations of cosmology and cosmogony. The mystical number symbolism probably originates in neo-Pythagorean sources, according to Scholem (1962). It reaches its apex in the system called "gematria," which will be explained shortly.

At this point we need to ask ourselves: what is meant by this method of using correspondences and how does it work? The Qabalah is certainly not the only system which uses an intricate correspondence schema for categorizing and classifying, but it is one of the most methodical. As explained earlier, virtually any god or goddess, attribute or idea, number or image, myth or religion, philosophy, symbol, flower, gem, element, color, and so on *ad infinitum* can find a specific place on the map of the Tree of Life. Qabalah is therefore a very embracing tradition. But correspondences are simply a method of psychological association. Astrology has a system of correspondences. Religious rituals, from primitive rites to more sophisticated ones such as those utilized in the Catholic Mass, use correspondences. All peoples on the planet have discovered that certain colors, elements, stones, incenses, symbols, etc. are associated with a particular myth or ritual.

For example, the symbol of the dove belongs to mythological beings representing all these traditions: Aphrodite (Greece), Venus (Rome) Astarte (Caananite), Shekinah (Jewish), Sophia (Gnostic), and Holy Ghost (Catholic). Regardie (1970) tells us that correspondences are complex behavorial forms that have been built up over time and that have carved deep impressions in the collective unconscious of the race. The more the behavior (or ritual) which is associated with specific symbols is also repetitively associated with a particular state of consciousness, the stronger the collective memory becomes. Some esoteric sciences would have us believe that such impressions are actually written in the ether, or "akashic records."

Jung did much to add to our understanding of how the collective unconscious works and how it can be categorized. If we dream of a particular symbol or image, for example, and we have some knowledge of universal symbolic correspondences (or if we choose to discover more by doing some personal research on such a symbol), we add a deeper dimension or wider significance to other personal interpretations of the dream. Through myths, symbols, dreams, visions, etc., we come into contact with those numinous elements of the psyche we call Archetypes.

It has been noted by the Jungian scholar Stephan Hoeller (1975) and others that the Tree of Life contains most of the major Archetypes as well as the archetypal images that the collective unconscious is capable of forming. The Archetypes, which, as Jung discovered in his later work, are not the same as the images which spring from them, can best be identified with the pure Energy-Source of the Emanations or Sephiroth. Archetypes of this sort, says Hoeller, "are of sovereign numinousness and an unending fountainhead of power and inspiration" to human consciousness (Hoeller, 1975, p. 28). Archetypal images appear to us not only in myths and dreams, but in poetry, art, classic literature, and any kind of visionary experience. They swim continually in the sea of the psyche whether one is consciously aware of them or not.

The Paths on the Tree which connect the energy sources are packed with archetypal imagery and working any particular Path will thus evoke or balance different kinds of energy in the psyche. This is the principle at the bottom of the "Secret Doctrine" under the "Veil of Divination" spoken about by Waite, Case, Regardie, Fortune, and others. Balancing the energy-spheres in our own bodies and minds is how the Sephiroth operate on a personal level.

For example, the 19th Path balances the Spheres of Mercy and Severity. If we exalt the quality of strength or severity in our lives at the expense of tenderness or mercy, we become cold, callous, and unbalanced. If the scales are tipped in favor of the merciful side unbalanced by strength, on the other hand, we become mushy and malleable and are frequently victimized by those around us because we have no backbone.

The glyph of the Tree shows how these Paths are connected, what their Path numbers are (which are different from the Tarot numbers later assigned to them), and what the Hebrew letters are. The Paths begin at 11 and go to 32, the first 10 belonging to the Spheres themselves. The only numbers focused on in this book are the *original values* of the Hebrew letters themselves and the Paths on which they occur. A commentary on the *Sepher Yetzirah* refers to these Paths as "Intelligences" (Hebrew *Saykelim*), indicating the specific attribute of God they are attempting to describe.*

Although the aspirant works on all Paths of the Tree to maintain a balanced relationship with all of the Divine Emanations, according to one's birthdate and name, one can determine special meanings which the Tree reveals in terms of life symbols and personal revelation. This method of Qabalistic pathworking is not divinatory; it is devised strictly for the purpose of enabling you to tune in more deeply with your special needs, gifts, challenges, and purpose. You may use creatively the many correspondences which fit precisely with the archetype of the letter-number-Path.

Also, when you are very familiar with all the archetypal themes, images, and other correspondences related to a particular Path, you are able to "tune in" to the energy operating at any particular point in time by identifying the correspondences which pop up in your life with the specific Path they belong to. In the language of pictorial symbolism, which is perfectly understood by the subconscious mind because it is the one truly universal language, many secrets are conveyed which are only hinted at by the great masters and adepts who have written about the Qabalah and Tarot through the ages. The Tarot keys should therefore be meditated on; they will work in many ways for us, even though we are not consciously able to assimilate their multilayered symbolic content. B.O.T.A. decks, which are in black and white, can be purchased at most metaphysical bookstores for the purpose of bringing the keys to life by coloring them for meditation purposes.

The subconscious, which is already completely familiar with the major archetypes of consciousness underlying these images, will

---

* This document, called *The Thirty-two Paths of Wisdom*, was published in 1642 by Joannes Stephanus Rittangelius and is often attributed to him, but it may be much older.

begin to respond to the conscious intention to concentrate on the symbols and work for us on subliminal levels. It is the person who *reflects* who receives ideas from the unconscious. Likewise, the shape of the Hebrew letters can carve deep magical impressions an the mind when concentrated on for 3 to 5 minutes at a time. To a Qabalist, conscious thinking or conceptualization is brought about *by means of the letters* which, as the basic elements of thought, are the containers of all things of the spirit. For thousands of years, spiritual teachers of the Jewish and Christian traditions have asserted that the Hebrew alphabet is composed of "holy" letters of special significance and superhuman origin. Far more than tools for everyday human communication, the Hebrew letters themselves have intrinsic geometric forms and numerical associations which can point the serious student to a profound knowledge of life and to the intricate workings of human consciousness.

This is particularly emphasized in the numerical associations between the letters and names which are derived using gematria. In the Qabalistic word analysis called gematria, a letter of the alphabet is always associated with its corresponding number; when these are added together to form words, each word has a particular numerical vibration which expresses the essential nature of the thing. When two words have the same number value, they can therefore stand for each other; they show an inner relationship or mystical identity. This becomes apparent to anyone who studies the ancient texts in any depth and was expounded upon particularly well by the great Qabalist, Dr. Paul Case.

These pathworking lessons focus principally on the original archetypal images first associated with the Hebrew letters, and the progression of associations which "spin off" from the seed archetype. In the B.O.T.A. and Crowley decks, the letters are written at the bottom of the key. Unfortunately, Waite omitted them in his deck, perhaps because of his own rumored anti-Semitic feelings. The connection between the *Path letters* and the Tarot keys cannot be overlooked, however, if one is to get the "full picture," together with the hidden import of all the other images connected with the path.

You can determine your pathworking number by the simple addition of your birthday* or by adding the numbers of the letters of your name after changing them to Hebrew (see the chart at the end

---

*Example: January 21, 1939=1/21/39=1+2+1+1+9+3+9=26.

of this chapter). When working the Paths by this method of Qabalistic name and number analysis, however, you should not get confused by the many different numbers which may appear on your Path. If your birthdate is determined, for example, to break down (through addition) to 13, you would pay close attention to the ideas and symbols of the 13th Path; there may, however, be many other numerical associations or correspondences which will crop up there. We may think of the life-path as just that—a path or street wherein one walks to investigate the various points of interest located there. There may be different addresses (other number relationships) at several buildings or houses located on the path itself.

You should also remember that, to fully appreciate the Tree of Life and work constructively and creatively with all the potential energies of the psyche, you need to investigate other Paths besides the street you live on, particularly when your Path images correspond closely with those of another birthdate pathworking. Yoy may also use any other code which is meaningful to determine other Paths which appear to operate specifically in your life, such as the numerological method of working with your name, locating which Path corresponds to your astrological sign, which relate to Biblical phrases or words, which are created through other numerical sequences which pop up in your life (e.g., telephone, social security number, and so on). Qabalistic numerology can be a fascinating area to explore.

The pathworkings given at the end of each chapter are suggestions only. Once you understand the meanings and characteristics of any particular Path, you may write your own, especially if other mythological correspondences are meaningful to you. If you need help understanding more about how to create guided visualizations, see the works of Jean Houston (sacred psychologies), Robert Assagioli and Piero Ferrucci (psycho-synthesis), Carl Jung and disciples (active imagination or sandplay), Stanley Krippner or Strephon Williams (for working with dream images), or read Joseph Campbell, ancient myths, sacred texts, etc. Ideas will come, archetypes will manifest, imagination will flourish, and your personal story will begin to merge with the Larger Story as you discover what your personal Mythos is. The pathworkings you create can be long or short, only incorporate the correspondences which belong to that particular Path while you are journeying and be sure to create an opening and a closure.

The final meditation tool wherein the letter-Paths become important vehicles for learning is in correct pronunciation of the Divine Names. Each Hebrew letter is in Itself considered to be an expression or emanation of the Divine Spirit and it has long been believed that the pronunciation of a particular letter will awaken the essential nature which it embodies. In all religious and magical traditions, the name is the carrier of the essential *being*, and knowledge of the name means knowledge of the mystery of the name's possessor. Such belief is at the root of all prayer, mantra, and chanting.

There is a Qabalistic legend that every letter is ruled by an angel, which is considered to be simply a ray or outflow of the virtues of the Almighty. The letters form the words, and the words the prayers, and it is the angels who, by the designation of the assembled words, work the wonders at which ordinary humans marvel.

Sephiroth	Path	Intelligence	Titles	God-name	Attribute	Angel and Angelic Order	Symbols	Planet
Kether	1	Hidden	Ancient of Days Amen	Eheieh (AHIH)	Crown	Metatron Chaioth ha Qadosh	primal point, swastika	None
Chokmah	2	Illuminating	Abba, Supernal Father	IHVH	Wisdom	Ratziel Auphanim	line, phallus, rod of power	Uranus
Binah	3	Sanctifying	Ama, Aima Great Mother Great Sea	IHVH Elohim	Understanding	Tzaphkiel Aralim	yoni, cup, triangle	Saturn
Chesed	4	Cohesive	Infinite Love Divine Mercy	El	Mercy	Tzadkiel Chashmalim	pyramid, cross, wand	Jupiter
Geburah	5	Radical	Lord of Justice	Elohim Gibor	Strength, Severity	Khamael Seraphim	pentagon, five-petalled rose, spear	Mars
Tiphareth	6	Mediating	The Lesser Countenance, The Divine Child	IHVH Aloah va'Daath	Beauty, Harmony	Raphael Melechim	rosy-cross, cube	Sun
Netzach	7	Occult	Lady Triumphant	IHVH Tzabaoth	Victory	Haniel The Elohim	lamp, girdle	Venus
Hod	8	Absolute	Vision of Splendor	Elohim Tzabaoth	Glory	Michael Beni Elohim	versicle, apron	Mercury
Yesod	9	Pure	Treasure House of Images	Shaddai El Chai	Foundation	Gabriel Cherubim	perfumes, sandals	Moon
Malkuth	10	Resplendent	The Gate, Daughter, Bride	Adonai ha Aretz	Kingdom of God	Sandalphon Ashim	circle, equal-armed cross	Earth

Hebrew Letter	Meaning	English Letter	Joining Sephiroth	Numerical Value	Path	Tarot Image
Aleph	Primal Energy, Ox	A	Kether to Chokmah	1	11	Fool
Beth	House, Container	B, V	Kether to Binah	2	12	Magician
Gimel	Camel	G, J	Kether to Tiphareth	3	13	High Priestess
Daleth	Door, Opening	D	Chokmah to Binah	4	14	Empress
Heh	Window	H, E	Chokmah to Tiphareth	5	15	Emperor
Vav	Nail, Hook	W, U	Chokmah to Chesed	6	16	Hierophant
Zain	Sword	Z	Binah to Tiphareth	7	17	Lovers
Cheth	Field, Fence	Ch	Binah to Geburah	8	18	Chariot
Teth	Serpent	T	Chesed to Geburah	9	19	Strength
Yod	Open Hand	I, Y	Chesed to Tiphareth	10	20	Hermit
Kaph	Closed Hand	K, Kh	Chesed to Netzach	20	21	Wheel
Lamed	Whip, Ox-Goad	L	Geburah to Tiphareth	30	22	Justice
Mem	Water	M	Geburah to Hod	40	23	Hanged Man
Nun	Fish	N	Tiphareth to Netzach	50	24	Death, Rebirth
Samekh	Prop, Support	S	Tiphareth to Yesod	60	25	Temperance
Ayin	Eye	O	Tiphareth to Hod	70	26	Deception
Peh	Mouth	P, F	Netzach to Hod	80	27	Tower
Tzaddi	Fishhook	Tz, X	Netzach to Yesod	90	28	Star
Qoph	Back of Head	Q	Netzach to Malkuth	100	29	Moon
Resh	Face, Head	R	Hod to Yesod	200	30	Sun
Shin	Tooth	S, Sh	Hod to Malkuth	300	31	Judgment
Tav	Cross	Th	Yesod to Malkuth	400	32	World

Finals: Kaph = 500, Mem = 600, Nun = 700, Peh = 800, Tzaddi = 900, Aleph = 1000

Pathworking Intelligences and Their Corresponding Numbers

32. The Administrative Intelligence
31. The Perpetual Intelligence
30. The Collecting Intelligence
29. The Corporeal Intelligence
28. The Natural Intelligence
27. The Exciting Intelligence
26. The Renewing Intelligence
25. The Intelligence of Probation
24. The Imaginative Intelligence
23. The Stable Intelligence
22. The Faithful Intelligence
21. The Intelligence of Desirous Quest
20. The Intelligence of Will
19. The Intelligence of the Secret of All Spiritual Activities
18. The Intelligence of the House of Influence
17. The Disposing Intelligence
16. The Triumphal Intelligence
15. The Constituting Intelligence
14. The Luminous Intelligence
13. The Uniting or Conductive Intelligence
12. The Intelligence of Transparency
11. The Scintillating or Fiery Intelligence

Two Ways to Use This Book

1. Read it and put it aside.
2. Read it and use the Qabalistic exercises.

The first way will be helpful for those with only a mild interest in the topic, and also for those already familiar with much of the Qabalistic literature in terms of technique. The latter may find the information on the Hebrew letters, the Tarot trumps, and gematria intriguing, and the visualizations interesting or amusing.

For those unfamiliar with any prior Qabalistic history, a beginner's book (of which there are many) may be in order. Many are listed in the bibliography. The most essential and practical way to use the archetypes of the Tarot as pathwork is to carefully familiarize yourself with the images in the Tarot keys and to meditate on the Hebrew letters. Only slowly and persistently do associations fall into place until you have an "ah-ha" experience of personal discovery which only experiential work can bring. The best way to become intimate with the keys is to *paint or color them.* This initial technique cannot be stressed enough, and you will be reminded of it several times as you do the pathwork in this book. It is important to use the key-scales in the correspondence lists as the dominant color.

After studying each Path, mount the Tarot trump on a table by your bedside or on your altar. Try and meditate on it for several moments without closing your eyes. If you then want to do the visualizations or pathwork exercises, do so with closed eyes. (Perhaps someone can read the visualization to you, or you can read it to yourself, using a pre-recorded tape made earlier—your own voice is the best because it is immediately recognized by your subconscious.) However, you will first be using the archetypes of the Tarot trump as a "jumping off place" into the imaginative part of the experience. Then, when returning from the "inner psychic space," connect briefly again with the Tarot key. This will serve as a focal point for entering and leaving the world of the imagination, which for many will turn into an "actual" astral landscape. (All visions, in Qabalistic philosophy, are perceived through an astral landscape.)

Some of the pathworking exercises or visualizations given in this book are short and concise; some are longer and more involved. Once again—they are *guidelines only*. Once you learn enough about this aspect of Qabalistic work, you will be able to enter these realms and access information on your own. If you do so, be sure and write it down.

There are actually several ways to do pathwork visualizations—the involved "landscape" kind, wherein one starts in the physical world, goes through a temple or sphere of departure and ends up at another temple or sphere of destination. This is the most traditional. Paul Case and his foremost disciple, Ann Davies (herself a great mystic and psychic), suggest meditations on the keys which involve visualizations that stick more specifically with the symbols represented in the Tarot trumps themselves. Or you may, as a result of working on a specific Path over a length of time, simply find yourself already "on the way," so to speak; the angelic guides are very good at assisting one in doing this.

Very little is given in this book about the Sephiroth (or points of departure and destination). If you are unfamiliar with the attributes of the Sephiroth, you may be uncertain as to the "correct landscape" wherein you find yourself. Once you are familiar with the correspondences, however, you will immediately recognize the appropriate symbols, attributes, and *reasons* for the specific associations, which are of vital importance in Qabalah.

The next technique to use is to learn to chant or vibrate the Divine Letters or Divine Names. The pronunciation is given in the correspondence lists for each Path. The only way to really learn how to do this is by practice. It is *most* helpful to do in a group, where the vibration of the intoned Names takes on a powerful and magical quality indeed. Regardie has suggested playing with the voice until one actually hears the vocal cords "slip into" the vibrating aspect. This will sound very different from just saying or chanting the Names. If you have a pitchpipe, find the appropriate tone (also in the correspondence lists) and chant the Letter or Name in that tone.

Techniques for working with the correspondences could involve all the senses. By the end of the book, techniques will have been given that include developing the physical senses in ways which open up the corresponding psychic or inner senses. For now, it will be most helpful to simply meditate on the Tarot key and on the Hebrew Letter, using the other correspondences as you deem appropriate. You could burn the incense of the Path during the pathwork, for example, or dress your altar in the appropriate color, or gather as many symbols as possible around you which relate to the Path.

Once again, whether you believe the spheres are actual "places" or whether you are working solely with the energies of the subconscious, *symbols are the most vital key to unlocking doors.*

You will be amazed at the results.

Th	COSMOS	

Path 32
The Administrative Intelligence

Cosmic Consciousness   *Planet: Saturn*

CHAPTER TWO

The 32nd Path, Tau
The Universe
The Administrative Intelligence

The Hebrew letter Tau means "cross or mark" and also "sign or signature." It represents a *seal* or *witness*. *The Thirty-two Paths of Wisdom* says it "directs and associates" everything in the *universe*, which is the Tarot key attributed to it. It is the last of the 32 Paths. *The Thirty-two Paths of Wisdom* is the text most frequently interpreted and analyzed when working with the Tree of Life. We have noted that the 32 Paths are the 22 Hebrew letters and the 10 Sephiroth, although the latter are more often thought of as points of destination or destiny. The Sephiroth are rather Emanations of Pure Thought and Energy. The 22 actual pathways connecting the Sephiroth are the letters (and the corresponding Tarot archetypes), and the last letter in the Hebrew alphabet is Tau. It corresponds to the Greek Omega. For pathworking purposes, however, it is the beginning, because we are working our way, through finer and finer levels of energy, up to the Crown of the Tree.

The 32nd Path begins in the Sephira Malkuth, which is the Earth, and proceeds to Yesod, whose sphere is the Moon. It is here and now, in the physical body and on the physical plane, that we begin our serious spiritual journey. One of the lessons of this Path is to realize that the God-energy is just as alive and active in our present human condition as anywhere else we can conceive. It is our world which is the window to eternity, and Qabalists call Tau the "Palace of Holiness in the midst" (S.Y. 4:2), meaning it is the *center* from which everything else proceeds, much like a point of Light

27

extended in four directions from the center of a cross.

This image of the Tau cross is called by Qabalists of many schools "Light in Extension." It is "boundless to the East and the West; boundless to the North and South" (S.Y. 1:5). The earth itself is symbolized by this cross, which *marks* its four directions and its four elements. These elements are pictured symbolically in the corners of the Tarot key by the same astrological symbols we see in Path 21 (the Wheel) and which appeared in Ezekiel's vision. They correspond to the four aspects of the Absolute, IHVH, the Divine Name called the Tetragrammaton. The "sealing" of the Creation by means of the Divine Name is one of the most fundamental ideas in Qabalistic literature, dating prior to Talmudic times, and continues to be at the heart of Qabalistic ritual today.

The dancing figure in the picture is perfectly balanced in her position as the *center*, reflecting the self-knowing Spirit. Waite says it is "the soul in the consciousness of Divine Vision" (Waite, 1959, p. 156). In a Jungian sense, this is becoming conscious of the Self that stands at the center of the personality. To one working this Path, it is a profound symbol of individuation; the dancer is in constant motion in harmonious relationship to the elements of the world. Yet she moves in her own individual way, a vassal subservient to no doctrine or organization. The solid ground of her foundation is within her and, as she moves from that deepest source, she is able to creatively commune with the Universe surrounding her.

As the final Hebrew letter, Tau represents the end of manifestation and therefore completeness. There is a subtle nuance in the word (ThV), however, because when it is spelled out, it ends in Vav (V). Vav, which means "hook or nail," is also a conjunction meaning "and" or "also." Thus, in *The Book of Tokens*, Tau is called "the end which is without end" (Case, 1934, p.187), because it means "the end and ... " The other paradox Qabalists have noticed about Tau is that it is the last letter of the word *Bereshith* (Th), the first word of Genesis, which has been translated, "In the beginning." In the Tarot key, the wreath surrounding the dancer is in the shape of a 0, symbolizing the "beginning before the beginning," or the No-thing into which everything evaporates to (i.e., if a number is multiplied by 0) and which also increases growth in a manifold way (i.e., if added to another number). So it is this fluid ability to move back and forth between beginnings and endings that characterizes Tau's uniqueness.

Carlos Suares calls Tau "the cosmic resistance to the life-breath (Aleph) which animates it" (Suares, 1985, p. 60) without which the many varied forms of existence could not come into being. In this regard, the planet Saturn, which is known as the planet of limitation and structure, is attributed to Tau. Without the impacting of two opposed lateral forces (i.e., the positive and the negative), material creation could not exist. This is hinted at by the rods which the maiden holds in her hand signifying the positive and negative modes of force. In the Case deck, these are spirals which, spinning in different directions, manifest the principles of involution and evolution, or integration and disintegration.

In the Saturn myth, we see the first archetypal stirrings of these ideas of infinite space becoming constricted into form. Saturn (or Chronos), Father Time, was said to have castrated his father, Uranus (Space), thus creating a vehicle or form to contain Spirit. Saturn is thus a symbol for the law of limitation which gives a localized expression, or definite shape, to universal life.

The symbol of Saturn is composed of the cross and the moon (linking Malkuth to Yesod) and is also shaped like a sickle. He is Father Time who devours his children and is thus intimately connected not only to birth and the creation of Form but to the Great Reaper, death, and a return to the Source. In this sense, Case says that the Saturn myth expresses that mode of consciousness which swallows up all other modes of consciousness (Case, 1947). Those who can truely comprehend this mystery are said by Qabalists to be "The Lords of the Secret of Saturn," and the esoteric title given to Tau is "The Great One of the Night of Time."

The structure of the Hebrew letter Tau is composed of a shape which is also the letter Resh and a downward extension which resembles a Yod. The hidden meaning of this union is that the spirit or head (the meaning of Resh), which is Kether on the Tree, sends its force downward into the densest manifestation, our world, via Yod (Path 20), the Intelligence of Will. The dancing figure is surrounded by an oval shape, suggestive of the womb of the great Mother, Binah, which is Malkuth reflected on a higher sphere (and connected by the rulership of Saturn). The Sephira Binah is called "Black Saturn" or "Dark Mother," who is the giver of life through her *will to form* and also the thick darkness which is the eternal unmanifested Sea to which we return in depth and silence.

Our dancer is the Empress (Daleth, the door) as well as the

female magician in the Strength Key. She is Isis, the Egyptian mother of life, and the High Priestess (Path 13), who wears the Tau cross on her breast. She is Demeter, the mourning mother who descended into the chasm of the earth to locate her lost child. She is Madonna, mother of the world. In Hebrew, she is "Aima Elohim," the mother of God. She brings all things to completion by her dance of Life. This idea of completion is related to the Hebrew word *Shabbathai* (Sabbath), which is the root of the word Saturn.

This Path represents the first stage of mysticism as well as the early stirrings of the psyche opening to the unconscious and the inner planes. It is the first deep *instruction* offered by the Administrative Intelligence. In Hebrew, the word for "instruction" or "enlightenment" is *maskil* (MshKIL), which has a numerical value of 400, the same as the letter Tau. The number 400 also represents the total manifestation of the Sephiroth, which are the primal 10 Lights of Emanation reflected through the four worlds: Pure Idea or Archetype, the causal, the mental, and the physical. The secret connection here with Tau is that each of the Emanations contains all the others within it; thus $10 \times 10 \times 4 = 400$.

It is said that the Administrative Intelligence directs the operation of the seven planets and also "associates their activities and guides them in their proper courses." The seven planets refer both to the universe as it was known to the ancients and to the "interior stars" or chakras "in the midst"; i.e., in the human body. Each of these "planets" corresponds to one of the Hebrew "double letters," as explained in the *Sepher Yetzirah,* and also represents a direction: North, South, East, West, Height, Depth, and Center.

The Tau cross in Egypt was a device used for measuring the Nile waters and which was instrumental in building the pyramids, which the book of Exodus tells us were constructed by the Hebrews. This is because the Tau cross was a tally for measuring *depth* as well as a square for measuring right angles. Thus it corresponds to all possible directions. These directions, which are connected to the Tarot keys by the Hebrew letters, can be located by the earnest student and arranged in an archetypal "ladder" representing the human body's chakra energy centers. These seven points also represent the seven metals of the alchemists.

The goal of the Great Work in alchemy is arranging the elements or forces in nature to produce the Stone, and those who walk this Path by virtue of the birth date can be very adept at making their dreams and goals concrete. The true work of the 32nd Path, however, is locating that sacred point, embedded in matter, which is necessarily everywhere because it radiates from the center of one's own being. They thus become powerful *witnesses* to reflect that "still, small voice" which acts with perfect clarity in any given situation. Since Tau means "sign or signature," this Path signifies a pledge, or guarantee; thus is Tau the final *seal* and completion of the Great Work.

32nd Pathworking Correspondences

1. Intelligence: Administrative

2. Divine Letter: Tau, TV (pronounced Tah-oo) Value: 400, means "sign or cross"

3. Divine Names: ADNI (pronounced A-do-naiee). Aima

4. Incense: Storax, galbanum. Jasmine

5. Gems: Onyx, salt crystal, lead

6. Color: Indigo

7. Element: Earth

8. Animal: Crocodile

9. Plants: Ash, nightshade, cypress, narcissis, wheat

10. Planet: Saturn

11. Musical Tone: A

12. Magical Phenomenon: Vision of destiny, visions of rebirth, geomancy

13. Magical Weapon: Pantacle

14. Mythos and Related Symbols: Pan, Nephthys, Saturn, Brahma, Demeter (all earth goddesses), Shekinah, Virgin of the World, T-cross, Watchers at the Threshold, gnomes, a well, a cavern, a sickle, a fish-goat

15. Gift or Challenge: To fight despondency with trust, to discriminate between psychic and spiritual forces, to recognize that matter is holy

16. Rules: Skeleton

17. Tarot Arcana: The World

Suggested Exercises

Arrange the seven chakras* (represented by the planets) in a Tarot ladder. Tables are given in this book. Find the Tarot keys symbolized by their respective Intelligence. Then find out what other correspondences relate to these Tarot attributions. Here are how the chakras correspond to the metals of the alchemists, as well as their corresponding Intelligences. (This should be all you need to figure out the rest.)

1. Lead, Saturn, Administrative Intelligence
2. Iron, Mars, Exciting Intelligence
3. Tin, Jupiter, Intelligence of Conciliation
4. Gold, Sun, Collecting Intelligence
5. Copper, Venus, Luminous Intelligence
6. Silver, Moon, Uniting Intelligence
7. Quicksilver or mercury, Mercury, Intelligence of Transparency

This exercise can lead to many valuable insights if worked with over time. It is also useful in visualizations. Once you are familiar with the correspondences between the chakras, or body centers, and metals, colors, herbs, etc., it is also useful in healings.

---

*For those unfamiliar with the word, "chakras" refers to the principle "energy" centers in the spine, which are said to be the channels by which these energies are made manifest: 1. The "root" chakra (fourth sacral vertebra) is the reservoir of energy. 2. The spleen charka (first lumbar area) is the reserve center (which operates if the root chakra is, for some reason, dysfunctional). 3. The solar plexus (eighth thoracic area), which deals primarily with emotional energy. 4. The heart charka (first thoracic), the area of energy transformation. 5. Throat chakra (third cervical area) the expressive node of energy. 6. The brow chakra (first cervical or pituitary gland), which synthesizes and desynthesizes energy, and 7. The crown chakra (not located in the body, visualized as above the head), which acts as the main source of energy transmission. Many books have been written to specifically explain how these centers work. One of the best is *Wheels of Life* by Anodea Judith (Llewellyn, 1987). Key words to describe these areas are: (1) support, (2) action, (3) preservation, (4) will, (5) creativity (6) mysticism, and (7) integration.

Guided Visualization

Imagine you are sitting next to an old, arid well, concentrating on solidifying some dream that has been floating nebulously in your head for some time. You feel you are very close to perceiving all the answers to the many questions which have been plaguing you concerning the carrying out of this vision. But something still eludes you; it seems to be just on the edge your conscious awareness.

In your deep concentration you appear to lose consciousness of the world for a time, as you are gazing into the old well in reverie. Then, in a half-dream state, you seem to fall into this aged hole in mother earth. Much to your surprise, there is a tunnel carved out at the bottom. You decide to follow it for a while and notice that it soon comes to an old wooden door, which you push open curiously.

Immediately you perceive that there is a cube-like structure draped with lace upon which sits an oil lamp and a large book, much like a small altar. The air is permeated with a pungent odor, and you notice that there is incense smoke rising from the floor, which is scattered with sheafs of wheat. On either side of this altar are onyx pillars, and the cave walls have curious carvings in all directions. On one side is a bull, one has what appears to be an eagle's head, one a large cat, and one, which is barely discernible, is engraved with what looks to be the profile of a woman, or perhaps a man with long hair. You sense an aura of excitement and mystery in this place and move past the altar to explore the cavern further.

The tunnel gets blacker as you tread carefully, however, and you soon realize that the small lamp on the altar does not cast enough light to go much deeper. Before you can even think of what to do next, a figure appears that looks much like the carving you just left behind. This person (it seems it must be a female?) seems to be moving so quietly, you cannot even hear her footsteps; indeed, she seems to be gliding along beside you, clasping your hand gently to guide you through the indigo darkness. Soon you are able to perceive some small shaft of light at a juncture in the cave and you pause there, wondering if you should turn or keep on in the direction in which you were headed.

Your guide pauses also, as if waiting while you make up your mind. You approach the lit passageway and are amazed to see a small river, on the other side of which are strewn glittering gems of all kinds. In the waters, however, lurks a family of crocodiles, as well as other strange reptilian creatures you can't identify. Phantoms seem to float around the area studded with the precious gems and then disappear again. This is all very fascinating, yet it seems like something of a detour on your journey, and you decide to proceed on the original path.

Your guide moves quickly in response to your decision, grasping your hand and guiding you through the shadowy cavern. The air seems to be getting thicker and for a moment you wonder if this was the right choice, but you somehow feel a deep sense of trust in your angelic friend, who doesn't hesitate to move swiftly forward. You soon approach what looks like another underground stream, and as you get closer you notice that the air is even thicker and much warmer. When you are almost on top of this river your guide stops and you are able to slowly discern that it is not a river of water at all. It seems rather to be made of lead, it is so thick, and suddenly you realize it must be an underground lava stream. You gaze in awe at the swirling movements which appear from time to time, sucking downward into a deeper vortex. On the bank of this somewhat ominous scorching bed you perceive, with a start, the remains of a skeleton and, next to it, a silver sickle.

You are unsure what to do, but your guide motions to your right. You notice a small crevice in the cave wall that seems slick and cool; you move toward it. Suddenly, the figure sprouts glorious wings and disappears. Around the edges of this crack in the cavern are carved floral designs in the shape of a wreath, and, at the top, a cresent Moon. Not knowing what else to do, you step through the cave door.

Suddenly the world has changed; you can *see,* and what a beautiful sight it is! For a moment the thought crosses your mind that it must be the Garden of Eden. The flowers are profuse; the scent of jasmine assaults your nostrils. Immediately you become aware of a beautiful young maiden sitting in the midst of this garden, with a small circle of stones around her and with a lap full of what looks like narcissus. She motions to you with her eyes, which are deeply set and profound beyond belief, and you approach her gingerly. Once close to her, however, you cannot stop yourself from the compelling desire to touch her; the blood in your body is warm, and your limbs, so tired now from the journey, are longing to rest in her embrace.

She opens her arms and you lay your head gently on her lap of flowers, knowing somehow that this magical maiden has all the answers to every question since time began. You look up to speak to her, but suddenly you are stunned because she has instantly changed. No longer a fair daughter of the underworld, she is a mature woman with kind eyes and mouth, and for a moment she resembles your mother. Then another transformation follows, and her face is that of a rapidly aging woman with thick wrinkles and sagging skin. You want to draw back, but she continues to hold you in her grasp, and as you gaze into her eyes you recognize the face of Ancient Wisdom. A deep peace is transmitted to you in that moment, and then you are aware of someone tapping your shoulder.

You look up, half-expecting to see your guide interrupting you to tell you it is time to return, but realize it is only a passing stranger, also here at this well to reflect and pause on his journey. He is inquiring to see if you are all right. You awaken from your otherworldly dream with the sudden realization that you have brought back a clear image about your present condition; and, as you rise to leave, you smile at the newcomer at the well and drop in a small silver coin as a token of thanks for your vision.

Affirmations

1. *From my inmost central Self radiates the dance of Life Eternal.*

2. *I am identified with the Central Power which is the kingdom of Spirit residing in my body.*

3. *All form is a beautiful limitation of the infinite energy of God.*

4. *I will love the Indwelling Spirit with my whole heart, with my whole soul, with my whole strength, and with my whole mind.*

5. *I am one with the Imagination that forms the universe.*

Sh   JUDGEMENT

Path 31
The Perpetual Intelligence

Realization   *Planet: Pluto*

CHAPTER THREE

The 31st Path, Shin
Judgement
The Perpetual Intelligence

The path of Shin connects the sphere of Malkuth (Earth) on the Tree of Life with that of Hod (Reason). Shin is one of the three "mother" letters which indicate the elements of Air (Aleph), Water (Mem), and Fire (Shin). The holy text, *The Thirty-two Paths of Wisdom*, says of this Path, "The Thirty-first Path is the Perpetual Intelligence; and why is it so-called? Because it regulates the motions of the Sun and Moon in their proper order, each in an orbit convenient for it"

This Path connects and seeks to balance the energies of Malkuth, which is called the Kingdom or the Bride in Qabalistic literature and which is essentially the body (i.e., the temple of the Holy Spirit), with Hod, or Reason, the sphere of the Individual Mind, sometimes called Splendor. It is the sphere where the magical arts and sciences come together, and it belongs to Mercury, the planet which was later characterized as the god-form Mercury or Hermes.

This is an activating Path of the intellect rather than a Path of emotion, which would head the other direction on the Tree, toward Netzach. The meaning of "Shin" in Hebrew means "tooth," and the archetypal implication is that the task is one of "biting through," in order to achieve concrete victory through correct application of the mind. What is meant by "Judgement" is the process undergone by the Personality as it strives to become conscious of its own inner workings. It is called *perpetual* because such a process takes continual monitoring. As the aspirant moves closer to his or her desire or goal, the dross is slowly burned away by the redeeming Fire, which sometimes may not be experienced as pleasant. This is a

41

process that frequently takes place in the physical body, as indicated by its point of origin, Malkuth. What is indicated by the path of Judgement, however, is a resurrection, a rebirth. In this Path, the components of the Personality are critically analyzed and evaluated by the student. The seeker on this Path, however, needs to remember balance, for even though this Path leads towards the sphere of the mind, both the thinking and feeling functions are important.

Judgement is the Tarot Key where the divine forces descend to meet the aspirant to introduce him or her to the Mysteries, as he/she rises from the tomb of matter. Here is the time when the Personality answers the call of the angel whose Presence has been invoked by the Fire of desire. The archangel pictured here is Gabriel, "Might of God," from the root *gabroo* (GBR), "to conquer." Gabriel is related to the theme of resurrection and rebirth because he has traditionally been associated with heralding a change; i.e., annunciations. He appeared to Mary to announce the birth of Jesus and to Zacharias to announce the birth of John the Baptist.

In legend, it is Gabriel who guards and guides prospective mothers, as well as directs the spirit toward the mother and the home where it will find physical embodiment. In this sense, he truly represents the fiery influx of the "Breath of the Divine Spirit," which in Hebrew is "Ruach Elohim" (RVCh ALHIM). This designation of God has the same numerical value as the letter Shin; i.e., 300. Because of this link through gematria, the ancient Hebrew wise ones have called Shin the Holy Letter. Gabriel's trumpet is a symbol of the specialization of this Life Breath in sound.

The mode of consciousness assigned to the Perpetual Intelligence is directly related to extension, because the root word of "perpetual" in Hebrew means "to stretch," "to extend," or "to unfold" (MDD), hence the idea of an extension beyond the limits of the modes of consciousness common to most human beings. Judgement also implies completion, decision, termination. This is also implicit in one of the roots for "perpetual" (ThMIDI), which is ThM, a word which means "completion" or "perfection."

In the fourth dimension, represented by this Key, all things are the reverse of physical conditions. Thus, for example, in the Tarot picture, the man (i.e., consciousness) is passive and the woman (subconsciousness) *stretches* to receive the influence of the angel in her reaching arms. The influence of Gabriel's trumpet is received by her outstretched hands. Case, Crowley, and others have said she symbolizes the special fire of magic called *ob* (AVB). This word means "magic" and it also means "belly, skin or leather bag," again indicating a container that *stretches* and, in the case of a mother, one that stretches to an *unfolding* new life. The great Hebrew scholar Fabre d'Olivet has said that this root represents generative *force* and is the "Matrix of the Universe, the Orphic Egg, the Vessel of Isis," and to it are related all ideas of love, desire, expansion, growth, and propagation (1921, p. 288).

The value of the Hebrew word AVB is 9, the same as the letter Teth, the Strength Key (Path 19), where her magic force tames the lion. These ideas of strength or might refer us again to Gabriel, whose name, we recall, means "Might of God." He heralds the annunciation which is represented by the child, or the regenerated personality. This child's back is toward us because he represents a return to the Source. He signifies the balance the aspirant on this Path is attempting to achieve.

This card shows a stage of spiritual unfoldment when the personal consciousness is on the verge of blending with the forces around it. It is here that the student has flashes that his or her personality has no separate existence. The purpose of Shin (tooth) is to separate instinct from intellect, however, and to blend fourth-dimensional experience with intellectual conviction is the constant chore of the seeker traveling the 31st Path.

Fire has always been perceived as divine, belonging in the first place to the gods. A human being is the only animal that has learned to use fire and not be intimidated by it. Frequently, this is done by trial and error, as in the forging of metal. Fire is the essential element in any kind of transformation, including digestion, which breaks down energy (food) to be utilized in another way. Masters speak of using caution in choosing what one eats because at a certain stage in one's spiritual development, one has the opportunity to utilize these energies in a completely new way; i.e., that of creating a regenerated body (also represented by the child in the picture).

The other association with food and regeneration in this context is again "tooth," the vehicle for initially breaking food apart. A tooth is often the longest lasting part of us, again showing endurance and extension. The shape of the letter Shin itself suggests three flames arising from an altar and resembles a three-pronged molar. Here the tooth is a symbol of the collection and retention of knowledge imprinted on the most enduring part of the aspirant, the soul.

We have noticed that the value of Shin is 300, the same value as the Divine Breath of the Holy Spirit, which in Hebrew is called the *Ruach Elohim* (RVCh ALHIM). This points to the very close connection of this fiery Intelligence with the nature of the God-energy which in the Qabalistic trinity is said to be female. *The Book of Tokens* says of Shin, "This is the Fire of formation,/And by this Fire atonement is made" (Case, 1934, p.182). This is a reference not only to the activities of this Intelligence, but also to the association through gematria of Shin (value 300) and the word "formation" (*Yetzer*, or ITzR in Hebrew, also value 300), which points to the function of the female in the activity of forming new life. To a Christian Qabalist, there is an obvious reference here to the Fruit of this function, the Christ, as it receives the influx of Shin through the annunciation of Gabriel.

On this path, the seeker deals with critically assessing the fire of life, the "carrying of torches," as well as the other flames of passion and desires of one's instinct (which belong to the sphere of Malkuth), with those aspiring passions of the soul which seek above all else to know God with the mind (Hod).

In early humanity, fire was the liberator from the inertia that gripped one in hunger and cold. Inertia is also a vice of Malkuth (inert matter), the starting point of this path. The strongest implication of the final stages of this path is the beginning of the Knowledge and Conversation with the Holy Guardian Angel; that is, intuitive perception is begun to be felt through the aspirant's inner ear. The symbolic archetypal manifestation of this event of direct communication with one's inner Mind is that of the Holy Spirit descending in tongues of fire.

31st Pathworking Correspondences

1. Intelligence: Perpetual

2. Divine Letter: Shin, ShN (pronounced Sheen) Value: 300, means "tooth"

3. Divine Hames: Elohim, Elohim Tzabaoth (E-lo-heem Tzaa-ba-ooth)

4. Incense: Frankincense, copal. Lavender

5. Gem: Fire opal

6. Color: Scarlet red

7. Element: Fire

8. Animal: Lion

9. Plants: Red poppy, hibiscus

10. Planet: Pluto

11. Musical Tone: C

12. Magical Phenomenon: Visions of transformation, metamorphosis or renewal

13. Magical Weapons: Lamp, wand

14. Mythos and Related Symbols: Agni, Vulcan, Heru, Gabriel, Ariel, the Winged Watchers, salamanders, the Aeon

15. Gift or Challenge: To ground the intellect; to balance inertia vith activity; to strengthen memory

16. Rules: Organs of circulation and generation; also connected with fevers

17. Tarot Arcana: Judgement

Suggested Exercises

Color the Tarot key. It will mean much more to the subconscious than if it is left in black and white. Set it on your altar from time to time, or someplace where you can gaze at it attentively for 3-5 minutes. This key is good to meditate on when you want to bring something to completion or termination. Use the Judgement energy when doing group workings for intentions of renewal—a prayer group for a special intention of healing, for instance, or a ritual or meditation for world peace.

Research myths of renewal and rebirth: the Flood story, the resurrected Christ, the risen Osiris, the shamanic tales of disintegration and renewal, or others that appeal to your taste or tradition. Some other myths in this vein you may not be familiar with are: the decapitation of Orpheus, the descent of Inanna, the tribulations of Job, the rape of Persephone, the trials of Psyche, and the blinding of Oedipus. You may want to explore what happened to Zeus when his head split open, or to Prometheus' liver, or to Odin's eye or the shoulder of Eros. The archetypal themes of myths and how they relate to you are much more meaningful if you find out about them yourself.

Focus on what that myth or archetype *means* both in a universal sense and to you personally. How could such a fantastic tale relate to you in the most intimate core of your being? Research and contemplation on archetypal themes will yield many new associations and meanings.

Guided Visualization

After meditating on the Judgement Key, shut your eyes and visualize yourself approaching a winged being with flashes of fire for wings. This being has a glowing countenance and bright, discerning eyes, and, with a gentle, commanding gesture, beckons you to follow.

With a lamp in your hand, you approach your guide and descend toward a cave wherein glows a bright, hissing fire. Somewhere burns a faint odor of sweet incense. A salamander rustles from under a rock as you sit down to meditate on the fire. Visualize a bright spark of the fire alighting on your head, like a candle flame. Try to imagine it being drawn down into your body, cleansing and purifying as it pours through you. In the East, this is called the Diamond Body, or body of light. Imagine that, with this body of light, you can move swiftly through space. You are swimming through the stars, parting them as you go. You see a burning sun with an angelic figure inside of it. It has the shining image of the letter Shin on its forehead, and you bow in reverence.

See your body getting larger, so that galaxies are contained within it. As you wave your hands, worlds stream forth. You are, perhaps, witnessing the re-creation of time, space, and universes. Remain as long as possible in this feeling of being absorbed in your light body; then gently return to the peaceful fire.

After meditating in this card, experiment with your ovn visualizations by using this key as a starting place. What is important is to stick with the correspondences. Remember, for example, that the main theme here is fire. What particular importance do you attatch to this element? What associations does it stir?

When you begin to work with Letter Visualization, you could add an extra dimension to your imaginative pathwork by visualizing the Letter as a bright living flame above your head. In the same way that you imagined a spark of fire alighting upon your head and descending into your body to create a Diamond or Light body in this exercise, you will eventually become adept at seeing, and then *actually incorporating,* the Hebrew Letters into your body. This can be a very powerful exercise, hovever, and needs to be done in small doses, at first. Later, additional exercises will be given to help you add even more dimensions to the technique of working with the Letters.

Affirmations

1. *I am renewed, within and without. I am a child of the Divine flame, which can never be extinguished.*

2. *I am a new creature; today my insights will be new.*

3. *The flame of spiritual illumination now stimulates my inner eye of truth.*

4. *I rekindle my spirit with the gloving flame of desire to evoke transcendent thought forms which will lead me closer to my true Goal.*

R   THE SUN   ר

Path 30
The Collecting Intelligence

Regeneration   *Planet: The Sun*

CHAPTER FOUR

The 30th Path, Resh
The Sun

The Collecting Intelligence

Resh is called the "Collecting Intelligence" because from it are deduced the "judgment of the Stars, and of the celestial signs, and the perfection of their science ... " When we participate in applying the patterns inherent in such perfect Judgement, introduced to us in the previous Path, we share consciously in the reign of cosmic law. This is quite a task to ask of the humble pathworker, however, and on a more human level, the 30th Path is devoted to the refinement of physical sensation for the purpose of further regeneration of the personality.

Resh means "head or countenance," and it is in the human head that the controlling element of life is concentrated. The controlling element in our solar system is the Sun, the Tarot key which belongs to Resh, and in both the Waite and the Case decks, the Sun indeed has a shining countenance. Human consciousness is the form through which the Life-Power physically present in solar energy is perfected. It is the Collective Intelligence because it synthesizes and adapts all other forms of consciousness, administering the laws which govern reality. The sunflowers represent an operation of this solar force in the organic world. They turn toward the Sun, recognizing it as the source of their strength and growth.

The aspirant on this path attempts to cultivate vision, a practice which clears away mental, emotional, and physical obstructions to produce a deep inner regeneration. This is truly the path where the active work of alchemy takes place. Astrological references which point to this are the destination of the pathworking in Hod, whose

53

mundane chakra is the planet and god-form Mercury or Hermes and who presides over all alchemical activities, and the Sun, which represents the goal of the Great Work in the regenerated solar stone, gold (which it rules.)

This concept of regeneration is clearly indicated by the presence of the young child on a horse in the Waite deck, and by the two dancing children in Case's rendition. There is an overt reference here to the teaching of Jesus when He said that "Whosoever does not accept the kingdom of God as a child will not enter into it" (Luke 18:17). In this regard, Case says that "The intensity of the initiate's consciousness that he is truly the Eternal Child of the Eternal Father is the measure of his Understanding and the root of his Wisdom" (Case, 1985, p. 290). Since the words Understanding and Wisdom are capitalized here, we may infer that Case is referring to the two Divine Sephiroth, Binah and Chokmah, in the region of the Supernals, where the personality is no longer conscious of itself as a separate ego. There is a further link on this path with the Primordial Triangle: the letter Resh itself has a direct relationship to Kether, the Crown on the Tree, also called the "White Head." Resh crowns the word Kether itself by ending in R. In the Christian tradition, the part of the body which corresponds to Christ is the head, and, St. Paul also tells us that the head of Christ is God; i.e., Kether (I Cor. 11:3). The head is the part of the body that is anointed during initiations or rituals which recognize the student as being part of a greater "body."

The letter Resh has a value of 200, which is also the numeration of that which delineates our magical childlike consciousness: "belonging to spring" (QITz), also translated as "to awaken" or "to stir," as well as "summer fruit." Another word connected to the solar influence of Resh is "substance" (OTzM) or "essence" (value 200) which also means "strength" or "power." We awaken to our creativity by the power of the Sun when we identify ourselves with its essence.

This pathworking begins in the sphere of Yesod, which rules the Moon and imagination and has its destiny in Hod, Mercury, the sphere of pure knowledge and visionary inspiration. The Yesod energy is also connected with our sexuality and is called the *Foundation* of existence itself, whereas the sphere of Mercury-Hermes represents the synthesis of the female-male energies; i.e., as the hermaphroditic mythological being who has discovered the secret of the 2-in-1.

It is Hod, the eighth Sephira, that governs the forces of regeneration, and in the Tarot key, the radiating Sun has eight points as well as eight wavy lines in the Case deck and is the alchemical representation of the day-star. The wavy lines common to both the Case and Waite deck represent the feminine, the straight lines the masculine forces of the personality. Waite shows 11 of each, probably to indicate the 22 divine letters. Case has 48 lines issuing from the Sun's countenance, and 48 is the number of the Hebrew word *kokab* (KVKB), which also means "star" or "great prince" and is used by Qabalists to specifically designate Mercury. Thus in Resh do we see the alchemical fusion of the yang/Sun with the yin/Moon under the auspices of Mercury. This is called the "Operation of the Sun" by alchemists and is said to be "performed by the Sun and Moon with the aid of Mercury." The planet Mercury is the one associated with the *expansion* of forms in nature and that which gives impetus and momentum.

In *The Book of Tokens*, Resh is thus described: "Beneath the wings of the Great Sun thou dwellest," a Biblical reference to the "shadow of the wings" of IHVH (Case, 1934, p. 176). The numerical association is again 200, for the symbol of the winged disk, the *Kanaphim* (KHPIM), also adds up to 200. The transformation which gives wings to this solar principle occurs in the "walled garden" of the human body, which affects the dual components of the lower self. Thus we see the child (or children) riding or dancing in the garden under the guiding influence of the wings of the all-supporting Life-Principle. They are the new Adam and Eve (in the Case deck) or the "self-renewed spirit ... which bears the seal of Nature and of Art" in the Waite interpretation (Waite, 1959, p. 147).

This is a path of great discovery, because it leads to Hod, the sphere of activity of the mind. Some have described this as the point where deep contact with the Inner Teachers is formed. It is also a balance between mind and body, striking at the heart of the relationship between the intellect and the intuition, and if the initiate is ready reveals secrets known only to rare adepts.

Paul Case says that this process marks distinct physiological changes in the body of the initiate, much like master yogis of the East; that there are different constituents in his bloodstream and that the nervous system, brain, and glands function differently. These are alchemical transformations in the very crucible of the body and specifically relate to the reason the "philosophic gold" is considered to be the Elixir of Life as well as the miraculous Stone.

For those who are actively working with the energies of this Path, a feeling of the new and innocent is inevitable. Fresh insights unfold about the self. In particular, it is a process whereby most anyone can begin to "grow backwards" toward a recollection of the Source from which we emerged.

30th Pathworking Correspondences

1. Intelligence: Collecting

2. Divine Letter: Resh, RASh (pronounced Raash) Value: 200, means "head or face"

3. Divine Names: Eloah (E-lo-ah); Elohim Tzabaoth (E-lo-heem Tzaa-ba-ooth)

4. Incense: Heliotrope, cinnamon. Mastic

5. Gem: Chrysolite, gold

6. Colors: Orange, amber

7. Element: Air, fire

8. Animals: Sparrowhawk, lion, beetle, peacock

9. Plants: Rose, sunflower, laurel

10. Planets: Sun, Mercury

11. Musical Tone: D

12. Magical Phenomenon: Alchemy, plant and herb magic, healing

13. Magical Weapon: Lamen, wand

14. Mythos and Related Symbols: Helios, Ra, Christ as Philosopher's Stone, the Conquering Child, a golden chalice, griffins, dragons, the Red Flower of the Sun, the Golden Lion, a laurel tree, the wheel, unicorn

15. Gift or Challenge: To use clear analysis in looking at one's self; to balance thinking with feeling and intuition, to develop strength

16. Rules: Heart and circulation

17. Tarot Arcana: The Sun

Suggested Exercises

Use the energy of this path when you are refining some aspect of your personality which needs attention. When involved in therapeutic work, individually or in groups, keep an image of the Sun-Being before your mind's eye from time to time to help "throw some light on the matter." Create an image of this powerful energy symbol, in clay, watercolor or some other media. Or color the Tarot key and meditate on it for 3-5 minutes, focusing on clearing, cleansing, and lightening. Use it also when you are feeling heavy or depressed, or when you need to spark your confidence. Try to imagine that one of the young children in the Tarot key is entering your body, filling you with a childlike simplicity, innocence, and trust. It is also good to work with the energies of this path when you are working with herbs or tinctures.

Resh is a powerful letter to meditate on. You may stare at it for several minutes and then visualize it as above your head, sending out its light from the *tip at its bottom*. Imagine your head connecting with the Primal Head which hovers over you like a shadow, only waiting for your call.

Guided Visualization

You are standing in a temple with obelisks and crypts surrounding you and papyri containing indecipherable messages covering the walls. You look around and see that the room is full of busy priests reading hieroglyphs and translating manuscripts; in the dark corners, you discern alchemists bending over boiling pots. They do not seem to notice your presence. However, your gaze alights on one of them dressed in a particularly startling golden robe. He immediately looks up to meet your glance, then approaches you carrying a book. He introduces himself as your guide.

He leads you deeper into the temple, which strangely enough contains a dark stream of water. He tells you that this is the River of Forgetfulness. At this juncture, however, he opens the book in his hand and tells you that you are about to receive your real name. After he reveals it to you, though, you ponder the fact that it doesn't sound like your real name, although it seems to stir a distant memory. As you cross the stream, a large shadow looms ahead, and your guide says, "Stay away from the Black Double." He goes on to tell you that when you recognize the White Double, a magic formula will be revealed for regaining your real memory.

Suddenly you enter a doorway with a graven clay image hanging overhead. It is quite dark but you can discern that it is the emblem of a Sun beetle. As you pass through this doorway, someone says, "Herein lies the Sun of Osiris." Although it is very hazy here, there is a pinpoint of light which you follow. You pass a gushing, bubbling fountain guarded by a bright-transparent golden lion. Herbs are growing all around. As the light gets slowly brighter, you notice that you growing weary. You sit for a moment near a sweet-smelling bush. A golden cup lies nearby. You gaze into this cup and see a beautiful glowing rose, and as you stare deeply into it, you seem to enter into a deep trance.

The rose itself seems to continue to grow before your very eyes. Spilling out of its many unfolding petals appear to be worlds in transformation. Deep at the heart of the Golden Flower of the Sun is a tiny bright fire. Its flickering movements appear to be the controlling factor in the unfolding of the rose in perfect symmetry and glory. Suddenly, you realize that you have been lying down, and that someone has placed something on your forehead. You hear invocations being read by ghostly voices, and one from among them shouts, "O Sun of Midnight!" The image of the rose appears again before your mind's eye, and its rays seems to embrace the universe.

Suddenly a black cross image appears within the Sun rose and on it hangs a crucified God, whose image fills the Sun and grows beyond it. His face is bathed in glowing love, sympathy, and radiant beauty. Then he is no longer on the cross but radiant with shining robes and walking towards you. You recognize that he is the White Double. In awe, you watch this figure behind your closed eyes move lovingly toward you and then softly touch your forehead to anoint you. He says, "You too are the Logos" and then reveals to you a word which causes memories to flood across you in waves. Suddenly he disappears.

When you return to waking consciousness, you stand and notice that you have some kind of crown on your head. Your guide leads you back through a temple door, at the edge of which grows a laurel tree. As you enter someone tells you, "Welcome to the Foundation of all the worlds. May you be a shining star in one of them."

Experiment with the rose in this pathworking (or any flower or symbol which represents to you the Red Flower of the Sun). Where else could it take you? What secrets does it hold? What would your "real" name be? Why?

Affirmations

1. *As I walk in the Light, I don't forget to transform my shadow.*

2. *Seeing in perfect faith is the Foundation upon which I build my experience of Divine Splendor.*

3. *I am self-generated and self-created.*

4. *All the necessary transformations of my personality have already begun.*

5. *"Be ye transformed by the renewing of your mind."*

 THE MOON

Path 29
The Corporeal Intelligence

Organization   *Sign: Pisces*

CHAPTER FIVE

The 29th Path, Qoph
The Moon
The Corporeal Intelligence

The Thirty-two Paths of Wisdom calls Qoph the "Corporeal Intelligence, so-called because it forms every body which is formed beneath the whole set of worlds and the increment of them." Waite's translation uses the phrase "it is the growth thereof" instead of "increment" (Waite, 1960, p. 217), indicating a continued interest in the bodies which the Corporeal Intelligence forms. This is truly the path of body consciousness, in the literal sense of the intricate working together of the millions of cells of the physical organism.

The letter-word Resh, the path which immediately precedes this one, means, "head" or "face." *Qoph* means specifically *back of the head*. As the consciousness which shapes bodies, the Corporeal Intelligence is identified with Qoph because it is in the back of the head where the specific organ is located which is related to the structure, chemistry, and functions of the human organism; i.e., the medulla oblongata. This is referred to by masters and yogis of both Eastern and Western esoteric traditions as perhaps the most single important organ in the body, because it is the connecting link between the higher brain centers and the spinal cord and subordinate centers in the lower body. It governs respiration, heart movement, circulation, and many kinds of health maintenance, carrying on its functions uninterrupted whether we are awake or not. It is still actively working for us while we are asleep, and interestingly, the body activity assigned by the *Sepher Yetzirah* to Qoph is the *function of sleep*.

We know that those activities once considered "autonomic" or

65

"involuntary" (i.e., breathing, heartbeat, etc.) have repeatedly been demonstrated to come under the voluntary direction of masters and adepts who have practiced the discipline necessary to exercise control over these areas. These disciplines are almost always connected to an awareness of how the brain centers in the back of the head function. In Qabalah, the sphere of the Moon, or the *Foundation* (Yesod), is the "seat of the Vital Soul" manifested as this autonomic consciousness or subconsciousness.

The word *corporeal* or *bodily* in Hebrew is *gasami* (GShMI), which has a value of 353, also the value of the word for "delight" or "joy," *shimchah* (ShMChH). The root of "corporeal" (GShM) means "to rain upon." In the Tarot key we notice that a stream of "yods" (the Hebrew letter representing existence, the Intelligence of Will, and the *hand* of the Divine) are raining on the body of the earth. Many Qabalists refer to this rain as actual *blood*, and mythologies connect this theme with the menstruation of the Moon goddess, Artemis or Diana, who represents the life-giving properties of the childbearing woman. The words for menstruation and Moon are closely related: the root "mens" means simply "Moon," and it is an ancient archetypal theme which links these two ideas. Peasants in much of Europe had a common belief that the Moon menstruates as part of her cycle just as women do. The root of the word "Diana" means "divine or brilliant," and "Artemis" is derived from the root meaning "high source of water."

Earlier than the Greek and Roman Moon goddesses was the Babylonian mother-goddess Asherah, who is mentioned many times in the Bible. In *The Hebrew Goddess*, Raphael Patai (1968) tells us that Jewish women offered cakes to her as Queen of Heaven till the end of the Judaean monarchy. In ancient times, bulls were associated with Moon-worship because their horns resemble a New Moon. In Babylonian astrology, the Moon was connected with water and other kinds of fluids. This association of Moon, water, and the heifer must have still existed in Old Testament Judaic rituals, according to Patai, because under Mosaic law, ritual cleanliness could only be conveyed by waters mixed with the ashes of a red heifer. (See Numbers 19:2.)

In Hebrew, the word for "Moon" is *lebanah*, and in it are contained the words *laib* (LB) or "heart" and *nah* (NH), meaning "ornamental" or "beautiful," thus containing the hidden meaning, "Beautiful Heart." It is unfortunate that so many Tarot interpretations of this vital life-giving image are negative. It is true that, when it comes to the bleeding of women or the mysterious ways of the Moon, the ideas of *taboo, fear, uncleanliness,* etc. have dominated the human psyche (mostly men's) for a long stretch of our history. And both can be "bewitching," as anyone has noticed who has ever observed how lovers react to a full Moon or how a male dog will forego sleep and food to seek out a female in heat.

It is perhaps this association with our "lower animal" side—which many claim to be the interpretation of the dogs in the Tarot image—which dominates our negative thinking about the Moon key. More probably, it has to do with the original seed-thought linking the Moon, ruler of the night, with sleep, the time wherein we venture into the great unknown. As we saw, the letter Qoph is associated with the back of the head and sleep rather than the face, the Sun, and the light of day (Resh).

In both the Waite and the Case deck, the image of the Moon is shown with 16 large and 16 small rays, 32 in all, to represent the 32 holy paths of wisdom. Thus the esoteric interpretation is that the Moon itself is the radius which is our first point of contact with psychic and spiritual opening. In its association with the subconscious, the seat of the soul, it is our perpetual guardian which never sleeps. Case interprets the two dogs, one more wolf-like than the other, to be the poles of nature and art. In fact, *all corporeal existence* is portrayed in the Tarot key in an unfolding sequence (not, however, a derogatory one). At the bottom, near the pool, are stones and plants, symbolizing the mineral and vegetable kingdom; the crayfish, symbol of the first stirrings of consciousness; the animal kingdom, represented by the dog and wolf wailing their timeless lunar lamentation, calling to Artemis, the mistress of wild beasts.

It has been noted that the wolf is the *most faithful* of all animals and will fight to the death to protect its family. Then we see the cultivated field, representing the developement of patterns controlled through human evolution. Finally, there are the towers which mark the boundaries of the known, and beyond them the heights of consciousness represented by the mountains. The towers, as boundary markers, are those secret places to which the aspirant on this path withdraws to incubate his or her own dreams, to take refuge from the world and meditate. They represent the secrets which cannot be penetrated until we have risen above ground level, at least Moon-high or beyond. This great Beyond is presently available to most of us only when we sleep, but to the 29th pathworker, this source of inspiration, and the intuitive and psychic work which characterized trance or deep meditation is a natural fact of life. The paths which proceed toward Netzach, in fact, are all Orphic paths, and resemble that magical mythical poet, Orpheus, who charmed all of nature with the gift of his song.

We saw that the images of the dog and wolf remind us of the qualities of faithfulness, guardianship, and alert watchfulness. The dog is also sacred to Hecate, goddess of the Moon. One of the symbols in alchemy is a dog devoured by a wolf, which represents the purification of gold by means of antimony.

Another symbolic "dog theme" we find in mythology is the relationship between Anubis, the Egyptian jackel deity of death and resurrection (also a lunar god), and the watchful dog. The dog, like the vulture, is characterized in the minds of ancient peoples as a companion of the dead on their "crossover" journey. In Christian symbolism, the sheep dog plays the role of guardian and protector, much like Anubis, god of rebirth. In this regard, we notice the link with the sacrificed and risen figure of Christ, whose body and blood is considered to be the life of those who partake of it.

There is a legend that once a year during the Inquisition, on the day of Corpus Christi (i.e., the Body of Christ), the initiates of the Rosy Cross (Rosicrucians) would meet in the "House of the Spirit" to embrace their secret doctrine through study and ritual. One cannot fail to notice the connection between the significance of this event and its relationship to the *Corporeal* Intelligence. Case indicates that it is because of this intimate relationship between matter and spirit that all great rituals make eating and drinking central to their mysteries. The other connection to the Christos principle in this regard is that Qoph is one of the 12 "simple" letters to which an astrological symbol is assigned, and Qoph is the fish, or Pisces.

One of the important lessons of this Path, which is stressed in Qabalah again and again, is that it is not to our advantage to attempt to separate the "higher states of the mind" from the "lower gross" forms of the physical body. If we think of the flesh as being a heavy weight we are forced to carry around while we search for Spirit, we neglect to find the Spirit embodied in the Flesh, which is where the Christ principle has declared that it could be found. We also create the impression that the body is an enemy, whereas the aim of a true esoteric aspirant is to begin where nature leaves off and to go on to "perfect the work of evolution," which is how the alchemist works with matter.

This image of growth is indicated by the word Qoph spelled out (QVP), which equals 186, the same numerical value as the word *mosaph*, "to increase." It also has the same numeration as the "Tentative Intelligence" (NSIVNI) of Samekh, thus linking it to the 25th Path of probation and trial.

The value of the letter Qoph itself is 100, which is 10 x 10 (the number of Sephiroth multiplied by itself), as well as the value of *kaleem* (KLIM), "vessels" or "instruments." In this association, we get a clear sense of the relationship of the divine through its medium of expression, the instruments of the body, or the corporeal intelligences.

The 29th Path leads from Malkuth to Netzach, joining the physical and emotional natures. It sometimes has the tendency to carry with it powerful emotional complexes, and the balance here is to "use one's reason" when it is called for, especially in volatile situations, and to process one's psychic and emotional nature with others who *can* see clearly when we can't. The "shadow" crops up frequently on this path, as we deal with our various projections of what we consider to be humanity's "lower instincts." As Path 31 needs to be balanced with instinct and emotion, so Path 29 needs to be balanced with intellect and reason.

This is a path of flux and reflux, and a journey of evolution. Ascending through the 29th Path can be an experience in "psychic fecundation" as we encounter becoming birthed by the vibrant Sephira Netzach, one of whose goddesses is Aphrodite—the Awakener. Aphrodite, the goddess of love, was said to be born on the sea-foam; and the sea, like the Moon, reflects continual cyclical transformations. But in the aspect of Netzach as Divine Love and Victory, we realize at the destination of this Path that our birthright is to reclaim the Divine Mother who formed "every body which is formed beneath the whole set of worlds" (*The Thirty-two Paths of Wisdom*).

29th Pathworking Correspondences

1. Intelligence: Corporeal

2. Divine Letter: Qoph, QVP or QP (pronounced Kofe), Value: 100, means "back of head"

3. Divine Name: El. IHVH Tzabaoth (Yod–Heh–Vaw–Heh Tza–ba–ooth)

4. Incense: Ambergris. Amber or Rose

5. Gem: Pearl

6. Colors: Crimson, violet–red

7. Element: Water

8. Animals: Dog, fish, amphibians, bull

9. Plants: Poppy, hibiscus, oak

10. Planet: Moon

11. Musical Tone: B

12. Magical Phenomenon: Bewitchments, creating materializations

13. Magical Weapon: Magic Mirror

14. Mythos and Related Symbols: Vishnu, Poseidon, Hecate, Christ as Ichthys or Host, the sea, the cup, the mountain, the Fish-avatar, phantoms of twilight, the swan-maiden

15. Gift or Challenge: To balance instinct with reason, to stay grounded, to see the divine in matter

16. Rules: Legs and feet

17. Tarot Arcana: The Moon

Suggested Exercises

Use this key to find a balance between tradition and innovative insight and vision. Use it also to work with conflicts that you feel are making you a little "crazy." (The word "lunatic" comes from "luna," or Moon). Visualize yourself on a journey deep inside yourself. Imagine that you are getting smaller and smaller, like Alice in Wonderland, so you can squeeze into a tiny hole that leads inside your own body. You may need to explore the outside of your body to find an entrance which seems acceptable to the "tiny you" that is the journeyer. One fairly easy entrance may be the navel. Once inside, explore it thoroughly: where is the tension in your body caused by this conflict? Your body is a metaphor for your experience, so you should be able to find out all about the mythic and sensory dimensions of conflict as you examine your body. Is the tension hot, cold, heavy, light, damp, dry, smooth, rough? Does it suck you in or push you away? What color is it? Are different parts of your body at war with each other? Can you talk to the body part and will it talk back to you?

Another good technique to use in conjunction with this path is to keep a dream journal. It is useful not only in dealing with present conflicts but also in revealing a deeper meaning, purpose, and orientation in your life. Use it also to immerse yourself in surrealistic images of dreamland, and see how your creativity improves. Examining or interrogating fearful dream images is helpful in understanding them as well as eliminating them if they are recurring. Dreams can be as ephemeral as soap bubbles, but if your intention is strong, they can become very concrete. Many artists use dreams to furnish ideas for inspiration and create a work of art which serves as a metaphor for their ongoing stages of personal growth. Pay attention to the associations and synchronicities between your waking and sleeping selves. Most of us have far more precognitive dreams than we know, if we would only notice them in a systematic way.

Guided Visualization

Imagine you are wandering down the Tarot path between the two towers. At the edge of one sits an old beggar woman who holds out a cup. After you drop her a coin, she points forward, motioning you onward. Once on the other side, the landscape has changed. You no longer see the familiar fields of earth; you are on the verge of a vast unknown landscape with silver sands flecked with white crystal that dance in swirling rainbows in the winds. There is a vivid crimson mountain on the horizon. Then, as you walk, the very ground beneath you appears to change; the silver-white desert sands instantly become a lush jungle floor. The smell of vegetation springing up around you fills your nostrils with its intensity. Wild beasts crouch on the edge of your vision, slinking away as you approach. Off to the right you notice a small clan of cave-dwellers roasting a piece of meat over an open fire. Reptilian creatures you can't identify slither across your feet, and you realize that you are witnessing a scene from the dawn of humankind. As soon as this thought crosses your mind, the scene instantly changes again, and you are standing in a circle of large, round, and very tall stones.

The Moon is just breaking over the edge of the tallest one, and on the outside of the circle it is pitch black, which seems strange, because the inner circle is flooded with moonlight. As you marvel at the silver light cast into this magical space, you have a deep intuitive sense of what "moon-stones" are: vehicles for trapping energy during specific times for psychic opening.

Then you are instantly transported to a courtyard, this time not with wild, lush vegetation, but with perfectly terraced gardens adorned with varieties of flowers and birds you have never seen. You are on a path again, and soon you approach a couple dressed as if they are in a Shakesperean play, embracing closely, oblivious to your voyeur eyes. There is a crystal clear lake in the background upon which floats a stately white swan.

Suddenly, at the edge of this glorious garden of Aphrodite, you see looming before you the velvet red mountain which earlier had seemed so far away. You approach this jeweled stone structure, which seems to resemble a tower of crimson, in stark contrast to the rich green you just left behind in the lush courtyard. As you enter its

72

long shadow, you immediately perceive that you are transported up without the task of climbing. Once at the top, the scarlet and violet colors seems to fold into a huge wall of flashing copper. It looks like an enormous mirror, reflecting the world below. You spy a small door in this wall, over which hangs an icon of a copper angel with the name "Haniel" printed at its feet. You enter a small door and behold the most beautiful woman your eyes have ever witnessed; the purple eyes which fall back upon you hold you in an embrace you can hardly endure. She has a large luminescent pearl at her throat.

You are suddenly aware of flashes of small streaks of lightning jumping from her fingertips. She waves her arm at you and behold, a burst of fireworks envelops you, disappearing into your skin like cool kisses. For a second you wonder if this is how love is made in this mysterious and sacred place, and at this thought you are beckoned to the crest of her Rose Mountain and behold, under her outstretched arms is the world you left behind.

Amazingly, all times, all places seem to unfold in a single universal experience, and the thing that astounds you the most is that it is all happening *in response to the sparks which fall from the hands of the Lady.* They rain down upon the world below in an endless display of Love in the act of Creating. This obviously fills her with delight, as you comprehend that this is, indeed, how she makes her love. Such a profound vision stirs you deeply.

You leave with gratitude that such an act of creative exuberance has been shown to you, and as you stroll back through her magical garden you hear a voice distinctly speaking from somewhere inside your head. It says you must learn to build your own dreams and aspirations so strongly into your own flesh and blood that they ooze out of your body to become concrete in the world. You think on these things and, on your way back through the towers, old Hecate is there with her faithful dog and a smile of farewell.

Affirmations

1. *I kindle my spirit with the red flame of desire to evoke my evolving creativity.*

2. *Although my Personality may go through fluctuations, I am the Self that never changes.*

3. *I am a New Creature, growing a body of health and beneficence.*

4. *The God of Strength is reigning in my mind.*

5. *The Goddess of Love is reigning in my heart.*

Ts Tz Cz   THE STAR   צ

Path 28
The Natural Intelligence

Revelation   *Sign: Aquarius*

The 28th Path, Tzaddi
The Star
The Natural Intelligence

Tzaddi is called the "Natural Intelligence" because "by it is completed and perfected the *nature* of all that exists beneath the Sun." When we speak of something being natural, we often mean to distinguish it from something which is not. The lesson in this Path is that there is no such distinction; everything is natural, even that which we presently call supernatural, if we had the eyes to see. What once appeared fantastic, such as flying metal objects, or boxes that speak to us from our living rooms, are now perfectly normal, albeit they may still appear to be "magic" to very primitive peoples. Esoteric philosophy teaches that through a natural process of evolution, which is part of our divine heritage, we will continue to uncover the "secrets" of the present unknown and of nature, and supernatural events will cease to belong to the "super" realm because we will have entered into an understanding of *how their laws work*.

The word "tzaddi" means "fishhook." The connection with the paths of Nun (fish) and Mem (water) begins to unfold through meditation. Meditation is the mode of consciousness attributed to this Path, which links Netzach, frequently associated with the "raw forces of nature," with the intuition of Yesod. The Natural Intelligence is connected to the idea of meditation by the Hebrew root "TBO," which means "to sink down" or "to be laid deep,"an obvious reference to the fishhook. The adjective "natural" is also from this root (TBOI). This hints at the power of Tzaddi, which is arrived at by meditating on the qualities of nature.

The fishhook symbolizes the agency whereby one investigates the unseen, and also the patience required while "fishing for truth" in the depths of the psyche. The number for Tzaddi is 90, and early adepts who developed the Tarot keys drew the naked "water-bearer" (the symbol of Aquarius) with her leg at a 90-degree angle resting on the surface of the water. Ninety is also the numerical value for a Hebrew word (DVMM) which means "a great silence" as well as the letter-name *maim*, which means "water."

The process of meditation is symbolized by the flow of water from the vessels, in the same sense that meditation is described in Raja Yoga as an unbroken flow of knowledge on a particular object or idea. In the Christian context, this is known as "centering prayer." For a Qabalist, it is focusing on the symbols involved with a particular path or Sephira until one stumbles, as it were, on the Silent Source of all the seed-thoughts constellating around it.

In *The Book of Tokens* it is said of this Intelligence, "The Hook and the Gate and the Right Hand am I," indicating that it is Tzaddi, the *hook*, which draws us forth "from the death of error into the light of truth," as well as the *gate* and the outstretched *hand* to guide us through the portal. This is implicit in the *very spelling* of the word Tzaddi (TzDI), which consists of the letters that mean, in order, "hook," "gate" (the Daleth or *D*), and "hand" (the Yod or *I*).

The idea of meditation is generally considered to be a process of "unveiling," and the female figure is unclothed because she is the archetypal "Isis Unveiled," the Great Mother who also appears to us in the keys of the Empress, the High Priestess, and the Universe. But only here she appears in her *natural* radiant glory. To catch a glimpse of such a One was the sole objective of Actaeon in the powerful myth wherein he was willing to endure total disintegration to view the naked body of Artemis for a brief second. Mythological motifs and esoteric wisdom both tell us that seldom is the personality able to approach the divine unveiled. On this Path, she is described in *The Thirty-two Paths of Wisdom* as being in the process of making perfect everything *under the Sun*, a reference to Tiphareth, her Son-Sun. Waite says she is the Supernal Mother, Binah, the sphere of absolute Understanding, who communicates to her children below "in the measure that they can receive her influx" (Waite, 1910, p.139).

Meditation is the process wherein we participate in this dimension of understanding and, through it, we discover that a pattern can be discerned in the events of earthly existence which corresponds to a heavenly order. In this context, this Path relates directly to the often-quoted alchemical maxim, "As above, so below: grasp this and rejoice!" The Master Jesus reminded us numerous times that the kingdom of heaven is here, now, and within.

According to universal religious teachings, whenever we enter into a deep state of contemplation, we are sharing in a exercise continually offered by the Divine Power which creates everything. When we actually perceive this fact, we enter into a profound realization that it is not really the personal ego which is meditating; rather it is *we who are being meditated.* The great joy of this Path is the fleeting recognition we have of the continual meditation of the Life-power on Its own nature.

The Star is an apt symbol for the Eternally-abiding Higher Self which seeks, like the attentive water-bearer, to bring the personality of the ego into at-one-ment with the flow of life and nature. Such a stabilizing image of wholeness is frequently identified as a Jungian symbol of individuation, as well as the priceless alchemical philosopher's gold. Alchemical texts often picture a fixed star around which rotate seven smaller stars, similar to the Tarot key on this Path.

The image of the Star symbolizes enlightenment, or the fruit of the Great Work, while the stars circling around it represent the seven planets or planetary metals which the alchemists are seeking to renew. In the alchemical art, the idea is to "free the spirit" of the metal, uniting it with its golden essence. To one who practices the fine art of individuation, the process involves freeing the spirit of archetypal elements in the psyche, thus making them more conscious. For those practicing yoga or a similar system of focus on the body's internal energy system, they represent the seven chakras. The exercise explained in Chapter 2 is valuable for a student on this Path; that is, to locate the corresponding Path keys ruled by these seven circling planets and identify them with his or her own chakra system. Case indicates that using them as images for concentration will arouse the activity of the corresponding chakra centers naturally.

The vessels hint at another alchemical as well as psychological process—the seperation and reintegration of the primal forces that need to be dealt with on this Path. On one level, Netzach represents desires and feelings, and the Path of the Star seeks to balance these with the intuition and instincts of Yesod. Crowley states that it is in this Path that "the Universe is resolved into its ultimate elements" (Crowley, 1974, p. 109). Such a resolution makes the star the "Light-bearer," which is a title frequently attributed to Venus, the planet of love with its astrological association to Netzach.

The mythological figure of Isis-Urania has one foot resting on the water, similar to the angel on the 25th Path (Temperance). The water appears to be "fixed" or solid, not volatile or fluid. Paul Case refers to meditation as the alchemical process called "fixation of the volatile." If something is volatile, it is transitory, characterized by rapid change and difficult to capture or hold permanently, much like the ever-racing mind. Thus the picture hints at how the mind is made fixed through the meditative process.

The vessel flows out in five streams representing the purification and perfection of the five senses, as the water goes back to the pool, the source from which it came. This Path signifies the concrete manifestation of the laws represented by the 21st Path, the Wheel of Ezekiel (which also has a symbol of the Aquarian water-bearer), indicating cyclic return.

In the background is an ibis, a fishing bird, identified by the Egyptians as Thoth and by the Greeks as Hermes or Mercury. This is the archetype representing the "messenger" from heaven, also the interpreter or mediator. He epitomizes the spoken work and in astrology is characterized as intellectual energy. In Qabalistic analogy, he is attributed to the Magician, Path 12, which represents *conscious attention*.

The challenge of the aspirant on this Path is patience in fishing for the spiritual light in the murky waters of the individual psyche. The symbols of Tzaddi and Nun together form a powerful vehicle for concentrating the mind and balancing the energies of primal intuition, feeling, and the Higher Ego. It is this Logos residing in the Christos-center of Tiphareth, symbolized by the fish (Nun) of regeneration that is caught by the steady hook of transmuted devotion.

28th Pathworking Correspondences

1. Intelligence: Natural

2. Divine Letter: Tzaddi, TZI (pronounced Zah-di) Value: 90, as final: 900, means "fishhook"

3. Divine Names: Yahu, IHVH Tzabaoth (Yod-Heh-Vaw-Heh Tzaa-ba-oot)

4. Incense: Galbanum. Red Sandalwood

5. Gems: Chalcedony, crystal, also glass or mirrors

6. Color: Violet

7. Element: Air

8. Animals: Peacock, eagle, ibis

9. Plants: Olive, coconut

10. Planet: Uranus, Saturn

11. Musical Tone: B flat

12. Magical Phenomenon: Astrology, feelings of levitation, deep meditations

13. Magical Weapon: Censor

14. Mythos and Related Symbols: Juno, Athena, Aphrodite, Isis-Urania, the Water-bearer, a winged angel, water nymphs, mermaids, the man-eagle, the sistrum, the vessel, the Star

15. Gift or Challenge: Patience; the grace of deep contemplation, the ability to develop harmony in environment

16. Rules: Ankles, the circulation

17. Tarot Arcana: The Star

Suggested Exercises

This is a good key to use to improve your power of concentration and meditation. There are meditation techniques that abound in metaphysical and occult literature today, but perhaps one of the simplest and most profound is simply watching the breath. The more one focuses on the breath as a method of concentration while in silent meditation, the more one learns to use it as a focus throughout daily activities. If you have a hard time concentrating with closed eyes, stare at the Tarot key.

Contemplate it when you are seeking an answer to something. Bait the hook of your concentration and cast it into the still deep waters and be attentive with it there. Be specific in your need, in your questioning, or in your desire. Don't simply let your mind go blank or wander into some nowhere land. Bring your attention back to your question by staring at the key. Or devise a similar star symbol in your room to represent the *fixing* of your attention on your problem or need.

When one is fishing, one must angle for the fish. To angle correctly is an artful means of obtaining an objective. Working with the chakras by the method of the "Tarot ladder" (Chapter 2) is a way of mental angling. Another is following a sequence of prayer–meditations in such a way as to lead the mind toward a specific desired state.

It is said in the Western Esoteric schools that five minutes of concentrated attention is worth more than hours of meditation if the mind is not made fixed. It is difficult (for a Western mind, at least) to remain attentive or fixed if one seeks to "empty the mind." Our Western minds are developed in such a way as to continually need external stimulus, and frequently Eastern systems of meditation may not work as well for us as they do for those who created them and for whom they were devised.

If you can spend 3 to 5 concentrated minutes with this key, you will have accomplished much. If necessary, use one of the affirmations and try repeating it with focused attention for one full minute, then move on to another. After clearly baiting the hook with your problem or question, focusing on the clear knowledge that the universe has all answers and therefore must have one for you, remain patient, as one who fishes must learn to do.

A fish will not bite a hook that is constantly jiggling. When you feel your mind wandering, create a definite closure to the "problem-solving ritual" you have created. Keep paper and pencil handy for flashes of insight, which will definitely come, probably when you least suspect it. Pay attention to your dreams.

Guided Visualization

Imagine you are exploring a foreign land, walking contentedly down a sparse, thin path, the edges of which are adorned with an occasional olive tree. You sense the smell of salty waters in the air and you wonder if you will soon reach the sea. It is almost dusk and, since you don't know where you are and since the trail seems to die out, you question whether you should venture yet forward. Ahead lie some coconut trees, however, and so you press onward, following your intuition and a brilliant peacock which has just emerged from within the grove of trees. It seems to want you to follow it; in fact, it occasionally pauses, as if to let you catch up, then scurries onward again. In the golden twilight, it flashes its rainbow feathers, dazzling your eyes and encouraging you forward.

On the other side of a row of coconut palms is a large lake; several fishermen sit quietly by its side with poles sunk in the water. Others are in a cresent-shaped boat with their nets stretched over the still surface. A small fishing bird is strutting on the sandy beach looking for remnants of food. You inquire from a fisherman what body of water this is, and he replies, "This is the Live Sea, but once it was Dead."

Since it does not look like a sea—you can see the far shore—you are uncertain about his curious statement, but it seems so serene and beautiful here, you sit for a while and rest. The vestiges of the setting Sun have cast a golden glow over everything, and the air itself seems to be heavily cast in a deep sparkling mist.

Suddenly you spy what looks like a mermaid swimming toward you. She has a warm smile as she approaches. Amazed, you watch as the recognition dawns upon you that, indeed, this is a kind of water nymph. She pulls herself up to rest on a rock beside you and you breathe the sweet, intoxicating scent of sand mixed with salt which radiates from her, seeming to dull your senses and dim your sight. The stars are just popping out and you are not sure what to do. Is this magical maiden a mythical dream, a stretch of your imagination. She tells you her name is Echo and that she has brought you a gift from the depths. You must, however, focus on the water, not on her. "I am only a distraction," she laughs.

Daylight is gone now and the stars are reflected on the face of the

84

still, dark lake that the fishers insist is a sea. You seem to become mesmerized as your gaze is caught by the flashing stars in the water. The rest of the world seems simply to evaporate. Suddenly, you hear the faint jingling of bells and at the same time one of the stars actually rises from the surface of the water and glows brilliantly before you. It is so blinding, you avert your eyes, but then it seems to soften and take the shape of a magnificent man with the face of an eagle and the wings of an angel.

In awe you stare as it changes again into another mysterious kind of being, a woman with the body of a cow and the face of a goddess. Her body is laden with the teats of a nurturing mother, heavy with milk, and in her hair is a garland of flowers. She announces to you that she is mistress of music and sovereign of song and, in some miraculous kind of way, her numerous cow-teats open and spray a jet of intoxicating joy which pours over and through your body in a lavash spray of light and sound. Your senses merge as you drink in her milk with ecstasy.

It could be a second or an eternity later, but at some point your mind returns, stunned, to an empty night with only one bright star shining through the clouds. You are alone, save for a single fisher sitting with determination further down the shore. You walk toward him, dazed, and with no sense of time or direction. As you approach, you notice he has two fishes laying on the sandy shore beside him. He seems to radiate a deep kindness, and you decide to ask him the way toward the path which brought you here.

"Good catch," you mention, as you glance at his two small fishes.

"This is the Sea of Life," he answers, "from which one draws all that one needs, if one is not greedy. With these two fish alone, I will feed five thousand tomorrow."

You know in the depth of your heart that this stranger speaks the truth, for the miracle of the Sky-goddess is still alive and singing in your soul. He smiles again and, before you ask, he points toward the path from which you came. You wander back with a tune ringing in your heart and a rich sense of mystery, hungry to find someone with whom you can share your song.

Affirmations

1. *Nature is the result of the Eternal Spirit meditating in me.*

2. *The Divine Mother unveils all her mystery to the one who ponders her deeply.*

3. *I am moving to the degree of ripeness wherein I realize that Life power is conscious energy.*

4. *Universal wisdom solves problems through attention.*

5. *I feel that my own intent is pure and clear enough right now that I need to be given the means to fulfill it.*

6. *Every person I see is a star.*

| P PhF | THE TOWER | |

Path 27
The Exciting Intelligence

Awakening   *Planet: Mars*

CHAPTER SEVEN

The 27th Path, Peh
The Tower
The Exciting Intelligence

The 27th Path is called the Active or Exciting Intelligence because "through it is consummated and perfected the nature of every existent being ..." The Tarot key certainly looks exciting, albeit, at first glance, somewhat ominous. The Intelligence itself means "to be tumultuous." Exoteric interpretations of the card generally are somewhat pessimistic, offering at best words such as "upheavel" or "transformation." As usual, when we dive into the deeper esoteric meanings of the Path through Qabalah, new vistas unfold.

The letter "Peh" means "mouth"; in this case, the mouth of God. In the first chapter of the *Sepher Yetzirah* is the verse: "The Ten ineffable Sephiroth have the appearance of the Lightning flash, their origin is unseen and no end is perceived. The Word is in them as they rush forth and as they return, they speak as if from a whirlwind ..." (S.Y. 1:6). In Qabalah, this is called the Path of the Flaming Sword and is symbolized by the glyph of the Tree with the lightning flash proceeding from Kether through each Sephira in numerical succession. This is, in fact, how the Sephiroth are created, or manifested in a perceivable way.

In the same way, we are created and sustained; i.e., by the Word or Primal Vibration of the Original God-energy. For we do not live by bread alone, but by every word that proceeds out of the mouth (Peh) of IHVH" (Deuteronomy 8:3). In the Gospel of Thomas, Jesus said, "He who will drink from *My mouth* will become like Me. I

89

myself shall become he, and the things that are hidden will be revealed to him" *(Nag Hammadi, 1977, The Gospel of Thomas, v. 108; italics mine).*

In the Psalms, wherein all the 22 Intelligences or Letters praise God, Peh declares, "The revelation of your words sheds light, giving understanding to the simple. I gasp with open mouth, in my yearning for your commands" (Ps. 119:130).

Peh is the Power of Utterance, and in occult philosophy one imitates this divine power of the Word literally, by the correct vibration or intonation of the God-Names. In the Tarot key the lightning flash is the power of this Logos/Word in the process of manifesting. One of its titles is "Fire of Heaven." It begins at Kether, symbolized by the crown, and proceeds to ignite everything simultaneously by its flash. Dropping from it are 22 flames to represent the 22 Paths or Hebrew letters, which are the elements wherein the primal Word makes itself known. The letter Peh is itself the mouth or organ of speech whereby this Active Intelligence causes the Life power to manifest. All energy, in occult theory, is this continual utterance of the Word of Life.

In the *Sepher Yetzirah* this idea of the cosmic activity bound by the Creative Word is expressed by the phrase, "His word is in them when they rush out" (S.Y.1:6). This rushing out could be compared to the primordial explosion of the "cosmic egg" at the time of the Big Bang. We therefore see seeming destruction and chaos in the Tarot key. The "whirlwind" is actually the flashing light and sound at the same time; and lightning itself is really a whirling spiral motion, which Case predicted would be shown by science to be "double, consisting of an outgoing and a returning current" (Case, 1985, p. 202). Thus we have the image of the going out and in, mentioned in the *Sepher Yetzirah,* a theme also common to the eastern traditions, wherein the creation of the universes is compared to the exhalation and inhalation of Brahma.

To the aspirant on the 27th Path, Peh is a profound symbol of the power of speech and the *manifestation* of creative thought through the spoken word. As a vehicle for creative expression of the life principle, we are a microcosm of this intense Initial Cosmic Event. As soon as we *realize* this and integrate it on a deep level, so that subconsciousness is impressed with the truth behind the assumption, "As above, so below," we reflect this macrocosmic principle through the virtue of *Peh.* It is on this concept that all metaphysical principles concerning the efficacy of affirmation are based.

Why does the Tarot key seem to signify destruction? Esoteric teaching tells us that all action is disintegrative. The Active Intelligence began the world by a process of disintegration. The process by which human life begins is essentially the same: the male sperm penetrates the female cell and begins a process of division in the ovum. Power is released by disintegration, as is demonstrated repeatedly in nature; whenever one type of form appears, another disappears.

In *The Book of Tokens*, therefore, the commentary on the letter Peh is that "destruction is the foundation of existence," but that the tearing down is a necessary prerequisite for a "grander structure" (Case, 1934, p. 156). Gematria tells us that there is an intimate relationship between the words "yesod" (ISVD), or "foundation," and "union" or "assembling" (VOD), both of which add up to 80, the same as the numerical value of Peh. The process of cell division is the beginning of life and this process takes place in the sphere on the Tree known as the Foundation, to which are attributed the reproductive organs of the Heavenly Being. It is in the *union* of the male and female principles that the *foundation* of life as we know it is established, thus releasing the power of the creative word, Peh, which is continually made flesh as long as consciousness is attached to matter. This is a universal principle. The other link by numerical association in this regard is the Hebrew word *kilil* (KLL), which means "universal," "general," "total" or "complete," and also adds up to 80.

The lesson on this Path is the letting go of old forms so new ones can indeed appear. Peh joins Netzach to Hod, pure feeling to pure intellect. It is a precarious balance, one of three Paths going horizontally across the Tree. It is ruled by Mars, said to be the god (or planet) of destruction, which relates it to the Sphere Geburah and strength or severity. It is called the "House of God" or "Lord of the Hosts of the Mighty" (Elohim Gibor Tzabaoth).

In gematria these ideas are linked because the House of God (Beth ha-Elohim) adds up to 503, also the numerical value of the Hebrew word *garash* (GRS), which means "to cast out," "to thrust," or "to empty," which is the responsibility of the Hosts of the Mighty and which is also figured in the Tarot key. When old structures need tearing down, it is the responsibility of the Exciting Intelligence to send in its hosts to awaken us to new forms. The lightning flash is the symbol of our initial flashes of enlightenment.

We learn that to reach any goal we must first break down existing conditions which keep us from going towards it. We understand that the Mars force is not only a force which destroys old forms, but is the propulsive energy which drives us into action by continued concentration. Mars was not just a god of war; it was to Mars that the Roman farmer appealed for the fertility and prosperity of his crops.

An important feature on this Path is that, as it crosses the small abyss beneath Tiphareth going horizontally, it intersects the Path of Samekh, going vertically, in a perfect cross. At this balanced juncture, one is surrounded by Sephiroth on all four sides—by Tiphareth, the Son, on top; by Yesod, the Foundation, on the bottom; and by Hod and Netzach on either side. If there is confusion, or a hint of fear or peril associated with the 27th Path, this Cross of Light is an apt symbol on which to meditate for assistance. There is a Qabalistic ritual wherein the Christian sign of the cross is visualized as *light* intersecting within one's body (see end of chapter).

The cross is a universal symbol for integration and synthesis as well as for relationship In the pathworkings given by some occultists, the 27th Path is said to be worked with the thought of joining forces together, as in a partnership, or to alleviate quarrels in a relationship. It is a Path of triumph as it generally proceeds from Hod to Netzach, or Victory.

In the path of Tav, it is noted that the seven double letters point out the seven localities to which are assigned the planets of the ancients. The *Sepher Yetzirah* tells us that Peh is North (S.Y. 4:2), which is the place of the greatest symbolic darkness because legend states that the Sun never shone on the north side of Solomon's temple.

However, in Job we read that the splendor surrounding the majesty of IHVH comes from the north (Job 38:22). This is a hint to us that enlightenment may come from the deepest recesses of the soul, and the trials of Job, indeed, seem like a testimony to this. Likewise are the trials of the alchemist, who labors long with the dark matter (*nigredo*) before the light begins to emerge from it.

In examining the alchemical works of Thomas Aquinas, Marie von Franz notes that, in the fourth parable (on philosophic faith), the nigredo is called the "black earth," which, when purified by fire, is exalted, for "he exalteth the lowly, when he bringeth to the surface the soul deep and hidden in the bowels of the earth" (1966, p. 95). In Jungian terms this is an obvious reference to the shadow elements of the psyche. The nigredo is said by alchemists to come from the north, which is also the direction attributed to the earth in Qabalistic symbolism. In medieval number symbolism, earth is coordinated with the four elements, again symbolized by the cross. In alchemy, this is how the dense is separated from the subtle, for "earth is liquified and turned into water, water is liquified and turned into air, air is liquified and turned into fire, fire is liquified and turned into *glorified earth*" (1966, p. 93).

Although this may not be a Path of deliverance from oppression in the material world, it does signify redemption in the sense that one has the opportunity for freedom from old faults, vices, beliefs, and structures that kept one imprisoned in the past. The psychology of the unconscious has brought to our attention the fact that we have a built-in inner stability or compensatory element which seems to remove destructive elements within the psyche, one way or another, either through healing or wounding.

One of our responsibilities on this Path is to recognize this potential for renewal through suffering. Perhaps most important, it is a reminder to use with caution and creativity that great power known only to humankind: the spoken word.

27th Pathworking Correspondences

1. Intelligence: Exciting or Activating

2. Divine Letter: Peh, PH (pronounced Pay) Value: 80, as final: 800, means "mouth"

3. Divine Name: Elohim Gibor (E-lo-heem Gi-boor). IHVH Tzabaoth (Yod-Heh-Vaw-Heh Tzaa-ba-ooth)

4. Incense: Dragon's blood resin, capsium. Benzoin

5. Gems: Ruby, garnet, jasper, loadstone

6. Color: Scarlet

7. Element: Fire

8. Animals: Bear, wolf, horse

9. Plants: Absinth, rue

10. Planet: Mars

11. Musical Tone: C

12. Magical Power: Balance during transformations

13. Magical Weapon: Double-edged sword

14. Mythos and Related Symbols: Mars, Horus, Mentu, Path of Flaming Sword, fire, mouth, pentagram, lightning, furies, chimeras, towers

15. Gift or Challenge: To use words properly; to abandon structures that don't work; to weigh tension creatively

16. Rules: Muscular system

17. Tarot Arcana: Tower

Suggested Exercises

Focus on this Tarot key when you are feeling like your personality is becoming hardened, rigid, or resistant to change. Visualize yourself smashing the tower of self-created thoughts which keep you separated from someone you love. You can even act this out by building a tower of blocks, cards, books, or anything else and tearing it down with a powerful affirmation. Be sure what you are knocking down is your own faulty perceptions and not your projection of another person's faults. Use this key to overcome superstitions, rigid emotional patterns, structured ruts in your thinking, etc.

Visualize the letter Peh while you chant it or while you vibrate one of the God-names. Vibrating words of power is a profound technique that can be felt in the body in a way which one can only experience for one's self. Through continued practice, the Creative Word begins to reveal itself in our mouths and in our hearts.

Here is the exercise of the Qabalistic Cross:

Touch the forehead and say "ATOH" (Thou art).

Bring the hand down to the breast or heart area and say "MALKUTH" (the Kingdom).

Touch the right shoulder and say "VE-GEVURAH" (and the Power).

Touch the left shoulder and say "VE-GEDULAH" (and the Glory).

Clasp the hands together at the breast and say, "LE-OLAHM AMEN" (forever, Amen).

As this is being spoken the angels can be visualized in their respective quarters, and an attempt should be made to consciously *see* light intersecting inside the body with the motion of the hand and the intonation of the Hebrew prayer. The more one practices, the more powerful this technique becomes, building a strong protective aura around the etheric and physical bodies.

Guided Visualization

You have decided to trod the path toward Absolute Victory through Truth and you realize that it is not an easy one. At the onset you seek a guide, and in deep contemplation the archangel Michael appears to you in red and golden robes, surrounded by flames of orange tinged with green. Together you set off. At the beginning he tells you, "Think how tiny the spark is which sets a huge forest ablaze. The tongue is like such a flame. Blessing and curse alike can come out of the same mouth. The flames of the tongue encircle your course from birth. Every form of life, four-footed or winged, crawling or swimming, can be tamed by humans; the tongue is more difficult to train. Therefore, guard it carefully, and if you must speak in time of distress, say this word only—and say it only once."

And as he reveals to you the secret word of power, he presses into your hand a small red rock, which he says is the dried blood of a dragon.

As you walk along, you notice that the path zig-zags; as Michael walks before you small flames drip from his feet and catch parts of the trail on fire. Suddenly, you realize that this is truly the path of the flaming sword, and at this very thought clouds gather densely around you and flashes of lightning begin to dance in the sky.

Soon you come to a dank, bloody-looking river; the stench is overwhelming and fumes exude from the water, which itself appears to be in flames in certain places. Because Michael has both fire and water built into his very nature, he walks mildly across, neither sinking nor getting burned. Fear suddenly grips you as you see him moving ahead without even glancing back to take notice. You want to cry out in panic, anger, and frustration, but something makes you catch your tongue. Surely there is an answer to this dilemma . . .? Perhaps you can just trust that you too can walk across.

No sooner does your foot touch the burning waters, however, than you feel your spirits as well as your body sink. Quickly you retreat. Determined now to call back your guide, you search fervently ahead for a sign of him, but, aghast, you discover he has disappeared. With a fierce suddenness which startles you and throws you into an even deeper panic, a monster from this fiery depth plunges upward, with eyes like burning volcanoes and a huge gaping mouth vomiting flames. Slimy green scales cover its body, which sizzles as it sinks again into the foul waters. Again he rushes up and roars out at you that he will let you pass only if you solve the riddle of evil in the world and explain it to him.

Suddenly, your mind is racing. Why do innocent people suffer? Why do evil persons prosper? Why doesn't God do anything? Why doesn't someone help you right now? Rage, fear, and anger burn inside you and you want to scream your confusion and outrage to the winds. Frustrated and frightened, you turn to retreat—only to gaze with horrified eyes at a fierce wolf, apparently half-starved and half-crazed, plunging hungrily toward you. Immediately you call upon your word of power and the wolf bursts into flames, fire rushing from his sinews, his bones turning quickly to embers, his hair into rays of light, and whirlwind, thunder, and lightning surrounding him. He has suddenly become transformed into another angelic figure with a sword at his hip; he announces that his name is Haniel. He tells you that all your fears and miseries have been thrown into the flame of his compassion and mercy like a twig thrown into a fire. Gently, he enfolds you in his soft velvet wing and you feel a deep graditude and peace. He tells you to throw the dragon's blood into the river but first to take a small bite of it into your mouth.

You do so and watch, amazed, as the river of fire disappears, only to be replaced by a garden of lush vegetation and radiant color. Sitting in the midst of this enchanted fairyland is a maiden draped in a soft green gown trimmed with sapphires and emeralds. She looks briefly up to notice you and says, "Tragedy is purification through terror and pity. Let its seed germinate in you and you too will become an angel of compassion." Then she vanishes into the green world of nature which surrounds her.

Bewildered, you sit down beneath a large elder tree and ponder her words. Slowly you feel the bite which you have ingested begin to stir with a gentle heat deep inside your belly. It seems to rise and bathe the area around your heart, and then you realize that, through it, a transformation has taken place—some new quality has been integrated. You begin to feel that, from this moment on, whenever old feelings of fear, anger, or despair begin to attack or plague you, you can access this feeling of warmth, understanding, and love from this seed. By evoking this feeling, you you will be able to take the necessary actions to act with renewed strength. The seed of fire is like a crystal through which a ray of truth passes through you and into the world.

As you rise with a renewed sense of hope about the fragile beauty of this gift called life, Haniel slips his hand into yours to guide you safely home.

What would it be like for you to take a bite of the hardened dragon's blood? How would it feel in your body? What would it mean to your soul? What is your "power word"? How can you use it?

Affirmations

1. *No form separates one Portion of the God-ness energy from another.*

2. *I am an unbroken thread, linking past to future and passing through changes unchanged.*

3. *Today I break down all structures of error and false knowledge of separation I have built up in my mind by wrong thinking.*

4. *The Reality manifesting in one point in space is the same as the Reality manifesting at all points in space.*

5. *The light flashes in a world of darkness, but the darkness does not swallow it up.*

6. *I am the mouth that breathes the Word of God.*

O THE ADVERSARY

Path 26
The Renewing Intelligence

Mirth   *Sign: Capricorn*

CHAPTER EIGHT

The 26th Path, Ayin
The Deceiver
The Renewing Intelligence

The letter Ayin means "eye," and the 26th Path relates directly to the function of the eye, because the Hebrew word which means "vision," "appearance," or "revelation" (ChZVH) also adds up to 26. This word is also translated as *covenant* and is from the root *Chavvah* (ChVH), which means "Eve," or "first woman," also translated as "life" or "mother of all the living." Twenty-six is also the numeration of the Divine Name IHVH.

On the Tree, the Mother of all the Sephiroth is Binah, the third sphere, or the Holy Ghost in the Christian Trinity. To her is attributed the planet Saturn, and the symbol of this planet also appears in the right hand of the horned goat figure hovering over the "first couple" in the Tarot key. To the letter Ayin is attributed Capricorn, whose symbol is the goat and whose ruler is Saturn.

The position of this Path on the Tree is between Hod, the sphere of Splendor or the Divine Mind, and Tiphareth, the Christos-sphere and the center and pivot of the entire Tree. On a path of evolution, we proceed from the sphere of the intellect to the seat of the Divine Imagination and Beauty, centered in the Heart. In a process of involution, or descent, however, the Path goes the other way; from the Logos, which the Christian Gnostics identified as Christ, "all things came into being" (John 1:3). We notice that this Path of descent follows directly from the one above it proceeding from the Divine Mother, Binah, through the archetypal first couple again, Zain, the Lovers.

The 26th Path is called the "Renewing Intelligence" because the

Holy God renews by it all the changing things which are renewed by the creation of the world" *(The Thirty-two Paths of Wisdom)*. Another translation (Waite, 1960) of this Intelligence is that it "reneweth all which is *capable* of renovation in the creation of the world" (my italics). The subtle nuance in the latter rendition is interesting. It seems to imply that we must make ourselves receptive if we are to be renewed.

The number of this Intelligence (MChVDSh) is 358, from the root word, ChVDSh, "to renew," "to be fresh," "to erect anew." Qabalists frequently note that this is the same numeration as that of "messiach" (MShICh), or the Messiah. The word NChSh, which is also 358, means "omen," "to divine," or "to foretell," as well as "the constellation of the dragon or serpent." The image of the serpent biting its own tail is a symbol of infinity; i.e., Saturn or Father Time consuming itself endlessly. In the *Sepher Yetzirah,* the Celestial Dragon is placed over the universe "like a king upon the throne" (S.Y.6:2), and refers to the Primal Energy that sustains creation. In classical Jungian terminology, the dragon or serpent is the mother image, mirroring the maternal principle of the unconscious, an unknowable mysterious womb. The serpent itself is an archetypal symbol of renewal; from early times it has been noted that it has the unique ability of sloughing its old skin and growing a new one.

The serpent and dragon symbols were sacred to the matriarchal traditions for many thousands of years and signified wisdom and secret knowledge. In the east, it is still a numinous symbol of the Kundalini forces which reside at the bottom of the spine, to be awakened in deep meditation. Those who have experienced a Kundalini awakening report that it is usually felt as a hot, fiery sensation in the rear of the spine or back. In the Tarot key we see that the flame in the goat's hand which reaches downward to the earth is almost connected to the "tail" of the Adam figure, which rises, flame-like, to meet it.

Ayin, it is said, hides many mysteries, and the association in gematria for this is that the letter Ayin and the word for "secret" (SVD) both equal the number 70. All of the preceeding seed-thoughts connected by Qabalistic gematria can be ponderous to decipher, and although many explanations have been given concerning this key, much must be left to the individual to reflect for him or herself. Suffice to say, the Christian connotation of the horned-goat is the Devil or Deceiver, and this card is indeed named that. But esoteric philosophy will have us reach beyond the *appearance* (we recall this is ChZVH, 26) of things, to question the very nature of thought which, however subtle, intriguing, and vital, perverts the wholeness of that which lies just beyond it.

The eye, as the organ of sight, sees the surface or appearance of things. It cannot see inside the human body, for instance; it cannot see inside the molecular structure of anything without the aid of special instruments. Through the function of the eye, we are made aware of the phenomenon of this remarkable universe. This material world is called in the East *Maya*, Illusion or Deception. It is considered to be a dream from which we will someday awaken. Western esoteric theory sees it slightly differently. According to Qabalah, the world of appearances is not in itself a world of deception; rather illusions arise from our own perception, from our own tendency to take things at *face value*, to look *at* them instead of *into* them.

Looking into the nature of things is how we attempt to discern their hidden meaning. "Things are hidden only to be revealed," Jesus said (Mark 4:22), and our responsibility as we walk this Path is to attempt to uncover the veil behind the appearances, using our lamp of wisdom. Jesus also said that "the *eye* is the lamp of your body" (Luke 11:34), and it is this very vehicle which *deceives* us so easily that we must use it to adjust our vision. In this way, we *see things afresh.* (i.e., MChVDSh, 358) and are renewed.

The *Sepher Yetzirah* tells us the story of what happened when Abraham was first able to pierce the veil and *see*:

> And after that our father Abraham had perceived, and understood, and had taken down and engraved all these things, the Lord most high revealed Himself, and called him His beloved, and made a covenant with him ...
>
> —*Sepher Yetzirah* 6:4

The esoteric title of Ayin is "Lord of the Gates of Matter" (which is frequently associated with the concept of the devil, when it is used in contradistinction to *spirit)* and also "Child of the Forces of Time." Waite has said it is the "Dweller on the Threshold" (1959). These images all refer us back to the Capricorn-goat of the devil card and its ruler, Saturn. As Binah, Saturn creates all of the worlds. As Time, Saturn sustains the creatures who people these worlds. But Saturn also eats its children, meaning that, while the creation of form is necessary for manifestation, eventually all appearances dissolve, and we return to the Source. We enter again into the garden from which we were cast out. We are on the *threshold* when we trod this path back to its Source in Tiphareth, on the Way of Return.

As the 25th Path goes into the sphere of the Son-Sun, or the Divine Heart through mysticism, so does this path lead to the same sphere through intense search and questioning; it is the way of knowledge, or Juana Yoga. It is the path of the hermeticist. Frequently, one working this Path is obsessed with finding God in the Tao of physics, in the mysteries of the Cosmos, within the veil of matter. Eliphas Levi said, "The Infinite is the inevitable absurdity which imposes itself on science."

In Ayin we learn to use the intellectuel eye of Hod to see anew the Light of Beauty illuminated in Tiphareth. The symbol of Pan the goat-god is a guide on this Path's journey. In classical mythology, Pan was fathered by Mercury-Hermes, the great giver of Knowledge and Truth. Before he was carried up to heaven (where he became the zodiacal Capricorn) he was the deified goat-king who was a master of "divining and fortelling" (in Hebrew, we recall that this word is HChSh, 358). Since he knows the future, he is thus an apt symbol for pointing us on our way.

Rather than making this world the "scapegoat," we need to trust that we can pass through it nimbly, as a mountain goat, jumping from one height to another. We need to be *watchful* and attentive, lest we be deceived by our own worst enemies: our fears and projections of what we *think* these appearances really *are*. On this path we need to learn not to be so "Saturn-heavy," so serious-minded. Case once said that the deadliest personalities are those who have no gift of laughter.

The ascent on the path of Ayin is a process of transferring consciousness from the concrete mind to the abstract mind, from the ego to the Higher Personality. This Personality, residing in Tiphareth, is the source of consolation during the discouragement we sometimes encounter as we walk through the world of deception. It offers us lamps that we may see. It is the reassuring image that we need to sustain us, to anoint us, making us united with it in its freedom from the chains of faulty perceptions, and wrong thinking.

There was a common medieval Christian legend that went like

this: After the expulsion from the Garden of Eden, Adam managed to sneak a limb from the Tree of Knowledge, upon which had lain the serpent who had tempted Eve. This branch or staff was destined to have a miraculous history. It became the famous rod of Moses, around which twined the Serpent of Bronze, and which was the magic wand with which Moses parted the Red Sea. It was also the staff used for healing, so all who gazed on it were delivered from the plague. This archetypal image is still found in the physician's caduceus.

This was the rod used to strike the rock in the wilderness that gave forth water. It was later kept in the Ark of the Covenant in the Holy of Holies of Solomon's Temple. In time, it passed into the carpenter's shop of Joseph of Nazareth. Eventually, it came into the hands of Judas, who turned it over to the Romans, who used it for the cross. It thus became the Tree of Salvation. In the Tarot, this is the image of the Hanged Man, Path 23. As Dwellers on the Threshold of this path, however, we must make note that "Eden is not only a mirror of Paradise above it; it is a reflection . . . wherein all the events of redemption are seen in reverse" (Watts, 1968, p. 55).

Qabalists point to the fact that, behind the image of the devil-serpent (NChSh, 358) is the Messiah (MShICh, 358) who delivers. As if one gematria co-relation was not enough, Qabalah gives us yet another: both Ayin (when spelled out) and the word *deliverance* (HTzLH) add up to 130. Case makes note of the fact that, although the chained figures in the Tarot key are "slaves of necessity," they could easily lift the loose chains from over their heads and walk away. All they need to do is to wake up and *see*.

26th Pathworking Correspondences

1. Intelligence: Renewing

2. Divine Letter: Ayin, OIN (pronounced Ah-yeen) Value: 70, means "eye"

3. Divine Name: IHVH Eloah (Yod-Heh-Vaw-Heh E-lo-ah). IAO

4. Incense: Musk, civit. Cinnamon

5. Gem: Black diamond

6. Color: Indigo

7. Element: Earth

8. Animals: Goat, ass

9. Plants: Hemp, thistle, orchis root

10. Planet: Saturn

11. Musical Tone: A

12. Magical Phenomenon: Making wishes that come true

13. Magical Weapon: Lamp, chalice

14. Mythos and Related Symbols: Lord of the Gates of Matter, the Great Magical Agent, Set, Shiva, Saturn, Pan, yoni and lingam, the eye, the serpent, dragon, satyr, fauns

15. Gift or Challenge: To balance intellect with aesthetics, to ponder the heavy questions with an air of lightness, to see deeper than the present form or condition

16. Rules: Knees

17. Tarot Arcana: The Deceiver

Suggested Exercises

Use this path when someone makes you painfully aware of your worst faults. Imagine you are the chained figure who, thankful for the *realization* that you have been chained to matter, to a habit, to a concept, etc., can now remove the chain from your neck and freely work on your purification while you continue to evolve.

Use this image also when you need to ground. The archetype of the Lord of the Gates of Matter and Time is one which can help orient you to the here and now when you become too "airy-fairy" and unable to focus on what is at hand. It is sometimes fine to "have one's head in the clouds" but, if one does not have one's feet also on the earth, there is little sense in being there.

Finally, understand that it is the energies of this key at work in all magical rites. It is our utmost task as Qabalists to at all times keep our consciousness pure and free from the desire for raw power that can motivate some seekers on the magical paths, the hermetic paths, or the paths of knowledge. Robert Wang once commented (1983) that what distinguishes the student magician from the aesthetic monk is a greater curiosity. Use your curiosity to unlock the secrets of matter for the greater good of all and your goal will necessarily be found in the Great Giver and Keeper of all the mysteries, the Divine Son in Tiphareth.

Visualization

Imagine yourself as all of these things in order:

A crocodile
A donkey
A goat-fish
A devouring typhon
An old serpent
A dragon with wings
An eagle in the sun
A mother giving birth
A child running in the wind
A shepherd playing a pan-pipe
A lamb being roasted
A corpse under the earth
A pile of dry bones
A lake of fire
A huge, enclosing Heart
A Fountain of Light

Affirmations

1. Everything I see is the raw material for transmutation.

2. I regard every appearance of evil as an opportunity for the demonstration of good.

3. My body is aglow with the vitality of Gaia.

4. Today I behold the earth with the eye of Genesis, and I see that it is good.

5. I am free from the bondage and baggage of the past.

6. "Behold, I make all things new."

Path 25
The Intelligence of Probation

Verification   *Sign: Sagittarius*

CHAPTER NINE

The 25th Path, Samekh
Temperance
The Tentative Intelligence

The 25th Path on the Tree of Life is called Samekh, the Intelligence of Probation, and is the Path wherein, according to *The Thirty-two Paths of Wisdom*, "the Creator trieth all righteous persons." It leads from Yesod, called the "Foundation," or the sphere of the Moon, to Tiphareth, called "Beauty," or the sphere of the Sun. On the Qabalistic Tree, the Moon sphere represents the Personality, and that of the Sun the Higher Self. The astrological symbol associated with Samekh is the Sagittarian Archer, who is represented by Diana, the Huntress and Moon Goddess.

As Goddess of the Moon, the archetypal image of Diana (or Artemis) governs the astral currents associated with Yesod (or the Moon energy), as she governs the tides of oceans and women's blood cycles (on the earth). She is literally the *support* of these fluctuating energies and, in Hebrew, the word Samekh means "to prop," "to support" or "to establish." She represents complete control and restriction over all natural energies, and the purpose of one who trods this path is to understand how this manifest universe is managed within specific circumscriptians. It is in this way that one comes into contact with the Higher Self (represented here by the Sun), which is called the Knowledge and Conversation of the Holy Guardian Angel.

The basic meaning of this Path is *verification*, and the Tarot key associated with it is the Angel of Temperance. This key represents the way wherein we may confirm the accuracy of our beliefs and theories, so that we may establish the truth, which is a continual process of trial and error. The "Intelligence of Probation or Trial" represents the central idea that we may verify for ourselves the teachings of Ageless Wisdom, and this is the continual effort of the student on this Path.

The mental state evoked by concentration on the Temperance key is that of "practicing the Presence of God." The angel pictured here is Michael, whose name means "Like unto God." On his brow is a solar symbol and light radiates from his head. One foot is resting on water, symbol of the fluid cosmic mind-stuff, or that which is contained in the etheric records; the other rests on the earth, symbol of concrete manifestation.

When the Personality is brought into contact with the inner divine light, rising on the path of Temperance means giving birth to the Divine Child, which is a symbol for Tiphareth, the sphere of "Ben" (Hebrew for "the Son"), or the human incarnation of illumination. This divine child in each of us begins to come alive in our consciousness as we trod this path from the sphere of Yesod, the *foundation* or "Womb of creation," which governs the cyclic energies underlying matter, to Tiphareth the Sun, which governs the vision of the harmony of all things. It is in this aspect of the Great Work that the aspirant combines and harmonizes all the various elements which constitute his or her personality.

Sometimes this is not an easy task, and this Path has been called the "dark night of the soul" by some, pointing to the tempering process and trials brought about through this exchange and balance of opposites. In the alchemical work there are invariably dark stages before the golden ones, and metals (as human personalities) are subjected to repeated tests and trials before pure gold is attained. In this Path, we must subject our theories of spiritual philosophy to the laboratory tests of day-to-day experience.

In Hebrew, the word which means "to try by fire" is *bawkhan* (BChN), which adds up to 60, the value of the letter Samekh. The other word which relates to this path through gematria is "vision" (MChZH), which also equals 60. When the aspirant has successfully worked this Path, the philosophical gold of enlightenment, which represents *verified* truth, begins to be distilled from the dark nigredo of matter and its thousand illusionary visions. "Temperance" really means regulation and the measured proportion of constituent parts. Throughout one's work, theories that have been carefully weighed and measured become *established* and *supported*, as suggested by

Samekh. The letter Samekh represents the probation or purification of the student's personality, that it may become a fit channel for the Holy Guardian Angel. Thus does the Law of Verification bring about the *establishment* of the foundation of the Divine House of God through clear insight and true vision.

The *Sepher Yetzirah* tells us that the attribution given to Samekh is Wrath, but a good Qabalist will subject this interpretation to *trials and tests* for true *verification*. Paul Case tells us that this word (RVGZ in Hebrew), used frequently in the Bible, is a blind. The definition means "quivering" or "vibration." It has a numerical value of 216, the same as the word which means "force or strength" (GBVRH), thus linking it to Strength and the 19th Path. We will examine the numerical associations more in depth there. For now, we note that all of the vibrations which light can be broken into are represented by the rainbow over the angel's head. Science tells us that what we call color is made of varying vibrations of light; all matter is luminiferous and thus has a color vibration.

In its Chaldean form Samekh is the third of the three serpentine letters in the alphabet. It resembles a snake with its tail in its mouth (the reversal of the symbolism of Teth, Strength) and symbolizes completion or eternity. The angel in the picture has the unutterable Name of God YHVH (or IHVH) written on his breast, identifying him with the eternal One Reality which cannot be spoken about but only experienced.

In the Waite deck, the essence of life is being poured from one chalice to another. In the Case deck, the symbolism is more complicated. The vase of etheric fluid which the angel holds falls on a lion, symbol of Leo and Fire, to temper it. It transmutes the animal nature (again represented in Strength) by the powers of human consciousness. The torch in his other hand falls on an eagle, symbol of Scorpio and Water, thus tempering it.

One of the secrets of alchemy was supposed to in the knowledge of how to unite Fire and Water. In the Midrash, a Hebrew collection of tales and myths, it is Fire (Shin) and Water (Mim) that have to be united so that heaven may come to be. In the ancient Qabalistic text, the *Bahir*, it is said, "Heaven is called *shamayim* because fire and water existed before it" (*Bahir* 1:99). If we look at the word "heaven" (SMYM), we see that it is constructed, or created, from the letters meaning "Fire" (the S or Shin) and "Water" (MYM).

On one level, Water, representing etheric mind-stuff, and Fire, representing the sexual or kundalini energy, together form astral visions, images in the mind's eye. When distilled, properly verified, and grounded, or established by the human will, the consciously-controlled vision becomes the "channel for the Higher Self" rather than the endless myriad forms of visionary experience brought about by a peek into some astral doorway. The rainbow symbolizes the different vibrations of light into color when Water is mixed with the Air or Life-breath in the upper atmosphere. Thus is manifested the rainbow of promise, which was placed in the heavens as a sign of God's covenant, "I set my bow in the clouds to serve as a sign of the covenant between me and you and the earth" (Gen.9:13). The colors of the rainbow also relate to the colors of the planetary chakras of the human body. A rainbow was seen by Ezekiel (1:28) surrounding the throne of God and by John in the Revelation, where he records an angel descending from heaven with a face that shone like the Sun (Rev. 10:1).

The keynote of the astrological sign of the arrow in the archer's bow points to aspiration. The entire objective of one who trods this Path is the ever-new, uplifted aspiration toward the Sun, which is the human made perfect. This Path is called the "Path of the Arrow," which refers to the single, straight course leading from the Foundation toward Kether, the crown. It is frequently associated with the path of the mystic and represents a complete change in both the mode and the level of consciousness. A new way of looking at things has begun and is characterized by a total absorbtion in activity.

The path by which Tiphareth is to be attained is also the entrance into what is knovn as the world of Briah, the Qabalistic world of Pure Mind, or that belonging to the adept. The adept is one who has simply realized that there is nothing in the cosmos but vibration, and all forms of vibration can be modified and rearranged by concentration and will.

25th Pathworking Correspondences

1. Intelligence: Tentative, or Intelligence of Probation

2. Divine Letter: Samech, SMK (pronounced Sahm-ekh) Value: 60, means "prop or support"

3. Divine Names: El. YHVH Eloah V'Daath (Yod-Heh-Vaw-Heh E-lo-ah we Da-ath)

4. Incense: Heliotrope, ling-aloes. Olibanum

5. Gem: Jacinth

6. Color: Blue

7. Element: Fire

8. Animal: Lion

9. Plants: Rush (the plant used for making arrows), Iris

10. Planet: Jupiter

11. Musical Tone: A flat

12. Magical Phenomenon: Divine intoxications, transformations

13. Magical Weapons: Arrow, chalice

14. Mythos and Related Symbols: Apollo, Diana, Michael, the Eternal Child, the Dark Womb of Being, rainbow (Iris), centaurs, the Androgyne, Christ as Crown (or the Holy Guardian Angel), bow, thyrsus, the straight path, the archer

15. Gift or Challenge: Endurance, discrimination

16. Rules: Hips and thighs

17. Tarot Arcana: Temperance

Suggested Exercises

Working intently with the 25th Path will cause you to act with assurance in your pursuit of spiritual truths, as well as other life endeavors. It will evoke from your inner consciousness an urge to do something about what you already know; to shoot at some definite mark. It reminds your subconsciousness to work on subtle inner centers of your body and refine your senses and emotions.

Perhaps the most important element in the Tarot key is the Divine Name hidden in the angel's cloak. This Name has been translated as "I Am" and much refreshing identification with the limitless source of all Power can be gained by simply concentrating on the letters. The translation of this Sacred Name in Hebrew is frequently used as a chant by Qabalists, and is pronounced Yod-Heh-Waw-Heh, although you may want to *experiment* with the intonations and vibrations of this powerful Western mantra.

Color the Tarot key and mount it on your altar. It will mean much more to you when embellished with the rainbow colors from your mind's eye. Research the myths of the rainbow and sort out its various archetypal meanings and themes: its meaning to Noah, its appearance to Ezekiel and in the Revelation, the rainbow bridge of Odin (Germanic) or Iris (Greek), or the sacredness of the rainbow to the Incas. Contemplating the implications of these myths can deepen your understanding and appreciation of this powerful archetypal image.

The rainbow-chakra meditation is popular in many esoteric traditions and belongs to the energy of this path. To revitalize all your internal energy center, simply visualize red at the bottom of the spine, orange in the second chakra, yellow in the solar plexus, green at the heart, blue in the throat, indigo at the third-eye center, and violet at the top of the head. You may also practice Color Breathing in conjunction with this technique. It too is very simple: sit in a comfortable chair before an open window, exhale all the air from your lungs, and, in an upright position, breathe the color into the visualized body part. It is helpful to hold your breath for several seconds as you imagine the color flooding the area. This is a valuable aid in extending consciousness and sensitizing the psychic faculties.

Remember that color is really *vibration* and rays or vibrations of color can be consciously used to vitalize, heal, and expand your energies. Case suggests (1947) that this word for vibration (RVGZ) can also reveal hidden meanings when the Tarot keys corresponding to its letters are laid next to one another and studied. (They correspond to the Sun, the Hierophant, the High Priestess, and the Lovers.)

Guided Visualization

Imagine that Gabriel, the angel who resides in Yesod, is bidding you goodby on your journey toward Tiphareth. He waves you onward with a rush from his wings, which allows you to fly as if you had wings yourself. He calls out, "Envision the Sacred King," and you begin to wonder just what this King will look like. As you are flying through space, you pass through many astral visions and elemental tricksters: centaurs, a pegasus, gnomes and fairies...a maiden with golden hair, a mermaid with wings...You dismiss them all with a glance, knowing the King cannot be so ordinary as to be dressed in the fairy tale figures of your childhood. You begin to wonder what indeed constitutes *real* vision, and suddenly, from distant space comes a voice like an echo: "A seer is one who understands what she sees." As this thought is crystalized, the archangel Michael appears, in bright red garb with the sigil of the Sun on his forehead, calling out "Be sure to stay on the straight and narrow path."

You follow his advice, although you slow your flight somewhat when you come to clouds wherein many lovers lay languishing together in the golden rays of the Sun. Their eyes are locked and their hands and breasts touch and you feel a momentary tug, thinking about the past ecstasies and wounds of love, and you wonder...if the King has anything at all to say about Love, surely He must be hiding somewhere here...? At this thought, however, you seem to fall several degrees and for a moment you panic...what is keeping you in flight, anyway? So you shut your eyes and search for understanding, and immediately the image of a chalice appears in your mind's eye.

When you open your eyes, then, the archangel Raphael is there, dressed in mauve and gold. Gently the Healer touches your heart and a tiny burst of joy flutters through it. This gives you a resurgence of power in your flight. You suddenly begin to soar straight upward with him and soon discern a gleaming wreath dripping with blood. The realization dawns on you that somehow, you are being propelled, shot like an arrow into this bright red crown that glows more brilliant the closer you approach it. Refusing now to look either left or right, you focus on the center of that crown and begin to make out the chalice you had seen earlier in your mental vision, only this time it seems as immense as the sky itself and from it issue streams of vibrant, pulsating lights of many rainbow colors. The center of this light is golden and forms a column of concentrated Life-energy, and is offered by a hand reaching out from behind the rainbow-hued clouds. On reaching your destination, you reach humbly for the gracious gift, knowing you have successfully climbed the stairway to heaven.

The symbol of the chalice will come up again in other pathworkings. What would the gift of the chalice mean to you? Are there myths of chalices, grails, or golden cups that stir memories or evoke moods in you? How can you develop your own ongoing grail myth? A powerful focus for concentration is to envision a *pillar* of light descending from the grail or crown at the culmination of the vision. The more clearly one is able to envision this pillar on this path of the *middle pillar* on the Tree, the more prepared one will be to later incorporate this as a technique within one's body.

Affirmations

1. *The great I AM is Here Now, working in me and through me to flood my life with the pattern of divine substance.*

2. *Through the central gate of my balanced being, I enter the Sun-filled sphere of eternal Harmony and Beauty.*

3. *I direct the purified fire within my body and soul with the arrow of my will toward the supreme Good.*

4. *Recognizing everything to be a reflection of the One Life, I perceive every appearance of adversity to be, in truth, a mask worn by that Life, to test my power to know it.*

 TRANSITION

Path 24
The Imaginative Intelligence

Transformation   *Sign: Scorpio*

CHAPTER TEN

The 24th Path, Nun
Transformation
The Imaginative Intelligence

The value of the letter "Nun" is 50, which is a multiple of 5, the archetype of universal life (the letter Heh). In Tarot, however, Nun is attributed to the Death key. In *The Thirty two Paths of Wisdom*, it is called the Imaginative Intelligence, because it "gives a likeness to all the similitudes which are created in like manner similar to its harmonious elegancies." Although these ideas may seems disparate from one another, Qabalah teaches that, when we bring opposites together in the cauldron of our understanding, a new synthesis emerges. In alchemy, this is called *conjunctio*, or the *coincidentia oppositorium* in the Jungian sense. Only from thesis and antithesis can synthesis be born, and in the conjunction of all one's many selves lies the only possibility of supreme peace and rest.

The esoteric title of this key is called the Child of the Great Transformers. It is one of the three paths leading from the personality level to the Higher Self. It balances the energies of Netzach, that emanation of the God-energy dealing with art, feeling (particularly love), and nature, with Tiphareth, the Sun center and Supreme Ego, or potential Christ-center.

Nun is one of the Hebrew letters that has a different form and number when it appears at the end of a word. Nun Final has a value of 700, a number which Carlo Suares says expresses the very principle contended for in the interplay of all energies of the universe, because it is the "principle of indetermination in which life itself is at stake" (Suares, 1985, p. 59). Nun represents one of the five psychological archetypes, the activities of which take consciousness inward instead of outward. The others are the remaining final letters (final Kaph, Mem, Tzaddi, and Peh).

In the *Zohar*, 700 is considered a "complete number," symbolizing a profound mystery of male and female. This is also the number of the Hebrew word *Melekim* (MLKM), the Kings, which is the angelic choir associated with the Sphere of Tiphareth, the Sun. In Tiphareth, we see the marriage of the opposing principles of anima and animus in a whole androgynous Being.

There are many other mysteries connected to this final Nun, 700. This number is the name of Seth, who was the third son of Adam and the first of an unbroken line of ancestors traced in St. Luke in his genealogy of Jesus the Christ. The *Zohar* tells us that Seth (ShT) symbolizes an end, because it is composed of the last two letters in the Hebrew alphabet (Shin and Tau). For Qabalists, "end" represents the completion or fullfillment or consummation, all ideas which constellate around the image of Death as Transformer.

Because death is the greatest mystery, Paul Case, Aleister Crowley, and other Qabalists tell us that this key contains some of the most profound secrets of any of the Paths. This is connected to two other Hebrew words with the value of 700: the "mercy seat" or the golden *cover* of the ark of the covenant (KPRTh) and the *veil* of the Holy of Holies (PRKTh). Both words connote what was *concealed* in the ark, hinting at the great mystery which was not to be understood with any of the senses.

The word "Nun" itself means "fish." The archetypal image of the fish, we know, was intimately connected by the early Christians with the figure of Jesus, a reference to the Sun center.

This was perhaps due to the fact that the initials of "Jesus Christ, Son of God, Savior" in Greek spelled *ichthys,* or fish. In Hebrew, Nun also means "perpetuity," "eternally increasing" or "prolific" (ideas associated with the propagation of fish) and was the name of the father of Joshua, the successor of Moses, who delivered the children of Israel into the promised land. The words Joshua and Jesus are spelled the same way in Hebrew (Yeheshua) and the name means "one who liberates" or "Jah liberates."

Nun also means "to sprout" or "to generate" and is connected with procreative power. This is apparent in the Tarot key, because the Death card corresponds to Scorpio, which rules the organs of reproduction. All these ideas constellate around the central theme of universal life, death, and transformation through the great power and mystery of generation and regeneration. Nun signifies the interpenetrating and continuous increase of Truth in the consciousness of the individual who opens her/his heart, mind, and will to the eternal influx of the Wisdom and Love that eternally liberates.

In this Path are concealed occult powers that, when subliminated, lead to illumination. This is represented by the eagle, which replaces the scorpion as the symbol of Scorpio at a certain stage of initiation in many of the mystery schools. This is the same eagle pictured in the keys which relate to Ezekiel's vision (Paths 21, the Wheel, and 32, the Universe) representing the Water (Scorpio) element in these four directions. It is the element of Water which dissolves forms and in alchemy this stage is most important for the completion of the Great Work. It is in this Path that the student learns the power of dissolution, of breaking up old forms, so that a recombination of elements leading to new births can blossom.

Viewed in this way, the old connotations of death take on new meaning. It is seen as a part of an ongoing process, without which nothing could continue to exist. It is obvious, if one thinks about it, that physical dissolution is a process that has definite advantages for the human race. Likewise, it is through the death of countless organisms that a human life is supported. It is through this ongoing dissolution that we are able to see and participate in the unity of all things.

In gematria, the word for "unity" has a value of 13, the same number attributed to this path in many Tarot decks. It is an apt number for representing the Death card for many, because 13 was generally supposed to be considered unlucky, in some superstitious corner of consciousness. But such are the blinds for those who have not yet uncovered the deeper secrets of this Path. The Path number itself, 24, breaks down to 6, and 6 is the number of the Divine Sun (Son) emanation which is the destination of this path (Tiphareth).

When forms break down, energy is released to be utilized for further development, as we know from the second law of thermodynamics. Nun, governing the organs of reproduction, indicates that the sexual or kundalini-serpent forces are directly related to the liberating, transforming powers of dissolution. Yogis, Christian saints, and others who lived or understand the mysteries connected with this Path have been known to use these forces to modify the metabolism of their bodies.

On a psychological level, this is the Path wherein the personality is beginning to leave behind the "desire" nature of Netzach and become absorbed in the all-embracing Love of Tiphareth, the universal consciousness. Personal love becomes transformed and projected onto humanity. Perceptual changes occur in the aspirant about nature and the meaning of life and what constitutes the real Self. Old concepts continually die as the student seeks to reconstitute his or her world view. The challenge here is the surrendering to the unknown, whereas it is easier to cling to the familiar.

We re-create our world by continually adapting our world-view to changing circumstances, and this is the challenge of the student on this Path. Nun is called the Imaginative Intelligence because it is through the process of imagery that we are able to control the circumstances which surround us, to inspire us with new options. To a Qabalist, all changes are first changes in mental imagery. This is hinted at when *The Thirty-two Paths of Wisdom* says "it is the ground of similarity." This also relates again to the reproductive function, the mystery of this path, which creates likenesses in human beings. In this context, we may meditate on the mystery of being created in the image and likeness of God.

In most Tarot decks, the ground upon which the Reaper is trodding is strewn with bodies or parts of bodies. This suggests that the veil of life (recall the *veil* of the Holy of Holies) is perpetuated (recall the word *perpetuity*, a meaning of Nun) in dissolution and change. The skeleton itself is an apt symbol for movement and change; all movements in the human body depend on it. It is this flexibility which allows us to seek ever new methods of liberation and should therefore be revered instead of feared.

In most Tarot keys, revitalization is hinted at by the profusion of the growing plants, as well as the heads popping up out of the soil. The link with the verb, Nun, "to sprout," is evident in keys which capture the essence of this idea. In the B.O.T.A. version there is, in addition, a seed planted in the sky.

The skeleton can also be a symbol of initiation; when we have a hunch about something, we feel it "in our bones." The bones of the human body not only allow us our flexibility but also create our stability; therefore, we see that the skeleton is also a form of *conjunctio*—joining in itself these opposites. Finally, in the Tarot keys of both the Waite and the B.O.T.A. decks, there is a river flowing in the background toward the east. Although death is usually associated with west and the sunset, here the sun is rising.

Through the miracle of fear and attatchment transforming itself into love and freedom, represented by the Christ-consciousness in Tiphareth, do we approach with confidence the Sun gleaming at the end of the Reaper's path.

24th Pathworking Correspondences

1. Intelligence: Imaginative

2. Divine Letter: Nun, NVN (pronounced Noon) Value: 50, as final: 700, means "fish"

3. Divine Names: Elohim Gibor (E-lo-heem Gi-boor). IAO

4. Incense: Benzoin, opoponax, geranium. Heliotrope

5. Gems: Snakestone, red coral, carnelian

6. Color: Blue-green

7. Element: Fire

8. Animals: Scorpion, fish, sun-beetle

9. Plants: Cactus, capsium, pine, anemones

10. Planet: Mars

11. Musical Tone: G

12. Magical Phenomenon: Visions of the Primeval Beginning; a flaming fire

13. Magical Weapon: Sword of discrimination

14. Mythos and Related Symbols: Ares, Khephra, Joshua, Kali, Cybele (all dark Goddesses), harpies, the Midnight Sun, the crone, treasures of the depths, the pit, the ocean

15. Gift or Challenge: To balance one's emotional life with one's higher aspirations; to surrender to ongoing change

16. Rules: Reproductive organs

17. Tarot Arcana: Death

Suggested Exercises

While working with the energies of this card, you may want to research the symbols and rituals connected with death in other cultures and traditions; e.g., the Tibetan Book of the Dead, the Egyptian Book of the Dead, the primitive encounter with death, the deaths of great heroes and gods in various mythologies. Including other interpretations and methods of incorporating and understanding this profound phenomenon helps us enlarge our own vision of it and decrease our fear about it on a personal level.

A helpful meditation is to color the Death key and mount it next to the Star key, Tzaddi. Together, they represent the fish and the fishhook. By contemplating the images for about five minutes each with eyes open and closed, seed thoughts begin to emerge that are deeply personal and at the same time archetypal and transpersonal, concerning the relationships between life, death, and meditation (or, the state in between). A useful exercise is to simply imagine yourself as a dead corpse and then to visualize yourself leaving your body. Where would you go?

You may find yourself searching for the Beloved; that is, one of the world's great teachers or gurus who, as a result of your personal search, is attached to your heart. Identity with the Christos principle in Tiphareth allows us to connect with the Larger Story, the Archetype which always tells us that death is really a glorification. The great master and poet Rumi wrote:

> I said to my heart: How are you? It said, Increasing, for, by God, I
> am His Image's House, Like Jesus, Thy Image goes into the heart
> to Bestow a new spirit-like Divine revelation.*

What is most important here in analyzing the 24th path of Death or the *Imaginative Intelligence*, is the *image:* that which we adopt as an ideal, we gravitate towards. The idea we have of our Beloved promises us release if we can but imagine it properly, for It has an *irrestible tendency* to imagine us in a way that is fundamentally *liberating*. This is the secret meaning hidden in the name Jesus, which means "God liberates."

---

*Chittick, W., *The Sufi Path of Love,* 1983

Guided Visualization

Imagine that you are traveling on a path next to a flowing river which curves slightly upward. Many reeds grow along its bank and stir gently in the wind. It is not yet dawn and you want to approach a certain point so as to behold a lovely view in the early morning light. As you press forward, stumbling somewhat in the pre-dawn shadows, listening to the sounds of the soft hum of the river rippling over stones and a few awakening birds, you are suddenly aware of a shift in your perception.

You thought you were alone in the wilderness, but you stop and become alert. All of a sudden you are aware of a possible presence; is it benevolent? For a moment you are afraid. Then, before you can realize what is happening, you are completely enveloped in a dense mist, so that you can no longer see your way. You immediately brush against a rosebush, and, with the slightly intoxicating scent of roses, you are simultaneously pricked by its thorns. You step back, unsure of what to do.

Again you are aware of a presence; at the same time, apprehension grips you as you feel your foot slide gently into the water. You quickly withdraw it, but you are suddenly keenly aware that you have entered marsh; every direction you step you begin to feel yourself sink in. In a concentrated, calm manner, you make yourself pause; it is impossible now to see anything, so you remain very still and try to get your bearings.

Then, like out of a dream, a shape begins to take form in the thick cloud surrounding you. In wonder you stare, knowing that this is not a Being from the earth you live on. Your fear vanishes, however, as the angelic figure, which communicates only with her deep-set penetrating eyes, allows you to perceive that she is only here to assist you, to act as your guide. You know that any time in the future when you are in a state of doubt, fear, or confusion, you will remember this moment and bring her back to consciousness to help you in your turmoil.

She beckons for you to step forward into what you know to be cold, deep water. But because you are certain somewhere in the depths of your being that it is absolutely safe and correct to do so, you follow her as she leads you still deeper into the blue-green watery womb. Suddenly you are under the water but, amazingly enough, you can still breathe. And there is the faint beautiful form of your host still in front of you. You continue to follow her with only a slight twist of your body; it is as if you are moved by your will alone. You glance at your feet and behold gems sparkling like the sun on the river floor.

As you move, you are aware that you seem to be dissolving into the water itself; there are no boundaries that you can feel between yourself and the luminous velvet waves that you appear to be moving though. There is a great sense of at-one-ment with this realization and perhaps a vague rememberance of what it was like to be enclosed in your mother's womb at the dawn of your own creation.

Then your gliding reverie seems to be disturbed as you begin to feel yourself moving much more quickly; you have become caught in a current and are no longer moving of your own volition. You try to make out the form of your guide, but she seems to have vanished; for a moment, apprehension again seizes you. The ongoing current drags you forward and you can do nothing but surrender to it. You are suddenly aware of great sea anemones with huge gaping mouths, open as if to suck you in should you brush against them. But you are moving much too swiftly. Through the silver, misty waters, however, other forms begin to take shape; in your rapid whirling you see many-hued fish swimming quickly by; a long emerald-green serpent slides against you and is gone. Fear pounds in your heart, and you wonder if the serpent may turn again toward you, to engulf you in one swallow; then the thought enters your mind that you may, indeed, be dead already.

In a flash, however, you are ascending out of the watery depths; the gleaming image of your guide is again before you, but only for a second. You see her point to a huge glowing disk at the end of the water's edge, and then she is gone. You gaze again at the brilliant ball of light and for a moment you imagine that there is a definite image imprinted on its surface. Squinting to behold it through the bright streams of light, you notice that it is shaped like a golden fish several hues darker that the Sun itself. You know you must approach this beckoning light within the Sun, which is no longer in the sky but at the very edge of your conscious awareness. With each step you are overcome with the awe and beauty of the Presence of this dazzling Light. It seems to be enclosed in a giant temple of pure crystal which reflects its brightness in thousands of rainbow hues.

You find yourself gazing into its intense white center, however, with the steadfastness of an eagle staring into the sun. You have a longing to enter into its Presence which is more immense than anything you have ever experienced. You know it is into this brilliant temple of light that your angelic guide has vanished, and with absolute certainty and the wonder of a child, you follow her there.

Affirmations

1. *I, here and now, dissolve all negative forces which I, knowingly or unknowingly, have ever given to my subconscious mind.*

2. *Probing deep waters pierces the veil of past illusions.*

3. *I am rejuvenated by the cosmic inflow of perpetually renewing life-energy.*

4. *That which I sow does not quicken unless it die.*

5. *Perfect love casts out all fear.*

 M SUSPENDED MAN

Path 23
The Stable Intelligence

Reversal   *Planet: Neptune*

CHAPTER ELEVEN

The 23rd Path, Mem
The Hanged Man
The Stable Intelligence

Mem is one of the three "mother letters" and means "water" or "seas." Its esoteric title is "Spirit of the Mighty Waters." Water is considered to be the First Principle in alchemy, that which underlies everything else. It is the most *stable,* most primordial of the elements; i.e., that which we first encounter in the womb and that which holds and contains us until we are developed enough to encounter the elements of earth and air. We have the image of the Hanged Man in the Tarot Key representing this Stable Intelligence, because he is inseparable from this Unity that water represents. He has no separate existence; he is "drowned" in the Universal Consciousness. We notice that the tree upon which he hangs suspended is in the shape of a T cross, but he hangs only by a cord at his ankle. The cross, we recall, represents Path 32 and the Universe; the symbolism is that he is suspended from the world by a thread. The key represents suspension of personal will and absolute surrender.

The path connects Hod, Splendor, where the Hanged Man points his head, and Geburah, the fiery energy of Strength and Will, where he rests his feet. The most implicit symbolism in the 23rd Path is that of *reversal*, or suspension of ordinary consciousness and ordinary activity, and immersion in Superconsciousness, or the collective unconscious.

Mem, or water, is a universal symbol signifying this "other

consciousness"; in many cultures it is considered to be "maternal" and life-giving. It is the intuitive, motivating, female side of the personality; the potent female images connected with its life-giving functions are rain, milk, and blood. Immersion in water signifies a return to the source, and, in this sense, Mem represents baptism.

When the Great Sea which is our Source is conceived as reflecting our limitless inner life and we learn to dive deep into it as meditative and contemplative traditions of all religions teach, we lose the sense of ego. Water is considered to be the element that *dissolves*, and this is definitely a path of dissolution. What is implied in any kind of transformation or baptism is a surrender of what went before, of one's prior life. Mem renews, like Tzaddi, the path of meditation, and Nun, the transformation by death. These images are also intimately related by the Hebrew words which connect them: "Mem" = water, "Nun" = fish in the water, and "Tzaddi" = the fishhook which is immersed in water. To a Christian Qabalist, these are obvious references to the figure of Christ.

The Thirty-two Paths of Wisdom says the 23rd Path is the "Stable Intelligence" because it "is the source of consistency among all the numerations." In Hebrew, the word for stable is *khayam* (QIIM), and it has a numeration of 160. The Hebrew letter Mem has a value of 40, which reflects "the fourfold elemental division" of the nature and Name of Tetragrammaton, the divine four-letter Name, IHVH. Each of these letters contains one of the four elements and thus everything created is a part of it. This is explained by Paul Case, who says, "To commemorate this fourfold manifestation of Life, the Divine Names in many languages are four-lettered. This is particularly true in Hebrew, and of the Divine Names in that language the most important is the Tetragrammaton, IHVH. Each letter of this Name represents one of the four aspects of Life called 'elements.' I stands for FIRE; the first H for WATER; the V for AIR; and the second H for EARTH" (Case, 1934, p. 125).

The number four in itself is a powerful number reflecting stability and structure, and when 40 is multiplied by four, we obtain 160, the Stable Intelligence. We note that, in addition, the legs of the Hanged Man form an inverted figure four. The word *sehla* (SLO), which means "rock," also has a value of 160, as does the Hebrew word for "tree" (OTz), which is the Qabalistic image that contains all of the Sephiroth and paths; i.e., *all the numerations*. The tree is an obvious vehicle for salvation and renewal, present in the archetypal image of the Hanged Man as well as in many mythological traditions.

The figure in Path 23 connects Hod with Geburah. Here Hod represents the deep concentration of the intellect and Geburah the Law of undeviating justice. The task of one who walks this Path (and this is not a favorite Path to tread) is to be a clear channel for the unfailing Law of the Cosmos through correct application of the concentrated mind. It is a Path that requires one-pointedness in dedication. We may not achieve our ideals immediately, but we sharpen our focus and continue to put one foot in front of the other.

The concept of selflessness is strongly implied in the Tarot key. Some occultists have noted that St. Peter, whose name means "rock," was crucified in this manner. Sacrifice is not a popular concept in an age which popularizes visualizations for prosperity, success, and a comfortable, harmonious life. And there is nothing in esoteric teaching that implies that we should not want these things, only that it is in our best spiritual interests to keep them in balance.

On this Path, however, desire is principally sacrificed to the *rational principle*. This is why the Hanged Man is on the side of the Tree with severity and intellect. Desire causes activity; we set wheels in motion by it. The opposite side of the Tree in this position is occupied by the Wheel, Kaph, which connects to our desire nature, represented by Netzach. When we sacrifice this principle, using the strength of the rational mind and will, the wheel comes to rest. And rest, or *suspension* of ordinary consciousness, is the principle function of the 23rd Path.

Jung noticed that in human history to "sacrifice" frequently meant to "make sacred," and the task of one who walks this Path is to sacrifice any ego-centered notions he or she may have that keep him or her from being holy, or whole. Part of this ego-sacrifice, and one of the most difficult chores for many of us, is to *suspend judgment.* Judgments concerning any of our fellow travelers should not belong to the sphere of the personality; it is reserved for that aspect of the Godness energy called Geburah, one of whose names is Divine Justice. The Master Jesus reminded us to suspend judgments when he inquired who was pure enough to cast the first stone, thus inviting us not only to question our own selves deeply but to trade one form of energy (i.e., the "stone") for another, the Stable Intelligence—both of which, we recall, have a numeration of 160.

It is in the Stable Intelligence that we find what we need for permanance, rest, security, completeness. The 23rd Path is one of utter resignation and trust in the Preserving *Life* Principle. The being hangs on a cross, suspended by a *thread* as it were, *removed and separated* from the ordinary experience of most human beings by his ordeal. The numerical value of these words testifies to this intimate association: 23 is the value of "thread or cord" (ChVT) as well as "parted, removed, seperated" (ZChCh) and is also one of the Hebrew words meaning "life" (ChYH). Furthermore, this is a voluntary and *joyful* process, for the value of "joy or gladness" is also 23 (ChDVH); and we note, as Waite did, that the face of the Hanged Man is one of "deep entrancement, not suffering" (Waite, 1959, p. 116).

In addition, there is a close relationship between the letters Mem and Tau. We noted that he hangs from a cross in the shape of a T, the symbol for the letter Tau, the final letter of the Hebrew alphabet. Together, these two letters form the word, *toom* (TM), meaning the "power of permanence" or "perfect, whole, sound and complete." It is the Divine Sacrifice which restores, perfects, and completes creation.

This power of the Dying God, the concept of the mythological sacrifice, is universal and cross-cultural. Before the historical drama of the Supreme Christian Sacrifice, the dying god was celebrated in seasonal rituals for many thousands of years. The Norse god Odin hung on the World Tree for nine days. The Sumerian Dumuzi, the Egyptian Osiris, the Phrygian Attis, the Greek Dionysos, the Syrian Adonis, the Roman Mithra—all were sacrificed and resurrected gods. The rites celebrating the dying and reviving gods were likewise all connected to the agricultural year and the intimate identity of the savior to the grain; i.e., wheat or corn. Common to all mystery religions of both the pagan and Christian cults was the belief by participants that they were eating the body of the God.

The commemoration of the divine passion of Osiris was celebrated in Egypt annually through a ritual mystery-play. St. Epiphanius tells us that in Egyptian Alexandria the resurrection of the god was celebrated the same day as the feast of the Visit of the Hagi, January 6th, which was the date of the birth of the new Aion, the personification of the resurrected Osiris in the form of the rising star Sirius (Sothis). During the event, the custom was to spend the night singing and praying, and at dawn a descent was made to a crypt and a wooden image brought up "which had the sign of a cross and a star of gold marked on hands, knees, and head" which was then carried around in a procession (Campbell, 1964, p. 339).

We notice that in both the Mem and the Tau cards (which create the word *toom*), the figures have a bent knee to form an inverted four or a cross symbol. This is actually a fylfot cross and shows an intimate relationship to the Crown of creation, Kether, because this is one of the symbols that belongs to this Sephira. The fylfot cross, or swastika, is the oldest wheel of life, and is found in almost every ancient cult all over the world, from the Christian catacombs to the Celtic stones. It is generally interpreted to be a representation of the solar or lunar wheel, and like both Mem and Tau is a symbol of the quaternary. It signifies the action of the Origin (radiating from the center) on the rest of the universe. In Qabalah, it symbolizes the four elements which are the latent aspects of the Tetragrammaton IHVH. If the fylfot cross is imagined as rotating in rapid motion, these elements are no longer differentiated (as they are in Tau, the Universe) but become indistinguishable from one another.

Thus the primary image of the Dying God is one of total absolution, and we imitate the message of this path when we live in submission to the ideals which it represents. This is particularly intimated by the idea in the Book of Formation of the restoration of the Creator back to the throne; that is, to lose the false personal "self" in order to find the true eternal Self.

23rd Pathworking Correspondences

1. Intelligence: Stable

2. Divine Letter: Mem, MIM (pronounced Mam) Value: 40, as final: 600, means "water"

3. Divine Name: El. Elohim Gibor (E-lo-heem Gi-boor)

4. Incense: Qnycha, myrrh. Rue

5. Gem: Aquamarine

6. Color: Blue

7. Element: Water

8. Animals: Eagle, scorpion

9. Plants: Lotus, all water plants

10. Planet: Neptune

11. Musical Tone: A flat

12. Magical Phenomenon: The power of sacred images; mirror gazing, talismans

13. Magical Weapons: Cross, cup and wine

14. Mythos and Related Symbols: Osiris, Joshua, all savior gods, Neptune, the Logos, Christ on the Tree, T-cross, undines, water nymphs

15. Gift or Challenge: To surrender desire to reason; to surrender intellect to Will

16. Rules: Organs of nutrition, the body's astral currents

17. Tarot Arcana: Hanged Man

Suggested Exercise

Use this key to concentrate on when you need to change the habits of your thinking, when you need to see something from a *different perspective*. Try reversing the whole way of perceiving a particular problem, situation, concept, or idea. Before we can attain to any degree of illumination, we must change our *point of view; we* must perceive that the Life-power is the only basis of form, not the material manifestations we rely on as being so "real." It is not money, posessions, security, etc., that is our true stability. Use the Hanged Man to focus on what True Stability is.

Focus on it also when you need to withdraw your projections in relationships; i.e., to suspend judgment. Meditate on the image of the Hanged Being suspended like a perfect pendulum at rest, not racing back and forth between two polarities. You may research some of the myths of the dying gods and see what kind of insights you recieve concerning the concepts of "sacrifice" and "the sacred."

A Qabalistic exercise connected with this path is the ritual of the Rosy Cross. A shortened form is as follows: Extend your arms in the form of one crucified and say, "Yod-Nun-Resh-Yod (INRI)." Keep the left arm extended, and raise the right arm vertically upwards, while you bow your head. Raise both arms, making a V over the head, then cross the arms at the breast. Then say "L-V-X—LUX—LIGHT." Conclude by folding the hands at the breast and say, "The Light of the Cross."

Through this exercise, you form the Latin letters which mean "Light" with your own body.

Guided Visualization

As a meditational image for this Path, imagine you are staring into a deep blue pool wherein, just behind the reflection of yourself, shines a luminescent glowing cross. You are not sure you see correctly, and as you lean forward to examine the flickering cross of light deep in the pool, you take a tumble and fall in headfirst. Immediately, a being appears who tells you that you are the diver their team has been looking for. You apparently have been equipped with diving gear, for you suuddenly realize it is strapped to your body and your guide, who is your age but much more lithe in the water, has one also. He descends rapidly, his white hair flaming around him like a halo.

You seem to be on an important mission. Suddenly you are on the sea floor immersed in a forest of plant forms with long stems, which you recognize to be the bottoms of lotus blossoms which adorn the pool at the top. You can see your guide disappear into the roots of these tall, stable plant forms, and cautiously you part the fronds and follow. Immediately, you are in another world, one where everything seems reversed. The earth seems solid beneath your feet but all the plants and trees have their roots in the air. Birds are flying, but upside down. You notice a small scorpion crawling by backwards. You stop to ponder the meaning of this strange universe and are startled by a great rumbling.

The earth is not moving, but it feels as if something is about to break open. You stop, hoping for the courage and under-standing to comprehend these strange events. Then the scorpion scurries by again, but this time it runns directly into and pierces your body deeply. You are amazed to notice simultaneously a crack in the sky, out of which falls a flaming serpent-shaped creature. Then another falls from another part of the sky, followed by three more. These flaming serpents seem also to have wings, and they converge on you all at once. Fear grips your breast and you search wildly for your guide. But the fiery beasts have already attatched themselves to your body, at each of your arms, at your lower extremities, and one at your head. You begin to feel yourself lose consciousness as you are enveloped by their searing fire, and you are suddenly acutely aware that you are *the angel of this sphere*.

148

Scales seem to fall from your eyes, and you realize that you are standing on top of a cross mounted on a golden triangle. A laugh escapes you as you seem to awaken as from a long, deep dream. At the foot of the tall glowing cross on which you are perched is a small door. With your newly discovered wings, you make your way down (depending on your frame of reference) to the ground and back to the door of roots where lies the entrance to the "right-side-up" world, where a weary traveler is sitting on the edge of a pool calling in despair for God to answer his anguished plea.

You fly down through the watery sky toward the place where your intuition is guiding you, listening closely to the words running through your body. *They are his prayers.* Your flaming wings part the water at a rock where he sits in the midst of a fierce raging in his heart. His prayers begin to feel like small arrows.

You realize he doesn't see you, but you perch on his right side and begin to chant gently in his ear, hoping he will stop his racing mind for a moment to listen. But you know he probably won't; he is looking for signs and wonders, and you will most likely end up going deeper yet, sacrificing even your angelic body, to help him understand that there is One who loves him infinitely. As you descend further down into the density that is his body, you speak to yourself, hearing as if another had spoken, listening to the voice of the Mighty One trying to reach His lost beloved: "I, the supreme Spirit who manifests through sacrifice, am divided up among innumerable souls. I live, suffer, breathe, and aspire through you. Though the vulger know Me not, it is your task to reconstitute Me completely within yourself. Uproot with flaming zeal the thorns which the enemy fosters in you. Then will I descend in my Power and my Glory. Then too, you shall be radiant at what you see; your heart shall throb and overflow, for the riches of the sea will be emptied out before you."

Are there specific kinds, or bodies of water that are very meaningful to you? What special gift would the sea, or your body of water, hold for you?

This is a path of total transformation. Make a list of the most profound or initiatory events of your life. What did they have in common? How did they alter your life?

Look up the words "baptize" and baptism" in a good dictionary and make a list of associations which relate to you specifically. Return to these ideas the next time you work this path.

Affirmations

1. *I am not the thinker, the speaker, or the actor.*

2. *In spite of appearances, the universal Will-to-Good cannot possibly be defeated.*

3. *I welcome the sacrifices I make today as part of my education.*

4. *My utter dependence on the one Divine Principle inspires me with its Strength and Splendor, its Power and its Glory.*

5. *My mind and will are linked in the permanent stability of the God-ness moving through me.*

L   JUSTICE   ל

Path 22
The Faithful Intelligence

Equilibration   *Sign: Libra*

CHAPTER TWELVE

The 22nd Path, Lamed
Justice
The Faithful Intelligence

The 22nd path is called the Faithful Intelligence "because by it spiritual virtues are increased, and all dwellers on earth are nearly under its shadow." The word "faithful" in Hebrew is *Amen*. This simple word, used daily by so many peoples of the world, has multiple meanings and is quite complex. Besides the well known "so be it," *Amen* (AMN) means: "to make firm," "to be constant," "to be nursed," "to hold fast," "true," "established," "fidelity," "faithful"; it also means "artist or artisan," and finally it means "to train or teach." The word *Amen* is auspicious to Qabalists because its number (91) is the sum of the two great Divine Names IHVH (26) and Adonai (65), or "the Lord God." *Amen* is one of the names assigned to Kether, the Prime Mover, and is related to the idea of the original motivational impulse from which everything else proceeds.

Amana was a river flowing in Damascus as well as the summit mentioned in the Song of Songs (4:8), wherein the Beloved, presumably Solomon, asks his bride to come down from the "top of Amana" because she has ravished his heart. "Amana," a derivative of *Amen*, means "a firm covenant" and implies a faithful union.

In *The Book of Tokens*, Lamed is called the "Teacher of teachers," whose "instruction is like unto a goad,/Which guideth thee through the long circuit of existence" (Case, 1934, p. 115). The letter name of Lamed (LMD) spelled out has a value of 74, the same as the "circuit" (SBIB) spoken of in the passage as well as the word "constantly" (OD) or "till eternity." These ideas demonstrate the nature of this Intelligence; i.e., that of a faithful, eternally abiding Spirit which continually teaches us the lessons we need to know on our homebound journey.

"Lamed" means "ox-goad," and the Ox is Aleph, called the "Great Ox of the Breath of Life." *The Thirty-two Paths of Wisdom* implies that the Faithful Intelligence of Lamed multiplies and distributes these powers of the Life Force in a way which is consistent with Divine Justice and in perfect equilibrium. Thus we have the image of the Justice key with scales and sword.

It is the energy in the 22nd Path which maintains the balance of the entire Tree, with its 22 archetypal constellations represented by the Major Arcana. An ox-goad is something which regulates the primal raw energy of Aleph, the unfathomable Beginning, in a way that we, who dwell in its shadow, can begin, using the language of symbols, to understand.

The conscious maintenance of balance is the assigned task of one who trods this path, as it requires continual adjustment of one's thoughts and actions. On a personal level, we are afflicted and spurred on by the goad of our own karma, until, through repeated efforts, we adjust our actions to reap rewards more attuned to the harmony of the Faithful Intelligence. Case implies this is definitely a path of action, and Goethe (also a seeker and occultist) observed that we only build character through contact with other fellow human beings in our ordinary daily busy world.

As a symbolic image, the letter Lamed represents a serpent unfolding, or the wing of a bird which raises, extends, and unfolds itself. Through meditation on the letter-shape itself, these associations can become more meaningful. The astrological symbol related to Lamed is, of course, Libra, whose ruling planet is Venus, represented by the dove, and in the Tarot by the Empress and imagination. Creative imagination is the foundation of Tarot practice; mental imagery is a frequently used technique in both metaphysics and psychology. But it is the controlling and equilibriating factor represented by Lamed which makes these creative powers manifest in specific forms.

The archetype of Our Lady of the Scales is the Egyptian Maat, goddess of truth, justice, and law. Her task was to weigh the souls of the dead to determine their fate in the afterlife. She did this by placing the heart of the deceased on one side of the scale and the "feather of Maat" (or truth) on the other. If one's heart was too heavy with guilt, one tipped the scales; if, on the other hand, one's heart was pure, perfect balance was maintained and one was admitted to the rewards of the heavenly kingdom. In Egypt, Maat was called the "Queen of Heaven."

Maat was the daughter of Ra, the Sun-god, and on the Tree of Life, this Path connects Geburah, the Law of Undeviating Justice, with Tiphareth, the Sun-King. Her sword points upward toward the Strength and Severity of the Law, but her scales lean toward the Beauty and Harmony of the Sun-sphere. She acts as a regulator of energy and a keeper of the balance. It is said that "Equilibrium is the basis of the Great Work," and in the *Sepher Yetzirah* the special function assigned to Lamed is work or action. Maat represents total equilibrium, yet at the same time constant motion. It is important to understand this concept of equilibrium, because it is inherent in the very nature of Qabalah. It is said that the God-energy "formed, weighed, and composed with these 22 letters every created thing" (S.Y. 2:1), and this path is closely associated with the regulation, measurement, and distribution of such a profound work. On a practical level, this may mean dealing with words through writing or speaking.

As the "ox-goad," Lamed is charged with the responsibility of reconciling and mediating the most powerful forces of the Cosmos; Aleph is the "mother" letter which represents this primal Life-Force through the element of air. The *Sepher Yetzirah* says air "derived from the Spirit is as the tongue of a balance" (S.Y.2:1) between the other two mother letters, Mem (water) and Shin (fire). We saw elsewhere (Path 25) that these two letters together form the word "heaven" (ShMYM.) Aleph is the connecting link to these primal energies and Lamed is the connecting link to Aleph.

Together Aleph (A) and Lamed (L) form another important relationship: the word "Al" or "El," used frequently in the Old Testament, which means "God, the most high." It was El Shaddai (God Almighty) who originally formed the covenant with Abraham (Genesis 17:1). So we understand the Aleph-Lamed connection to represent the vital idea of the primal driving force being adjusted to suit our individual needs in terms of our relationship to this Energy. Since Aleph represents the beginning of things, and one of the symbols of Lamed is a feather or a bird's wing, this name (AL) conveys the idea of the might and power of the God-energy (Aleph) being borne up by the outspreading force of Lamed. In this connection, we note that most angelic names end in "al" or "el."

On a psychological level, the process most frequently encountered on this path is one of self-assessment. The soul is weighed on the scales and adjustments are made by the sword of Geburah. What is not necessary and useful for our spiritual growth is cut away. The use of the sword is the "narrow way of attainment." Hence Jesus is represented as being identified both with the dove of peace (the archetypal bird of Venus) and the sword (Zain), which eliminates through discrimination (John 9:39). Both of these symbolic images are represented in this key. Libra is further associated because it governs the kidneys, the organs of elimination, thus cleansing the bloodstream of impurities. In alchemy, the Great Work is accomplished only through much elimination and purification.

The other prime prerequisite for the accomplishment of the Great Work is faith. The 22nd Path is called the Faithful Intelligence not only because it is faithful to us, but because we have a responsibility—if we want to have a relationship with it—to increase our own faith. This Path tells us we must have confidence in the principles on which we base our lives. No one else can give you faith in yourself. Jesus testified many times to the great healing power of faith (Luke 17:19), including its ability to do the impossible (Matthew 17:20).

Finally, we recall that one of the meanings of the word *Amen* is "to teach." The ideas of karma and education are strongly connected to this path. This implies the active *work* (karma meaning action) of developing abilities and applying them to the direction of others through the process of education. To educate in this way is not simply to be possessed with accumulated amounts of information, but to apply the inspiration of Superconsciousness (represented by Aleph) in all our affairs. And though many of us are not educators, in some sense we are all teachers at various points in our lives.

This path is one of working with knowledge, both within and without, and implies particularly intuitive knowledge gained through spiritual practice. Poise is also one of the meanings attached to Justice and one of the important elements to be developed while working the 22nd Path. Through correct personal assessment, the development of poise, learning from past actions, and repeated attempts to "weigh the facts" in our present situation, we begin to establish true justice in our lives and in our surroundings.

22nd Pathworking Correspondences

1. Intelligence: Faithful

2. Divine Letter: Lamed, LMD (pronounced Lahm-ed) Value: 30, means "ox-goad".

3. Divine Names: El, Elohim Gibor (E-lo-heem Gi-boor)

4. Incense: Galbanum, benzoin. Rue

5. Gem: Emerald

6. Color: Emerald Green

7. Element: Air

8. Animals: Elephant

9. Plants: Aloe, tobacco

10. Planet: Venus

11. Musical Tone: F sharp

12. Magical Povers: Works of Justice and Balance

13. Magical Weapon: Scales, sword

14. Mythos and Related Symbols: Themis, Yama, fairies, harpies, the Feather of Maat, wings of birds and angels, the Heart of Innocence, Nemesis

15. Gift or Challenge: To adjust and fine-tune the personality, to develop poise in the face of changes

16. Rules: Kidneys

17. Tarot Arcana: Justice

Suggested Exercises

When you feel out of balance, the energy of this key can help restore equilibrium and poise in your life. Meditate on it when you have the opportunity to *reflect* on the karmic seeds you are sowing and have sown. Try to pay particular attention to every action you do for the course of a day or even an hour and observe how balanced you are in each situation. Imagine you are observing this situation as an outsider, an impartial witness to yourself.

Also, meditate on the Justice Key when you are being judgmental with yourself. Being too hard on oneself can create useless guilt, which, in turn, inhibits one's faith. The great Qabalistic teacher Ann Davies often reminded her students that one's first responsibility in one's relationship with God is to hold fast to the *faith* in that relationship, to "rest in God," and to therefore act with confidence. Use the Justice key to tap into the limitless power and guidance of the Great Wings.

When working this Path, try to keep polarities in perspective and put your energy into the pole which has been neglected. Watch the pole of "uncomplaining martyrdom" or "suffering for justice's sake." This could be your own self-deluded need to invite even more unpleasant experiences into an imaginative subconscious that loves to work for you. On the other hand, if you are experiencing "bad karma" for reasons you may or may not understand, use this key as a meditative tool to allow new insights on how even this can be a finer adjustment to tune you to a deeper understanding of this wonderful education called life.

Guided Visualization

As a meditation for this Path, imagine that you are standing outside the temple of Maat, or the gate of heaven, waiting for judgment. You are truly uncertain how That which has been the silent Observer of all your actions in your life will respond to you once you enter. So you murmur a fervent prayer for assistance in maintaining balance and poise in this tense situation. At once, in response, appears the angel Khamael with a flaming sword which he at once strikes deeply into your heart. For a moment, you are enveloped in searing pain and then, miraculously, you see emerging from your own body, at the tip of his sword, heavy dark matter which apparently has been instantly stripped away. Suddenly, you feel as light as a feather and you know he has done you the most cherished favor an angel or being anywhere could do. You are suddenly ushered into the judgment room where hangs a pair of scales made of pure gold. On one side glows a wafer of radiant light, the other side is empty. In resignation and fervent thanksgiving, you offer your heart to the Powers That Be.

What is the darkness which Khamael would pull out from your soul? How would it weigh on the scale if it had been left in?

Affirmations

1. *All the activites of my life are held in equilibrium.*

2. *Good Luck is karma working itself out. Today I will wish it on everybody.*

3. *I am faithful to my spiritual ideals and my signature to this vow is my recitation of the word Amen with full consciousness.*

4. *Although I reap what I sow, I can still use discrimination in what I eat.*

5. *I am poised and prepared.*

6. *My faith is "the substance of things hoped for and the evidence of things unseen."*

K WHEEL OF FORTUNE **כ**

Path 21
The Rewarding Intelligence

Rotation   *Planet: Jupiter*

CHAPTER THIRTEEN

The 21st Path, Kaph
The Wheel
The Intelligence of Desirous Quest

The 21st Path is called the "Rewarding Intelligence of Those who Seek," or the "Intelligence of Conciliation." On the Tree, it links the spheres of Netzach, which represents the desire nature, and Chesed, Divine Mercy, one of whose attributes is memory. The word "quest" in Hebrew is *meboquash* and is from the root MBVQH, meaning hunger or emptiness. With an ending of Shin (Sh) instead of Heh (H), it means, "sought, requested," or "request" as well as "quest." The implication for the path is that, after a deep hunger, which the world is not found to have satisfied, the soul's undefined yearning turns to something higher, stirred by dim memories (represented by Chesed) of richer experiences which are only found in the inner life.

The *Sepher Yetzirah* says this Intelligence is directly connected to riches as well as poverty (S.Y. 4:1), and it is up to the individual seeker to determine where to search for those riches necessary to satisfy one's quest. The injunction "Seek and you shall find" varies considerably, from the one on a material quest to one on an intellectual or spiritual one. Kaph is a Path of considerable effort and exertion (as anyone who has trod it knows) and requires keen discretion in determining what indeed is "spiritual" and good for one's soul. The link with this association through gematria is that the letter name Kaph (KPh), which means "palm" as well as the "closed or grasping hand," has a numerical value of 100, the same as "exertion" or "effort" (MDVN).

The hope that our spiritual quest has the opportunity to find itself in Chesed, however, is also linked in gematria because "quest" (MBVQSh) has a value of 428, as does the Chasmalim (ChShMLYM), or the angelic choir who have attained to Chesed, also called the "Brilliant Ones." This angelic vision was recorded in Ezekiel 1:4, where he talks about the beings "enveloped in brightness . . . which gleamed like electrum" (ChShML). The figures into which this cloud of the Chasmalim then proceeded to manifest in this vision are the same as those pictured in the Tarot key: the human, the lion, the ox, and the eagle.

These symbols are commonly associated with the heavenly host known as the kerabim (cherabim). The kerabim have different names, like the Sephiroth, according to their various attributes or ways of manifesting. In Ez. 1:4, they are called the Brilliant Ones, Chasmalim, which belong to the sphere of Chesed. In Ez. 1:16, they are called "wheels," or Auphanim, which belong to the sphere of Chokmah. The kerabim are said to represent the powers of the letters of the Tetragrammaton (IHVH) on the material plane. The word kerabim means simply *cherub*, from the root word *cheri* (KRV), "to announce or herald."

Kaph, the Wheel, is layered with mystical import and is closely linked to *prophecy and visions* (ChZH), demonstrated by the fact that numerically they have the same value: 20. Interestingly, the famous legendary visionary Christian Rosencreutz, who supposedly founded the order of the Rosicrucians, was often called, "Brother Kaph." Also linked through the numerical value 20 are the words "fraternity" (AChVH) and "penetration" (ChZH). The *fraternity* of the Rosy Cross was known for its *deep penetration* into occult secrets veiled in symbolism such as we see in Ezekiel, as well as many other biblical passages.

Paul Case has said that the work of this path is for seekers only. "It is not enough to hear the word of liberation. Active and assiduous inquiry and search are necessary" (Case, 1985, p. 255). The emphasis on other Paths may include meditation (Tzaddi), concentration (Beth), imagination (Daleth), receptivity (Cheth) sacrifice (Mem), or mysticism (Samekh), but the work in Kaph is to ponder and probe the eternal riddle proposed by the sphinx which sits on the top of the Wheel; i.e., what does it mean to be a human?

The sphinx at Thebes which confronted Oedipus with this question was a symbolic figure representing the conjunction of the various elements in Ezekiel's vision, for she had the head of a human, the body of a bull or ox, the claws and tail of a lion, and (in most artistic renditions) the wings of a bird. Besides being an elusive archetype of the Supreme Enigma, she is simultaneously a symbol which unites the four elements, the four directions, and other quaternaries. She is the stable element in the midst of cyclic change, and in Egypt and Greece was viewed as the guardian of the gateway of the mysteries of life and death.

The four creatures of Ezekiel also appeared in the vision of John (Apocalypse 4:6-7) where they unceasingly honor the One. In the Masonic and Rosicrucian fraternities, they represent Leo, the lion; Taurus, the bull; Aquarius, the human (or angel); and Scorpio, the eagle, which are the 5th, 2nd, 11th, and 8th signs of the zodiac. These numbers add up to 26, the number of the Divine name IHVH (Yahweh), the initials of which appear in Hebrew on the outer rim of the Wheel.

In some decks, the images of these creatures are drawn with the heads only, but, in the Waite deck, they are all shown with wings and holding books, presumably referring to the four evangelists. Various mystical traditions of the middle ages tell us the attributions of Christ were defined as human by Matthew, as passionate by Luke (symbolized by the lion and fire), as a beast of burden by Mark (represented by the bull and earth) and in a mystical way by John (symbolized by the eagle and flight.)

Fundamental to the mysticism in this key is the cyclic nature of life and the various ways of viewing any particular person or situation. The Wheel represents the recurrence of the seasons, the repetitive activities of all human beings, the regularity of astronomical movements in the skies, the rotation of human fortunes. In Hindu philosophy, the idea is to get off the wheel. In the Western esoteric tradition, the philosophy is to be "in the world but not of it," thereby freeing consciousness to be at rest (symbolized by Path 23), perceiving the God-energy inherent in matter as well as in spirit but not identified with its endless revolutions and cycles.

These cycles of life and nature follow specific laws, which humans are obviously subject to until the time when the soul reaches adepthood (symbolized by Beth, the Magician). Then the normal laws of the world yield to her or his command as witnessed by masters and yogis of many traditions. The *law* in the Wheel of Fortune is represented by the word TORA (also spelled Torah), which is the body of wisdom and law contained in Jewish scripture.

It is printed alternately with the word Yahweh (IHVH) as one reads the Wheel in a counterclockwise direction. Qabalists, who are fond of word permutations, have noticed that reading the other way, one derives the word ROTA, which is Latin for wheel, and TAROT, which embodies the archetypal images on the wheel of life.

The Wheel is a symbolic synthesis of all cosmic forces, as well as the passage of time. But, in addition, the Wheel of Fortune represents the pattern of the individual's evolving destiny. In the process of involution, it is the Divine Mercy and Beneficence of Chesed descending into matter, drawn by the Desire and Love of Netzach. As a symbol for personal destiny it is closely linked to Kaph, the palm of the hand, which traditionally has been associated with holding one's destiny or fortune. It is also linked to the Tau cross (the World), and specifically relates to Kaph, the palm, which is the part of the body whereby Spirit is nailed to the Cross of Matter.

The letter Vav, which means "nail," is the third letter of the Tetragrammaton (IHVH) and is also connected in this regard. Together these three letters form a particularly powerful image for the Christian qabalist: TVK, T = cross, V = nail, and K = palm of the hand. This Hebrew word, *took* (TVK), means "center," "within," or "in the midst." It is the root of the word which means "retribution" (TVKChH). In addition, it has the numerical value of 426, the same as the Hebrew word meaning "savior" (MVShIO).

Because this is the path of the Desirous Quest, the myth which particularly belongs to it is the Quest for the Grail. The Grail, which for countless ages has been a metaphor for regeneration, was the cherished object of the Knights of the Round Table, an image which reflects the wheel. There was a legend that the cup which later was to hold the blood of Christ was originally fashioned by angels from an emerald that dropped from Lucifer's forehead when he was flung into the abyss. The myth points to the analogy that the sin of pride or desire is redeemed through the very Grail which was formed from it. The emerald, as Qabalistic correspondences tell us, belongs to Venus, the goddess of Love and Desire (and an attribute of Netzach), who in a different mythology was also called the "Light-bearer." This light- bringer, or Morning Star god or goddess, was noticed by ancient peoples to be also the same dying Evening Star and thus it is an archetypal representation of the ceaseless cycles of life and death. Christ also, however, identified himself as the Morning Star (Rev. 22:16), returning us again to the metaphor of regeneration.

The serpent descending on the left side of the Wheel represents the vibrating force which keeps the cosmos manifesting on a material plane; i.e., the serpent of Maya, illusion, or the serpent in the garden which birthed us from unconsciousness. In both a Jungian and a metaphysical interpretation, it is not inherently "evil," yet is an ambivalent figure because it is inevitably connected to dualities. It is related to Paths 19 and 26 (Teth and Ayin). The serpent is also called "Typhon," who was the fire-breathing monster which personified volcanoes and typhoons and who was also the father of the Sphinx.

Ascending on the other side of the Wheel is the figure of Anubis, an archetypal image in Egyptian mythology who was the mediator between this life and the next. Anubis was the guide and guardian of the soul when it left the body in astral travel or in death. The three figures of Anubis, the Sphinx, and the Typhon also represent the three alchemical elements of mercury, sulphur, and salt. These are the symbols at the ends of the spokes on the inner wheel which point to the letters A, T, and O. The fourth symbol (pointing to the R) represents the alchemical process of dissolution.

Teachers of many traditions tell us that in both alchemy and yoga, we learn to dissolve the various forms of appearance around us, to distill their essence, assimilate that into ourselves, and project that back into the world in new creative forms. The object of the quest, whether it be the alchemical labor or the individuation process, is the "quintessence," and the symbol for this is the eight-spoked wheel. For the Gnostics this was a symbol for Christ and, in the Greco-Egyptian world, for Hermes or Thoth.

The work for one who treads this Path is not to get off the wheel. It is to find the quintessence at its center. The Wheel of rotation will move unceasingly forward and we will either be victims of circumstance or masters of it. Qabalah teaches that the secret of mastering circumstance is to be found through the realization that the "center," the *took* (TVK), the very *heart* of that Wheel, the Primary Point of First Unity, is our only safe habitation. When we are identified with the Ruling Power which keeps in balance the wheeling activities of the cosmic cycles, we are simultaneously at the Beginning and the End of our Quest, because they are really the same place.

21st Pathworking Correspondences

1. Intelligence: Desirous Quest, or Intelligence of Those Who Seek

2. Divine Letter: Kaph, KPh (pronounced Kaff) Value: 20, as final: 500, means "closed or grasping hand"

3. Divine Name: Abba. El

4. Incense: Saffron, cedar. Pine

5. Gems: Amethyst, lapis lazuli

6. Color: Royal Violet

7. Element: Water

8. Animala: Eagle, ox, lion, jackal

9. Plants: Hyssop, oak, poplar, fig

10. Planet: Jupiter

11. Musical Tone: A sharp

12. Magical Powers: Political or social ascendency; centered spirituality

13. Magical Weapon: Scepter

14. Mythos and Related Symbols: Arthur, Ezekiel, Athor, Hermanubis, Jupiter, Zeus, Brahma, Pluto, winds and storms, the wheel, the revolving heavens, a grail cup, the Round Table, sphinx, typhon

15. Gift or Challenge: Practice in mastering circumstance; balance in mood swings, patience

16. Rules: Blood, also connected to gout

17. Tarot Arcana: Wheel

Suggested Exercises

Use this key to focus in on the following questions: How is the law of reciprocity at work in my life? Am I taking in more than I am giving, or giving more than I am taking in? Either way, how do I feel about it? How do those around me feel about it? Am I a victim of mood swings; am I "hanging out" on the rim of that wheel, being crushed by its every turn, or am I finding my way back towards its center?

The energy of meditating on this card will help balance emotional tone, curb impatience with a world you are fed up with, pick you up when you are feeling bored, tired, or victimized. It will help to reorient perspective. Use the time when working this Path to restructure your life so that it is not so scattered, to make lists of what you need to do to organize your thoughts in a coherent way, to write down events in your notebooks and analyze the patterns and cycles you are moving in.

A good exercise to enlarge your esoteric understanding of this Path is to make a list of all the symbols you can find in the picture and then look them up in a symbol dictionary. You may also attempt to discover how many of these same symbols appear in the other Tarot keys, what their meanings are there, and what the relationsip is between the cards as Paths on the Tree.

Guided Visualization

As a meditational contact image for this path, visualize a bright luminous cloud, almost metallic, like gold or silver, flashing in the Sun. It takes on fantasy shapes that dance, gleaming and shape-shifting in the brilliant light—a sphinx, a dragon, an eagle, a cloud again. Then you sense that from this whirling cloud radiates a powerful presence, an angelic brilliance.

Suddenly, from out of its center reaches a hand offering you a golden chalice. You realize it is the long-lost Grail and you reach humbly but eagerly toward it. When it falls gently into your grasp, you gaze deeply into it. The inside of this jeweled chalice is rich, royal violet, deepening into infinity at the vortex at its bottom. You can see the ceaseless flow of life eternal moving within its swirling center. It all appears to fit together in a grand pattern of perfection somehow; just holding the sacred cup seems to produce the missing piece of the puzzle of life that has always perplexed you the most. Gaze long into its hidden mysteries and meditate on what it reveals to you.

This is the place in your journey to contemplate deeply what your real desire is.

How clearly are you able to visualize it?

Affirmations

1. *I command control over my thoughts, my tongue, and my sensitivity.*

2. *I am one with the Limitless Light, condensing itself into a single point.*

3. *Today I am an instrument of blessing.*

4. *In the Living Wheel of my Father-Mother God, I live and move and have my being.*

5. *I am moving and still at the same time.*

THE HERMIT

Path 20
The Intelligence of Will

Response   *Sign: Virgo*

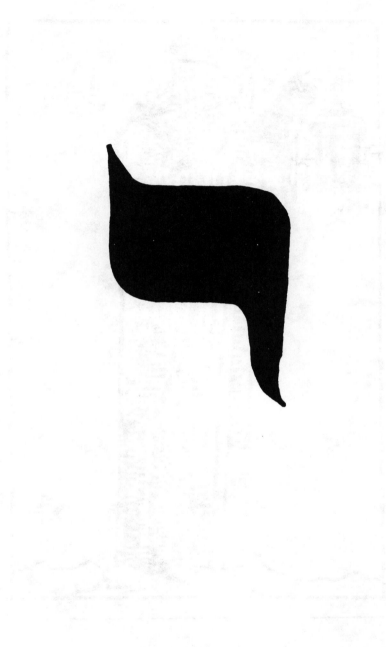

CHAPTER FOURTEEN

The 20th Path, Yod
The Hermit
The Intelligence of Will

The word *yod* means hand, particularly the open or extended hand. This is the 20th Path on the Tree and is called the "Intelligence of Will." Yod is spelled YVD, which equals 20 when its letters are added up, as does the Hebrew word DIV, which means "ink" or "fluid darkness." Twenty is also the numeration or value of "vision" or "prophesy" (ChZH). The word for "middle" or "breast" also has this numeration. Through gematria, we see an intimate connection between these seed-thoughts if we meditate on them. They are also connected beautifully in the Hermit, the key which connects the sphere of Chesed, or Mercy, with Tiphareth, or Harmony. It is truly a balanced, middle path wherein the great Seer grasps in his hand the Lamp of guidance in the inky darkness.

Yod is the tenth number in the Hebrew alphabet and, to Qabalists, ten is the number of all potential. No number exists beyond ten which cannot be broken down into a number smaller than ten. In addition, the shape of the letter is similar to a "primordial point"—the starting point, in fact, of the development of every other letter, as well as every creature and every form. Yod contains and includes in itself the germinal form of the Ten Sephiroth and also represents the Ten in their final point of development. The point symbolizes light and fire; its shape resembles a candle flame slightly on its side. This spherical light modeled on the point also represents the "golden" body that dwells in the hearts of all humans.

In Qabalah, the Primordial Point is identified as *abba* (i.e., the father) and Yod represents the "point" of the phallus, particularly the sperm which projects from it. Yod is the first letter of the most sacred Divine Name YHVH (Yod-Heh-Vav-Heh), which has been translated as "I Am" and also "I Shall Be." The word *yehi* (YHY), "become," joins the letters Yod and Heh together in a special relationship. Heh is considered feminine and the *Zohar* says that in Yehi is contained the mystery of the union of Father and Mother.

This Path represents the self-sustained original beginnings of manifestation. *The Thirty-two Paths of Wisdom* says "it is the means of preparation of all and each created being, and by this intelligence the existence of the Primordial Wisdom becomes known." The Hermit has attained the perfected state of oneness with the Primal Self. It represents adeptship. Great teachers and masters have always been identified as "God's hands," and when scripture speaks of the "hand of God," it intimates power, or an identification with the Master Power. All these ideas constellate around the primary image of union, the state which is the constant goal of the student on this Path.

The idea most strongly associated with the work here is that of *responsiveness.* The human sense which is attributed to the Path of the Hermit is the sense of touch. On a very literal level, this too represents the longing of the soul for completion, or union through the sexual act. In the mystical Song of Solomon, as well as in many narratives of Christian mystics, we see reflected the relationship of the aspirant and the Divine Object of its ardor.

The Hermit is definitely a solitary figure here; he is *not*, however, lonely. One of the diffficulties encountered in walking this Path is fighting off the collective fear we have of introversion. This is particularly pronounced in our society, where even the idea of a hermit is slightly frowned upon as reflecting an antisocial attitude. Throughout his or her pilgrimage, the student continually bumps into many others on many different paths and frequently forgets his or her own inner mission in an attempt to find an antidote for isolation. We want to be seen, touched, reacted to. The path of individuation is often a difficult one, as it continually prompts us to rid ourselves from the "herd consciousness," at any cost. It also painfully reminds us that, even though we may be intimately close to another human being, they can never walk our path for us; we can only become self-realized alone.

This is a Path of great determination. The hermit turns his or her back on much of what the world has to offer in search of wholeness; and once that vision is found, the task on this path is to extend an open hand to the next wayfarer. The Hermit is on the top of a mountain. His long journey has ended and he humbly holds out his light for those groping in the darkness below. This reflects the idea of the enlightened Master who is not content with his own illumination, but patiently waits for each and every seeker to join him in his at-one-ment with the Source of all.

The Intelligence of Will forms the patterns of all things, and one who reflects, or channels, this Will can identify with Christ, who sought not personal will, but the will of the One sending him. When one is so totally identified with the Primal Will through great concentration, one becomes the *Thaumaturge* or arch-magician, as was Moses. These ideas of "will" and "channel" are linked in Hebrew gematria; the word for "will" is *rawtsone* (RTzVN) which also means grace, as well as delight; and the word for "hollow," "conduit," "channel," etc. is *tzinnor*, TzNVR. Both words have a numerical value of 346. In Qabalah, the concept of the Thaumaturge is therefore one which represents the highest vehicle or channel for the God-energy, not simply a wonder-working magician.

The zodiacal sign attributed to this path is Virgo, whose ruling planet is Mercury. Virgo represents the virgin, ever pure and innocent, an uncontaminated channel for the Higher Good. Mercury is Thoth or Mercury-Hermes, the magician who is frequently quoted as uttering the famous maxim, "As above, so below," bringing divine Idea into manifestation through the power of the will. A magician never attempts to coerce life. His or her magical attunement is to be found in perfect obedience to the real nature behind the veil of appearances. He or she is a natural receiver, again reflecting the idea of *responsiveness*.

Virgo rules the intestines, and one of the practical "secrets" of working this Path well is to carefully choose one's food with the intention of building a finer vehicle for the Divine Life to manifest in. Subconsciousness, as we know, is not only amenable to suggestion, but it takes care of all our unconscious body processes, such as breathing, digestion, etc. Taking both of these factors into account, we can utilize this wonderful part of our psyche to make suggestions about doing its job more perfectly, and also to convey to us intuitively what it most appropriately needs to best carry out its various tasks (such as the right foods, exercise, therapy, and so on).

The Path of Yod signifies most specifically the ability of the open, extended, and creative hand. Our hands are the creative instruments by which we operate in the world. The theme of creativity is further emphasized by the relationship between Yod and the primal creative "animus" fire of the Logos. To the Greeks, the word, or logos, was spermatic; and to the Jews, this principle was embodied in the great hermit figure, Moses, who spoke with God.

This is a powerful Path for working with the creative word or creative acts of will of any kind. The Hermit shows us the relationship between the Light and the rays of creative fire which constitute our many diversified paths back to Its source.

20th Pathworking Correspondences

1. Intelligence: Intelligence of Will

2. Divine Letter: Yod, YVD (pronounced Yood) Value: 10, means "open hand"

3. Divine Name: IChIDH (Yek-hi-dah, the Indivisible One). El

4. Incense: Narcissis. Cedar

5. Gem: Peridot

6. Colors: Yellow-green, gray

7. Element: Air

8. Animal: Lamb

9. Plants: Lily, snowdrop

10. Planet: Mercury

11. Musical Tone: F

12. Magical Phenomenon: Parthenogenesis, Initiation

13. Magical Weapons: Lamp and staff

14. Mythos and Related Symbols: Moses, Adonis, Isis, The Orphic egg, the First Matter, the Great Teacher, Christ as Ruler (Supreme Will), the Light in Extension, a virgin clad in linen, a prophet, a mermaid

15. Gift or Challenge: Balance between detatchment and responsiveness

16. Rules: Intestines

17. Tarot Arcana: Hermit

Suggested Exercises

Use this key to remind you that your one true Self is already, right now, all that your individual personal will longs for. Contemplation on it will serve to bring to mind the fact that you are ever under the watchful presence of the divine indwelling "I AM" principle, which eternally holds out the light, even though you may fail to take notice of it. Let the figure remind your subconscious that it can build the perfect human in you by your ability to become ever more purely attuned and responsive to it. When examining the images that are created on the physical plane by your desire and will, pay particular attention to how they *feel* in your hand. This conscious awareness suggests even more deeply to your subconscious its power to manifest.

This is the Path to work with to develop clairsentience, which is a psychic ability to perceive the unknown through touch. This is related to the principle of cosmic feeling. When we touch a table, we recognize it as hard; when we touch water, we feel it is soft. Likewise, spirit dissolves the body and the body havens the spirit. Through clairsentience, we touch the world soul.

You may develop this extrasensory perception by doing this exercise: Turn on the faucet and feel the water running over your hand. Then try to imagine this stream of water not only on your body but running into it. Feel it pouring in through your skin; feel it passing into your heart or some other internal organ. When you can visualize what it feels like to have liquid *poured through the inside* of your body, imagine pouring this liquid back out through your body, projecting it to someone who perhaps needs healing or love. Imagine this stream as golden, light-filled, and holding your highest designs of good for that person.

Ann Davies, the foremost disciple of Paul Case, tells a story of how powerful this technique can be. She was naturally very clairsentient and had the capacity to enter a state of rapture with the God-energy (which she called the Higher Self) by visualizing the Hermit key. Once, she received a very strong intuitive message that a member of their Qabalistic group was crying out for help. So she threw herself into a "rapturous identity" with the "heart of the universe" and poured out love to her for about ten minutes. She

180

later learned that, at that same time, this woman, desperate to the point of suicide, had mentally called upon Ann and immediately received such a surge of strength and peace that she lost all desire for escape through suicide. Ann frequently said that this gift from the Higher Self often came when she was engaged in spiritual work, and testified to the fact that she was truly in tune with the energy of the Hermit, who always acts as a channel for God.

Visualization

As a meditation exercise, stare at the Tarot key for several moments. Then imagine yourself flooded with a green-golden light. It acts like a kind of glow which bathes you and also directs your way through the dark night. Visualize what it would be like to climb this lofty mountain peak the Wise Old Man is standing on and, once near to him, crawl inside the cloak he opens to shelter you. As you shut your eyes and rest there, in the comforting presence of his inky darkness, you are soothed and protected.

As you are nestled there, however, you soon notice something dripping upon you from above your head; somehow this warm caressing fluid seems to sink into your soul like heavenly dew. Suddenly, you realize that this substance is actually coming from the *heart* of this benevolent figure who patiently extends his lamp. Then, from somewhere deep inside the dark womb of his mantle, you hear a voice say: "Through these drops of mercy arise the substantialization of the self and the regeneration of the species. It penetrates human egoism like a vivifying fluid. I have inscribed your name upon my hand; you are engraved as a deep wound upon my heart. Through my blood, mercy enters your world. It is a bridge all can cross, if you would but have mercy on one another."

What does Divine Mercy mean to you? How does it balance the attribute of Divine Justice on the opposite pillar of the Tree? What can you do in your life today to manifest this theme in a realistic way?

Affirmations

1. I am the eternal witness of all activity, which I perceive as a series of transformations of cyclic energy radiating from the One Source.

2. I am an embodiment of the Will of God.

3. I feel the Light in Extension radiating through me this very moment.

4. I walk the earth perceiving the divine in everything and everyone.

5. Though I do not see the end of the road, my feet are set firm upon the path.

 STRENGTH

Path 19
Intelligence of the Secret of Spiritual Activities

Suggestion   *Sign: Leo*

CHAPTER FIFTEEN

The 19th Path, Teth
Strength
Intelligence of the Secret of All
Spiritual Activities

Teth is the ninth letter of the Hebrew alphabet and therefore has a value of 9. From the end of the alphabet (Tau) proceeding backwards to Yod, all the letters have numerical values that are multiples of ten or more so they could be used for counting. From Aleph to Teth are the first nine single-digit numerals. Since these are the primary numbers from which all others are formed, they represent the original nine primal archetypal ideas. The number 9 carries the obvious ideas of conclusion, goal, fulfillment; also adeptship, union, and innocence.

In addition, Teth (and the number 9) represents the archetype of "primeval female energy" (Suares, 1985, p. 57). Teth means "serpent" and is synonymous with the primitive powers represented by the lion that need to be tamed by the virgin in the Tarot key. She is, in a sense, the archetypal "fire-goddess," and the fire which she, as a magician, has under perfect control is the burning kundalini serpent energy, clothed here in the symbolism of Leo the lion. Leo is ruled by the Sun, linking this path to Resh and also to the Divine Incarnation in Tiphareth. It indicates that the Solar Power can open up higher levels of consciousness beyond those reflected in the Sun.

In Hebrew occultism, Leo is attributed to the tribe of Judah and, in the Revelation of John (5:5), it is the Lion of Judah who has the right to open the seven seals and expose their powerful releases of energy. The shape of the letter Teth suggests a serpent biting its ovn tail, intimating that the serpent power feeds on itself, or is

187

self-sustaining. Kundalini is called the "coiled one." The energy released when the snake uncoils can be divinely intoxicating or devastating, as testified by many personal experiences and expounded upon in a vast amount of literature.

The serpent energy is definitely one of the most primeval archetypes and in all ancient cultures was intimately connected with the mysterious or divine feminine. In shamanic and matriarchal cultures, it is a symbol of wisdom. It was likewise to Jesus, who told his disciples to be "wise as serpents" (Matthew 10:16). The serpent-power is known in Tibetan occultism and Theosophy as "Fohat," or "vital electricity or magnetism."

Case describes this Fohat power as having affinities with both fire and water. It is like water because it moves in waves and like fire in that it tends to disintegrate and consume physical form (Case, 1985). The biblical phrase, "The Lord our God is a consuming fire" (Deut. 4:24), reflects this idea, as do many mystical treatises which speak about the "possessive" aspects of the God-energy when one is "inflamed" with prayer.

Lest one think this passage in Deuteronomy describes a jealous, masculine God, one need only examine the etymology of the Hebrew word for "consume" or "devour" as used in the text: "ABLH," a descriptive adjective which means "mourning" as well as "consuming," is used in the feminine sense, because in Hebrew adjectives ending in H are feminine in gender. This reflects the fact that it is the *Holy Spirit* of God (*Ruach* Elohim, which in Hebrew is feminine and belongs to the sphere of Binah) that mourns for us like a faithful mother. She is intimately connected to the Fohat or fire energy in the Pentecostal analogy of the tongues of fire.

As the vitalizing electric principle which animates the cosmos, Fohat is similar to the Eastern concept of Shakti, or the female that is the supreme *force* of the universe. This is its relationship to the title of the Tarot key, which is Strength or Force. Qabalistically, this implies the power of the serpent energy and its control by the feminine principle, rather than concepts of "courage" or "fortitude" as given in some interpretations.

Through gematria, these concepts are linked, because *strength* or *energy* (ChZPhIM) and Fohat both equal 165. When broken down to a single digit, this equals 3, the number of Binah and the Holy Spirit. In addition, the 19th *Path* is connected to the feminine principle of "life" or Eve (ChVH), which also equals 19. In folklore, Brigit was considered the "fire-goddess," and at Kildare, 19 priestesses or vestal virgins (some versions say nuns) kept perpetual watch over the sacred fire which was never alloved to go out because it was magically linked to the life-giving powers of the Sun.

In Theosophy, Fohat is in the cosmos what Eros, individual passion or love, is in the microcosm. This reflects its magnetic principle. In Alchemy and Qabalah, the control and regulation of this power is the foundation upon which all works of practical occultism are based. In this regard, Teth, the ninth letter, and Yesod, the ninth Sephira, are closely related, because the *foundation* (Yesod) on which all life is based is rooted in primal sexual energies, which, like the Kundalini itself, reside at the bottom of the spine. It is the transformation of this energy which is represented by the Tarot key.

There is a commonplace myth in Qabalah that no wild animal can harm an adept. He or she walks in peace among all humans and animals, bringing the concept of Eden alive in his or her own personal life. This is reflected in the myth of Daniel in the lion's den. The symbolism is that it is the enlightened individual who can control the "animal potency," which is the root of the manifested creation. A variation of this theme is the myth of Brigit, again the archetype of the fire-goddess, whose purity and strength was demonstrated by the fact that she walked from one city to another with a burning coal in her bosom and was not burned.

The 19th Path is veiled in many mysteries; *The Thirty-two Paths of Wisdom* (Waite translation) calls it the "Intelligence of the Secret of all Spiritual Activities." *The Book of Tokens* tells us that one of those "secret activites" has to do with number; i.e., to discover the many hidden secrets in gematria, as well as to use rhythmic counting in meditation exercises. In Teth, it is said, ""By this letter do I show—/First, that all things are brought forth through number,/And second, that all works of power accomplished by the wise/Have number for their foundation" (Case, 1934, p. 92).

On the Tree, Teth connects two of the most dichotomous poles in the God-energy: Divine Mercy and Divine Severity. Those who think life should all be gentleness and kindness fail to see that, without the equilibrium of strength and severity, the personality's shadow on this Path, we would not be balanced human beings and would degenerate quickly into spineless creatures with no *force*. Geburah and Chesed are the light and shadow of the world drama. One of the primary symbols of the Geburah pole is the sword; its corresponding planet is fiery Mars. It is what empowers the evolving soul to move through its most comfortable blocks toward its unknown and awe-inspiring destination.

In terms of the concept of the deity, both the matriarchal and patriarchal traditions had to move toward this fearsome aspect of the incomprehensible God-energy; the "Dark Mother" who is the terrible but necesssary destroyer—Kali, Cybele, Hecate, Sekhmet, as well as the feared Yahweh. In Qabalah "fear of the Lord" is represented by the word *pachad* (PChD), which also means "awe," and is attributed to Geburah. The symbol of the lion reflects this awesome truth: that, in the last analysis, our final fear is of death; hence we may understand that to tame the lion is to conquer our last adversary.

In mythology, this is reflected in the many legends of the venomous world serpent or sea monster on the edge of the boundaries of consciousness. European cartographers used to draw their maps with the "ouroboros"—i.e., the snake biting its tail—in the corner or edge of the map where the unknown began.

But in Qabalah, to move closer toward the Source is to move still closer to the elusive Unknown. The higher on the Tree, in fact, the less personal the Paths become, as the Ineffable can only be described in more amorphous kinds of symbolism which can only describe the personality less. When we try to portray the God-energy in terms of the Geburah pole, we simply project onto it our useless and dreaded dramas of violence born from fear. This is apparent in many Old Testament narratives, which probably describe the psyche of the writers more than the God energy they are seeking to personalize. Despite this handicap, we cannot overlook the fact that much of the Torah was written by adepts who carefully wove many great Qabalistic mysteries into their tales.

One of the Qabalistic "secrets" connected to this path is that an attribute of the Hebrew God, frequently translated in the Old Testament as "anger" or "wrath," is actually the word *rogaz* (RVGZ), which means "to quake" or "vibration." This is, of course, an attribute of Geburah and is very important in Qabalah because it indicates that the root of the Fohat or fiery serpent power is the very "trembling" which keeps existence vibrating on a perceivable plane. This is a common concept to Easterners, where the tone or mantra of God's outgoing breath is what sustains the universe. It also reflects modern physics, which demonstrates that matter is vibrating energy.

The order of angels which belong to Geburah is the Seraphim, which means *fiery serpents* (ShRPhIM). They are considered to be fiery spirits of love who are continually "inflamed" before the throne, as is the mystic who is on fire with love for the Deity.

The word *rogaz* has a numerical value of 216, the same as *geburah* and strength, power, or force (GBVRH), and also "fear" or "dread" (YRAH). Likewise, the word "lion" (ARIH), which because it ends in H is designated as feminine, also equals 216. "Auriel," which is derived from this root word, is the angel whose name means "lion of God." It also means "hero," as well as "hearth of God," reflecting its fiery energy. The "madonna" also has a value of 216 and intimates a renewal of this Life Force through the Leo power of the Sun (Son) manifested on the material plane. The last association in this regard is "blood of grapes" (DM ONBIM), or the sacred wine, which also equals 216. There is much material here for meditation.

The part of the body which Leo rules is the heart and the spine, which demonstrates the fiery life power of love which is controlling the arousal of the serpent energy of psychic pover in the spinal chakras. In the Tarot key, the "lion-tamer" is a magician because she has the same symbol over her head as the Magician. She subdues the animal nature in a way which is natural and has nothing to do with repression. In Alchemy, this is the Red Lion, which is a symbol of matter that has been ripened and purified. The chain of roses which holds the lion in check demonstrates her strength, which is of a contemplative nature. In reference to this key Waite says that the chain of flowers "signifies the sweet yoke and light burden of Divine Law, when it has been taken into the heart of hearts" (Waite, 1959, p. 103).

She gives the aspirant on this path "backbone" through her correct application of control and direction of desire. We can participate in this awesome mystique by establishing a relationship with this archetype, in whatever way possible, to insure that she will have the opportunity to do this in our lives.

19th Pathworking Correspondences

1. Intelligence: Secret of Spiritual Activities

2. Divine Letter: Teth, TTh (pronounced Teth) Value: 9, means "serpent'

3. Divine Names: Elohim Gibor (E-lo-heem Gi-boor), El

4. Incense: Olibanum, frankincense. Cedar

5. Gem: Cat's eye

6. Color: Yellov

7. Element: Air

8. Animal: Serpent, lion

9. Plant: Sunflover

10. Planet: Sun

11. Musical Tone: B

12. Magical Phenomenon: Taming wild beasts

13. Magical Weapon: Discipline

14. Mythos and Related Symbols: Ra-hoor-khuit, Bast, the Green Lion, the Fohat, the Kundalini, sword, fiery serpents, roses

15. Gift or Challenge: To fortify consciousness with trust. To exercise discipline in controlling "instincts"

16. Rules: Heart and spine

17. Tarot Arcana: Strength

Suggested Exercises

Focus on the Tarot picture will help evoke in your consciousness the realization that you are presently in touch with the limitless source of power which is ready to aid you in overcoming your worst fears.

When working with this Path try to realize that everything in the universe is conscious, intelligent energy. Practice thinking this for 5-10 minutes at a time, with everything your mind perceives: a tree, a mineral, a plant, the sky. Only by repetitious learning do we eventually have a re-collection of Divine Order instead of our "little sleep" of thinking of the universe as a blind mechanical force.

Teth rules taste and the tongue, and a good practice associated with this Path is to exercise close control over your tongue: both what goes in and what comes out of it. Gossiping is one of the deadliest sins to an occultist.

As a rejuvenation exercise for the Strength Path, spend a few minutes alone with the Sun. Imagine it as concealing an actual Entity living deep in its heart who wants very much to have a personal relationship with you. Lying or sitting so you are facing it directly, look at it *with your eyes closed*. Imagine its deep penetrating brilliance coming into your body through the tiny shade of your closed eyelids.

Begin concentrating on this bright light as you focus on your breathing, making note of the ingoing and outgoing breath with a repetitious count. It doesn't matter what the count is, as long as it is comfortable for you and the inhalation and exhalation are the same. After "Sun-gazing" in this way for a few minutes, squeeze your eyelids shut as tightly as you can and notice the changes in color produced by the conscious manipulation of the vibration of the solar rays through your tension and relaxation. Then consciously tense and relax other body parts, focusing particularly on those places which may be giving you some discomfort. Try to keep your attention on three things: your rhythmic breathing; the tension in your body held for a few seconds and then released; and the Sun's potent, healing, strength-giving powers pouring in through your closed eyes. At the end of this exercise, offer a prayer of thanksgiving to the omni-potent Life-giver behind all forms who has empowered you with Its fiery outpouring of ceaseless Love.

Guided Visualization

Imagine that you have been riding on a bright yellow ray of the Celestial Sun. It has deposited you at the gate of the temple of Chesed, the sphere of the saints and angelic hosts of the Chasmalim. You are anxious to enter, but the gates appear to be locked tight and no one is around to open them. So you lie down next to the temple door and drift into a dream.

In it, you see a picture of yourself radiant and glowing; it is such a profound transformation, in fact, that you think you must have awakened and found your way into the heaven of Divine Mercy and are now in your glorified body. You can see your own face, streaming with rays of light and ecstasy. Then, aghast, you watch yourself transform again, only now you seem to have taken on the body of a writhing monster which looks something like a serpent or dragon figure with the claws of a lion, flaming breath, and a long, slimy tail. You seem to be covered with rotting scales, and you feel so sickened and frightened to have discovered yourself in such a body that you are immediately filled with horror. You gaze wildly about, feeling a restless hunger that is searching for anything to satiate it.

One part of your rational mind is fighting to rid yourself of this wretched form, but then you hear a loud voice say, "Look well, for this is part of yourself. It is, in fact, the most deeply concealed part of your life. You did not recognize it, but you must learn to understand the necessity for contradiction that lies at the root of all things. This is the Guardian at the Threshold; that is, your lower self. You must learn how to bring it into subjection or it will forever control you."

With a start, you awaken to see a brilliant Being hovering over you. It is very amorphous, yet you can barely make out the form of an angel. She tells you her name is Tzadkiel. She has something in her arms, which is so flooded with light that it is hardly distinguishable. But as she begins to extend her hands to offer you this gift, it clearly takes on the solidity of a carefully woven chain of roses.

"Take this", she tells you, "and return to the place of your birth. When you discover again the monster which awaits at the threshold, throw the chain quickly over its head and focus your

194

attention immediately upon your heart. Then you may discover the powers that the visible world hides beneath her veil and draw great strength from them. Go now, for this is the task you must do before you return. Remember also that the eyes of the Master follow every move of your heart with great attention."

Gingerly, she places the roses in your hand and then disappears. The secret of the wreath in you arms remains as a testimony to your vision and permeates your body with its holy perfume, leaving you filled with a new resolve and steadfastness. You ponder her words and your dream as you realize that the night has passed; patiently, you wait for the rising Sun to return you to your home.

Affirmations

1. All the cells in my body are perfect flowers blooming under the watchful vigilance of my gentle suggestion.

2. Today I will allow into my consciousness only that which I truly want to manifest in my life.

3. Spirit beats my heart. Spirit vibrates in my body. Spirit is all there is.

4. Strength connects creative imagination to the wheel of the world.

5. I will formulate my desires like a perfect chain of woven roses to represent my highest ideals.

 Ch THE CHARIOT

Path 18
Intelligence of the House of Influence
Receptivity-Will   *Sign: Cancer*

CHAPTER SIXTEEN

The 18th Path, Cheth
The Chariot
Intelligence of the House of Influence

The 18th Intelligence is called the "House of Influence" from which "are drawn the arcane and the concealed meanings which repose in the shadow thereof "(*The Thirty-two Paths of Wisdom*, Waite translation). Paul Case says this House is the same as the House of the Holy Spirit, presumably because it leads directly to the sphere of Binah, the boundless ocean of Divine Understanding, to which the Ruach Elohim (Holy Ghost) is attributed. The "shadow"' implies the wings which shelter us. The angels of Binah are called the Aralim (thrones) while those of her counterpart, Chokmah (the Father), are the Auphanim (wheels). Both are strong archetypal themes, pictured in the Chariot key, which were evoked in Ezekiel's vision.

The path connects the Severity of the Law to the Limitless Understanding of the Spirit. One who walks it must have transcended all sense of "my-ness." Like the other Paths this high on the Tree, it is seldom personal in its implications, but rather describes the one who has already refined the body, mind, heart, and soul to be a clear vehicle to house the presence of the Indwelling Spirit. It is obvious that everyone houses this spirit at all times; otherwise we could not breathe or move. What is implied here is conscious awareness of purpose, and in this sense, it is a card of victory. Because of its connecting Sephiroth, the Path does imply the concept of unchanging law tempered by the ever-present beneficent Mother who repeatedly attempts to bring all Her children back to Herself.

The number of Cheth is 8, and it is called by Carlo Suares "the sphere of storage or field of all undifferentiated sub- stance" (1985, p. 57). As a noun, Cheth means both "field" and "enclosure or fence," and implies the various means of structuring consciousness into components we can perceive and understand. Other ideas associated with the number 8 are alternation, rhythm, vibration, flux and reflux, involution and evolution, and thus culture, education, and growth. To Cheth is attributed the element of water, and the *Sepher Yetzirah* says that the function which is its foundation is speech (S.Y. 5:1). Water, in both metaphysical and Jungian terminology, is said to be the element representing the "sea of the unconscious," and in this sense, Cheth does not represent speech as we know it, because speech cannot define the Unconscious. The functions of speech belong more specifically to the Path of Peh (mouth). What is implied here (as we traverse the Path on the Way of Return) is the restoration of "the Word to its creator," as the *Sepher Yetzirah* tells us, thus replacing the God-energy back on its throne (S.Y. 1:1), which is Binah. The speech referred to is called the "Voice of Silence" because it contains secrets that are never written or communicated by the human tongue.

The word "arcana" means knowledge revealed to initiates and is from the root "arc" or "ark" (ARVK), which was the great mystery contained in the Holy of Holies or the sacred temple. It represents the central spark which resides in the heart of all knowledge. It was in the Ark of the Covenent where the Shekinah, or Divine Presence dwelled. Shekinah is a feminine noun which means the "glory of God," and it is attributed to Malkuth, the Earth, where She is Binah manifested on a perceivable plane. One of Shekinah's names is "Apple Field," referring us back to Cheth. In Jewish mysticism, it is the Shekinah who is the voice of the Sephiroth, or, in the Bible, of Yahweh. Cheth can be imagined as the birth of divine language. At creation and at the drama of Mt. Sinai, the Shekinah is revealed through the alchemy of the letters themselves.

In the Qabalistic work, the *Zohar*, is recounted the legend of the way the letters were engraved on the tablets given to Moses: "Now they came forth, these carved, flaming letters, flashing like gold when it dazzles . . . pure and bright from the flowing measure of the spark. When these letters came forth, they were all refined, carved precisely, sparkling, flashing. All of Israel saw the letters flying through space in every direction, engraving themselves on the tablets of stone" (trans. D.Matt, 1983, p. 120).

The Thirty-two Paths of Wisdom tells us that the arcana that spring forth on this path come from the "cause of all causes." The Tarot itself is called arcana because it imparts truths through symbolic language which is older than any human tongue. This is why Cheth is called "occult speech"; that is, in meditation, symbols bypass the mind and influence us through the subconscious.

Our conscious activity, however, is influenced by the Law, and the word for this Intelligence, "Influence" (ShPO),which also means "to flow," "abundance," or "plenty," has a value of 450. Hebrew gematria tells us this is also the value of *looakhuth* (LVChVTh), the "tablets of the Law," which is the body of wisdom known as the Torah. This is the same Tora which rests on the lap of the High Priestess (Gimel), the manifestation of this archetype on Path 13.

Qabalists have also noted that 450 is the same as *peree etz*, the "Fruit of the tree" (PRIOTz), as well as *peshah* (PShO), which means "sin or transgression," and is spelled similarly to ShPO (influence), only the first two letters are reversed. This indicates our mistaken interpretation about this divine influence when we know nothing about it except how it is perceived through the senses, and coincides with the original definition of "sin," which means "to miss the mark."

The single most important message of this Path is that Spirit must be recognized behind the form, and that, as a vehicle for Spirit's *own intention,* the form must be directed towards its ultimate reunion with its Source. On an outgoing path, Cheth represents the "enclosure" which is the container for spiritual essence. On the path of Return, these forms begin to dissolve. The chariot rider in the Tarot key has images of lunar crescents on each shoulder, indicating the influence of the Moon and Water. One face is severe, one benign, the same as the chariot's drivers, showing us the two faces of reality when it has become constricted into form.

An important idea connected to Cheth is that, as a "fenced field," it *really is not separate.* A field is still a part of the same land which is outside of it. The wall behind the chariot represents the false restrictions we as a species create for the purpose of setting ourselves apart. It is generally through education and training by our elders that we become aware of such divisions at all, for the younger the child, the less aware he or she is of concepts such as "posession" or "trespassing." Indeed, the boundaries between an infant and its mother are sometimes said to be so thin that there is an uncanny "telepathy" between them. Yet it is by these very restrictions that we are able to create structures such as culture and education as we grow.

Descending from the Sea of Binah, Path 18 is one where life springs into manifestation through the great power of Binah's Saturn influence, whose limitation creates form. These ideas are related through their numerical association; i.e., 18, which also means "living or alive" (ChI) as well as "refreshment" or "running water," referring us again to the ocean of Binah and the limitless unconscious.

The chariot is the carrier for our own special journey toward individuation. On this Path, however, we need to beware of the lure of the personality's "inflation"; the many myths of the hero's journey toward his cherished ideal remind us frequently of his hubris. Although Phaeton, the son of Apollo, boasted he could drive the sun-chariot across the sky, he lost control and fell into the sea. An archetypal figure functioning in accordance with the Self gravitates toward equilibrium, represented by the superior control and calm expression exercised by the chariot driver in the Tarot key.

The chariot on its return path embodies the ideas of rest within movement. Because it has lost its sense of me-ness, it has no cravings which would lose it in the world of sense; it moves through the world in pure non–attatchment, which was the essential message of Krishna to Arjuna in the Hindu myth of the chariot driver on the battlefield.

The Hebrew word for chariot is *merkabah* (MRKBH).There is a whole body of Jewish mysticism called the Merkabah mysticism, which was primarily concerned with Ezekiel's vision. Other mystical schools rejected "throne mysticism" because it was not absorbed in contemplation of the true *essence* of God but on the visionary quality of Ezekiel's apparation. Many students of consciousness or metaphysics have noticed that any visionary phenomenon of the divine is reflected through the culture, religious ideals, and expectations of the corresponding mystic. The Divine Mother Kali or Radha will not appear to a Christian, though many apparitions of Her are recorded by Hindu mystics. Likewise, a Christian sees Mary or Jesus. One who is absorbed in contemplating the essence of God rejects any outside form as a quality of dualism. Thus it is common in many yogas to ignore such forms if they do appear. Although monotheistic, Christianity is still a dualistic religious system which reflects *relationship* rather than identity. There are, of course, exceptions, such as Meister Eckhart, Julian of Norwich, and others, who could not perceive the God-energy as a duality.

The Merkabah mystics stressed strongly the concept of prayer, particularly praise, as a basic form of relationship and attatchment to God. Many of the miracle-working rabbis of the Hasidic tradition also stressed prayer, devotion, fasting, and service, and were frequently reported to have visions and other deep forms of communion with the Shekinah. In the Zohar, it is said that "hearing" Binah is a form of rapport with her through her attribute of understanding. Often their sermons were thought to come directly from her, much like today we think of the phenomenon of "channeling."

In the teachings of the Buddah, of Krishna, as well as Pythagoras, the human personality is likened to a chariot. We are vehicles for the expression of the One Self, and our minds are the reins. Our thoughts cultivate the fields we travel as well as the fences we construct. Our hope as aspirants on this Path is that, whatever our personal belief structures, we remain receptive to the *influence* of the Divine moving through the vehicle of our lives in its own unique way.

18th Pathworking Correspondences

1. Intelligence: House of Influence

2. Divine Letter: Cheth, CHTh (pronounced Kh-a-th) Value: 8, means "field"

3. Divine Names: Ama; Ruach Elohim (Roo–ch E–lo–heem)

4. Incense: Onycha,lotus. Myrhh

5. Gem: Amber

6. Color: Amber

7. Element: Water

8. Animals: Crab, turtle, beetle

9. Plants: Water-lily, watercress

10. Planet: Moon

11. Musical Tone: D sharp

12. Magical Phenomenon: Enchantments, visions

13. Magical Weapon: Fiery furnace

14. Mythos and Related Symbols: Apollo, Krishna, Khephra, Odin, chariot, sphinx, fence, field, ocean

15. Gift or Challenge: Receptivity, the art of surrender

16. Rules: Chest, stomach, solar plexus

17. Tarot Arcana: Chariot

Suggested Exercises

Consult this Tarot key before making any important decisions. Color it and mount it before you, visualizing the Charioteer as your Perfect Master. Imagine yourself permeated with yellow-orange, or a bright amber. Use as many other correspondences as you can from this Path. It is particularly good to use this key in conjunction with chanting the Divine Name or Letter, in the tone that belongs to it, to tune into forces of *guidance*.

Meditate for as long as possible on the symbols in the Chariot key, keeping your ideas focused clearly in your mind. Then imagine yourself handing over the reins of your life to this Higher Power. Before ending your meditation, compose a prayer of dedication to this Charioteer. Write it down, and return to it from time to time, to renew your devotion to always lifting your consciousness, actions, and will to the Supreme Selfhood which is the Driver behind your personality.

Finally, it will be a useful exercise to research the chariot myths: the Sun Chariot as Great Vehicle in the Buddhist tradition, the myths of the "fiery chariots" (e.g., Ezekiel and Enoch) in the Old Testament, the solar chariot of Apollo, the vehicle of Krishna, the chariots of Venus, Diana, Cybele, or Pluto, or the chariot of the Magi in the Iranian tradition. Which one speaks to you? Why? What do they have in common? What are their differences? How can you make your own chariot myth?

Guided Visualization

Imagine you are sitting near a flower garden in the back of a fenced cottage yard. Being encountered in this space has always made you feel safe; you are resting and contemplating a small crab which has found its way from the sea nearby. As it moves, you realize it is also safe and secure within the walls of the home it carries on its back. For a moment, you wonder about the crab in you: do you have a hard outer shell to protect the most vulnerable side of yourself?

Meditating on this thought as you are sitting in the dusk of evening, you begin to imagine that the most hidden part of yourself, so long shrouded in its inner chamber, is suddenly set loose. This is almost like a jolt from the body itself as you perceive that the outer shell contains yet a finer one, very similar to the physical body as you know it but able to move freely from one place to another by thought alone.

As soon as you realize this, the etheric body too disappears and you feel yourself to be moving like a ball of light propelled by your mind alone, which is still quite awake, aware, and very much a part of you. You decide that what you would really like to experience in this journey is a deeper understanding of yourself. Immediately you are back in your light astral form and riding on a brilliant chariot driven by an angelic being with a crown of stars on his head and a large amber gem around his neck. The canopy of the chariot is deep blue, also decked with stars. You ask him where you are, and he tells you that you are on the Midnight Special.

Before you have time to question what he means, it becomes very apparent, as you appear to be riding higher off the ground and are almost immediately enveloped in the night sky. The stars and comets flying by are a glorious sight, but only for a few seconds, because you soon become enshrouded in a thick indigo veil which is darker than any kind of black you have ever imagined. The only light is that emanating a few inches from the flying chariot that seems to be racing through nothing.

This makes you slightly uncomfortable as you begin to wonder about your sense of *boundaries*, but you quickly recall that you can become anything you wish through the power of your mind, and so you imagine that you are entering the protective shelter of a peaceful temple. Immediately, the chariot stops, and your angelic guide disappears as you gaze at the stone shelter hanging like a mirage in the midst of the inky darkness.

On exiting the chariot, you step gingerly out into what you think is air but what actually appears to be a vast, black sea. You realize you can walk on this water as easily as you could fly through space, and you move quickly toward the old temple structure. Upon entering, you notice a crescent moon hanging over a silver doorway, which you pass through. As you come into this inner chamber, you are instantly overwhelmed by a vibration of such intense sorrow that you are tempted to exit immediately. But something makes you pause, and you notice a tiny church pew in the shadows which you decide to sit upon as you reflect about this strange experience.

You cannot shake the ominous feelings of foreboding and grief which permeate this place, however, and at a point when you feel that—for some reason—your own heart is actually starting to break apart, a figure enters and sits quietly down beside you. She is dressed in a dark blue cape which drapes her from head to foot. You are instantly eased by her presence and as you turn to look at her you realize that this simple woman with no adornments radiates the most gentle love you have ever felt. You ask her name and she smiles slightly and whispers, "Some call me the Queen of Heaven, others the Stella Maris, Star of the Sea." Her words carry such a tone of loving comfort, you immediately realize you would have endured any kind of suffering to be here, suddenly healed and whole in her presence. You lean gently against her warm, maternal breast and you have a sense that she has contained the pain of all creatures within the tiny physical structure of her immense heart. You feel that heart pounding in your ear and for an instant you know all the joys of heaven.

Then she begins to speak again and each word that drops from her mouth is like a flower falling. "This heart has wept tears of blood, for it carries the suffering of all human beings on earth, who are all my children and who belong to me. If you knew how much I loved you right now, you would weep tears of joy. Reveal to me all your sentiments and all your problems. I want to console you. If you would open your heart to me as the flowers in spring open to the sun, I could come into you more deeply and more fully. I could help you end all your fears once and for all. I could begin to vibrate inside your own heart with my overwhelming, ceaseless love.

"Know that in your daily storms of life I will be with you

everywhere. I am your mother. I can and will help you. You will see everywhere the light of my Flame of Love lighting up heaven and earth. I will help you, but *I need your help*. As I bless you with a solemn benediction from my heart's flame which reaches out to intoxicate you, so you too must reach out and extend this blessing."

Then she asks you to engage in a prayerful exercise with her, to help her alleviate some of the sorrow which she so willingly carries, as she yearns for her children to return to the loving awareness of her waiting arms. It is a simple exercise.

"First, be very still, and with your hand on your heart, imagine some of the energy coming out of each heartbeat into your hand. After concentrating deeply on this image for a few minutes, remove your hand and imagine the love and blessing of your heart pouring out towards the rising sun in the east. Turn slightly and feel streams of this blessing going out toward the south. Turn again and pour out your love to all beings in the west, and once again to all in the north. Then imagine your powerful blessing of love going down into the earth, to heal it and enrich it for all its growing plants and creatures. Finally, extend your soul towards heaven and complete this circuit of love by giving back to me a portion of this never-ending stream of love I offer to you every moment of your existence."

After experiencing such a deep communication with her and the world she holds in such reverence through the vehicle of the heart in this prayer exercise, you suddenly realize your consciousness is back in the tiny church, but the lady is no longer beside you. Filled with the awesome realization that to understand yourself, which was the purpose of this journey, means to reach out and enclose all others in your ongoing blessing of understanding, you leave softly with a deep sense of gratitude, humility and at-one-ment with all creation. As you step gently outside into the expansive sky, the tiny blue ball that is the place you call Home glows extremely brightly, and your chariot waits to take you there.

Affirmations

1. *The One Identity is the vehicle of its own expression.*

2. *I am not my body, because I do not possess what I am.*

3. *The chariot of my mind links reason and intuition in perfect clarity.*

4. *The I Am, everywhere present, is the internal directive principle I call my "self."*

5. *I maintain control over the circumstances that affect me by increasing my trust in the Holy Spirit within.*

Z THE LOVERS ‫ז‬

Path 17
The Disposing Intelligence

Discernment   *Sign: Gemini*

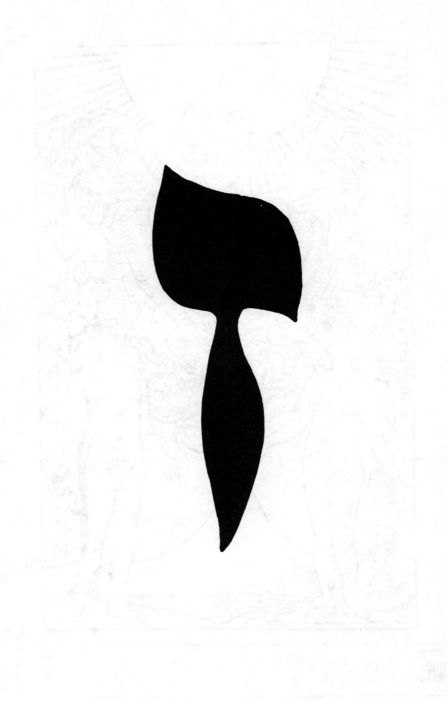

CHAPTER SEVENTEEN

The 17th Path, Zain
The Lovers
The Disposing Intelligence

The path of Zain is called the Disposing Intelligence because "it disposes the devout to perseverance" (*The Thirty-Two Paths of Wisdom*, Waite translation). The letter-word Zain means "sword" and has a value of 67 when spelled out. In *The Book of Tokens*, it is said, "I am the sword,/The sword which is understanding,/Dividing between the darkness and the light/At creation's dawn" (Case, 1934, p. 75). *Understanding* is the Divine Emanation of Binah, from which this Path descends. It also has a numerical value of 67. The Hebrew word *binah* (BINH) means "understanding, insight, prudence." Hence we arrive at the idea of the "sword of discrimination."

The "devout" of which *The Thirty-two Paths of Wisdom* speaks are those who have brought their feelings, thoughts, and actions into harmony with universal order, a process which requires keen discrimination. Zain implies this sword-like acuteness and sharp perception. Case explained that when both aspects of the human psyche, which he identified as the Solar and Lunar principles (the anima-animus in Jungian terms), are rightly perceived and rightly disposed, the human psyche becomes integrated.

A sword is something that cuts, divides, or separates. In the English Bible it says, "In the beginning God *created*," but a literal rendering of the verb *bara* (BRA) in Hebrew is "to cut out, to separate, to select," as well as "to engrave" or "to reform." In the Qabalistic design of the Tree of Life, it is Binah who is the Mother of all the other Sephiroth as well as all creation. To Her is attributed the

Divine Name "Elohim," the name of God in Genesis which brought forth the universe. We know this was done through a process of division and separation; i.e., darkness was separated from light, heaven from earth, etc.

In the word BRA (to form, or to divide), we see a hidden mystery of the Christian trinity because it contains their initials in Hebrew: B is for the Son (Ben), R is for the Spirit (Ruach), and A is for the Father (Abba). The creation process is, in fact, identified as plural in Genesis: "And God said, let us (Elohim) make humans in our image, after our likeness "(Gen. 1:26). The word Elohim combines a singular feminine noun (*Eloh*) and a masculine plural ending (*im*), thus uniting the female and male principles. Lest it be thought that Qabalah is not a monotheistic system, one need only recall that the concept of 3 in 1 (or 2 in 1) is a *mystery*.

In Qabalah, the world of "Atziluth," or the world of pure Idea, is composed only of the first three Sephiroth and is called the Supernal Triangle. Separating these three Spheres from the rest of the Tree is the gulf known as the Great Abyss. Below it reside the Spheres which are activated by Pure Spirit, seven in number, including Malkuth (the Earth). Seven is also the numerical value of the letter Zain, as well as the initials of "Adoni-Ha-Aretz" (AHA), which means the "Lord of the Earth."

The Abyss is an archetypal image that has haunted mystics, artists, poets, and scholars alike. Very little is spoken of it, or of the "invisible" Sphere residing there, *Daath*, because the Spheres beyond it, as well as the Abyss itself, are totally abstract and beyond comprehension. The "leap across the abyss" to the Divine Supernals is the most coveted desire of the sincere mystic seeking ultimate union, however, and the Paths which cross it are the 17th, the 13th, and the 15th.

Going in the "path of return," the 17th Path takes us from the Sphere of the Logos, or Incarnation in Tiphareth, to the Cosmic Mother, Binah. It is through the mediation of Binah that this primordial Energy flows the other way, spilling out from the preceeding Sphere known as Chokmah (Abba, the Father), through Her and across the Abyss. This is characterized in Genesis when it says, "and darkness covered the abyss, while a mighty wind swept over the waters" (Gen. 1:2).

When this principle of Divine Spirit swirled across the Abyss into manifestation, the concept of duality was born. This is symbolized in the Tarot key by the male and female in the primeval garden. The numeration of "created" or "formed" (BRA) is 203, which is also the value for the words "spring" or "well," a title given to Malkuth (BAR) and "dwelling," "exotic" "foreign land," and "stranger," "foreigner" or "pilgrim" (GAR), all references to Eden.

So it is through this process of division that everything is created. The Great Work of this path is the reversal of that process, an alchemical marriage of the dualities of form. In the Path of the Disposing Intelligence, "The Thirty-two Paths of Wisdom" says is found the "Foundation of Beauty in the Place of the Supernals." Beauty is the attribute given to the sixth Sephira, Tiphareth, the Christos-center wherein the dualities of anima/animus are blended in an androgynous whole. The path of Zain leads upward from the Sphere of the Sun to the Sphere of Binah, departing from the illusion of separate selfhood and arriving "at the realization that the semblance of separate individuality is but the effect produced by the One Self's power of *concentrating its limitless energy at any particular point in time and space*" (Case, 1985, p. 276).

As Zain is the sharp sword which divides the One into the many, so Zain is the "cutting edge" Path of return for those who have sharpened their *disposition*. By the Disposing Intelligence, we mean that pathworking energy which requires continual effort in discriminating, apportioning, arranging, organizing, preparing, and adjusting the personality to the highest ascent: that over the Abyss. "The Thirty-two Paths of Wisdom" tells us that men and women so disposed toward this faithful task are said to be "clothed with the Holy Life-Breath." This is the reason for the nudity of the figures in the Tarot key. Because they are clothed with Spirit, they have no need of false shame or embarassment.

The word for "spirit" or "breath" in Hebrew is *ruach,* a feminine noun which refers to the Mother, Binah, the destination of the 17th Path and and the Spirit of God which moved over the waters to first clothe the primal seeds of consciousness (Adam and Eve, with the breath of its Life. This profound mystery which philosophers and theologians have long pondered and debated reflects the most *intimate* relationship of the psyche to its primal beginnings. This intimacy is hinted at in the key (again by the nude couple) which clothes the whole philosophical paradox with the Garden of Eden allegory. Ultimately, as the Qabalist Carlo Suares says, the only transcendence is the intimacy with the unknown *as the unknown* which is "everlastingly present in an ever-present genesis" (Suares, 1985, p. 53).

There are a number of mysteries connected to this path; among them, Waite tells us, the mystery of the Covenant and the Sabbath. The covenant reflects that most intimate pact God made with the children of Israel. Case suggests to us in this regard to review what Ezekiel has to say about the "bond of the covenant," as well as the meaning of the word "Israel." In Ezekiel's vision of the dry bones, God told him to prophecy over them and the spirit would come into them and they would come to life and become the whole house of Israel. Previously, they had cried out, "our bones are dried up, our hope is lost, and we are *cut off*" (Ez. 37:11).

But God told Ezekiel to call the spirit of the four winds and breathe into them. And Ezekiel saw the bones come together with a loud rattling noise and join, and become alive with the spirit. God then promised Ezekiel that "never again shall they be divided" (Ez. 37:22) and "I will make with them an everlasting covenant of peace" (Ez. 37:26). If we then look at the definition of the word "Israel," we note that it means "He shall rule as God" or "a prince with God" or "one who prevails with God," referring to that aspect of human consciousness which is so intimately bonded with the principle I AM nature that it becomes an unobstructed channel for the expression of the Divine Life.

This idea of "everlasting peace" is nearly beyond human conception since we have never yet in the history of recorded humankind known anything like even a temporary period of total world peace and at-one-ment. But this is precisely the Path that takes us out of the world of creation and across the abyss back to our Source. The ideas connected with peace, rest, and retirement are reflected in the concept of Sabbath, the seventh day of rest. Zain is the seventh letter and represents the Path back from division to Unity. Next to the number 1, 7 is the number most frequently used to denote perfection, reflecting God's sense of completion and attainment after creating the first six days.

In the Tarot key, the angel symbolizes the Higher Self, the woman, subconsciousness, and the man self-consciousness. The principle lesson of this Path is that superconsciousness sheds its influence impartially on both aspects of consciousness, which are co-equal. In Zain, we see the perfect balance between these two aspects of the human personality as they harmoniously relate to the angel above. There is something of a secret in this relationship, however.

Behind the man is the Tree of Life; behind the woman, the Tree of Knowledge with its serpent of duality, good and evil. The Judeo-Christian concept, of course, always has been unkind to the woman in its interpretation of her as the cause of "the Fall," but Waite says, "she is rather the working of a Secret Law of Providence than a willing and conscious temptress" and, furthermore, it is only through her that "man shall arise ultimately, and ... complete himself" (Waite, 1959, p. 95).

Although he never explains how this happens (since it is in the nature of Arthur Waite to hint at secrets, but never divulge them), we find the psychological explanation in Case, Crowley, and other decks, which refer us to the concept of Spiritual Alchemy. The *Disposing* Intelligence in Hebrew is *he-regash* (HRGS), and its esoteric meaning is that the Sun and Moon together equal Shin, the quientessence or *spirit* of God. This is reflected in the Tarot keys ruled by the letters in this word. You may wish to investigate them.

How is this primary duality, first manifested in the Garden of Eden story, to be reconciled? How is the relationship between the two selves mended? One clue is in the fact that in the picture it is the woman who is looking up to the angel, while the man is looking at her. The self-conscious intellectual mind can seldom, by itself, become directly aware of superconsciousness. Subconsciousness does receive and transmit these powers, but only at the suggestion of the conscious mind. Whether through prayer, affirmation, visualization, etc., development comes about *in direct response of the inner to the outer.*

It is when both halves of the psyche veil nothing from each other that the true "Royal Marriage" occurs. Most often, what we experience is that consciously we want one thing, subconsciously we accept another. It is harmonious balance that is the true test of the 17th Path. The main idea of this key is that pairs of opposites, represented by the couple and the trees behind them, are really complements, no matter how antagonistic they appear to be at the time.

The astrological symbol assigned to the Lovers is Gemini, the twins, which signify the dual manifestation of an original single entity. It is important to understand that we do not achieve "oneness" with anything by simply wishing for it at the cost of repressed impulses, however. Conflict is the essential ingredient in all spiritual growth and must be faced squarely and courageously. Frequently, it is only through dealing with our shadow through conflict and suffering that we recover the deepest parts of ourselves.

A Qabalist does not view the "world of opposites" in quite the same way as the Eastern philosopher, who hopes to neutralize struggle by rising above it and thus eliminate suffering. In the same sense as Western Christianity, whose central image is the cross, Jung felt that it is through becoming conscious of our unconscious conflicts that we approach the alchemical marriage of our two selves. The sword of Zain is active on this path in cutting to the core of the personality; thus there is a strong implication of sacrifice.

There is a warning in any interpretation of the 17th Path that the sword can utterly destroy those who travel across the Abyss. This is natural if the ego is to be reconstituted; it must first undergo a total death. The numeration for the verb, "to slaughter, kill, sacrifice" is 17 (ZaBaCh), the same number as the path of Zain, and also implies a connection to Tiphareth, the point of departure and the Sphere of the Sacrificed God.

Together with the process begun on the 25th Path, Samekh, or Temperance, Zain works on the *conjunctio* or the Royal Marriage of the Self. These two paths form the vital *Solve et Coagula* formula of the alchemists (analysis and synthesis in Jungian terms), which means essentially: Analyze all the elements in yourself; dissolve that which is inferior, even though it may seem to break you; then, with the renewed strength obtained from the operation, congeal again.

17th Pathworking Correspondences

1. Intelligence: Disposing

2. Divine Letter: Zain, ZIN (pronounced Zah-yeen) Value: 7, means "sword"

3. Divine Names: IAO; Elohim (E-lo-heem)

4. Incense: Wormwood. Violet, myrhh

5. Gems: Alexanderite, tourmaline

6. Color: Orange

7. Element: Air

8. Animal: Snake

9. Plants: Orchid, hybrids

10. Planet: Mercury

11. Musical Tone: D

12. Magical Phenomenon: Feelings of being in two places at once

13. Magical Weapon: Tripod

14. Mythos and Related Symbols: Lord of Silence and Lord of Strength, Raphael, Adam and Eve, Lilith, Meru mountain, a gleaming sword, Castor and Pollux, the dark womb of the Mother

15. Gift or Challenge: Dedication, right discrimination

16. Rules: Lungs, shoulders, sense of smell

17. Tarot Arcana: The Lovers

Suggested Exercises

When working with this key, attempt to monitor yourself closely in terms of your impulses. Use your powers of discrimination to attempt to discern what is ultimately important in your actions and plans. Try to pay particular attention to your thoughts, particularly when you find yourself "talking to yourself." What did you catch yourself saying to your subconscious? We are particularly amenable to suggestions that begin with the words "I Am." If you are saying things such as, "I am afraid that ... " or "I am really stupid," etc., it may be time to seriously reflect on mending the relationship your conscious mind has with the subconscious.

It is perfectly all right to process these thoughts in a *concentrated, conscious way*, preferably with another person or group. The purpose of such work is to restore balance to the personality by bringing to light suppressed emotions, and such analysis is part of the process of Solve et Coagula. It is the unnecessary things we say to ourselves on a daily basis *without thinking* that can frequently cause us the most harm and confusion.

Zain is related to the sense of smell. This is the only sense that bypasses the thalamus, which relays information about the other senses to the cortex and goes directly to the limbic system. This is the part of the brain which is centrally located; much more primitive (older); and directly related to emotion, motivation, memory, and a sense of the transpersonal. If this part of the brain is electrically stimulated, in fact, subjects report mystical experiences.

Aromatherapy (healing with oils and using scent to change consciousness) has been around for many thousands of years, but is just now gaining popularity in the West. It is a science that uses subtle essences (actually scent molecules) to stimulate or activate the body's healing processes, primarily on the mental and emotional levels (which then filter down to the physical), although there is some evidence that aromatic oils also act directly on the physical body. Recent evidence also suggests that some odors are recognized only subliminally; that is, without our being aware of their effect on our behavior. Because it is fed directly into the limbic system, it has a close relationship to the subconscious mind and memory. Sometimes, only the hint of an odor will trigger a memory or an amorphous emotion.

In any magical tradition, and particularly in Qabalah, scents, oils and incenses are of prime importance in stimulating consciousness in a particular direction. It is recorded in the Bible that God gave the thaumaturge Moses specific instructions for making anointing oils and incense, (Ex. 30:22-38), and also that the apostles used it for healing (Mk. 6:13). Anointing would often produce the effect of the spirit taking possession in a very profound way (1 Sam. 16:13). In some magical rites, incense smoke is the basis for materializations or apparitions.

Note carefully the scents in the correspondence lists in this book, because a very ancient magical Qabalistic history has borne out their efficacy. Here are some other popular relationships used in aromatherapy today:

Amber: To stimulate the pineal gland (applied topically). For diseases associated with the heart (including emotional).

Cedar and Eucalyptus: For mucous conditions. Also antiseptic.

Frankincense: Cleanses aura or emotional body. Also used on the skin as a complexion oil.

Jasmine: Mood elevator, especially good for listlessness, depression, anxiety.

Geranium: Balances hormones through stimulation of adrenal cortex. Refreshing as a bath oil. Neuralgia.

Myrhh: A powerful healing and anointing oil. Strengthens pulmonary system, any body degeneration.

Patchouli: Skin care. Wounds.

Pennyroyal: Nausa, flatulence. Spasms. Toothache.

Rose: Insomnia. Blood circulation. Skin inflammation.

Sandlewood: Quiets ego, good for meditation. Infections.

Sweet Almond: Stimulant. Helps move nutrients under the skin when used as massage oil.

Ylang-ylang: Hypertension, anxiety.

Guided Visualization

Imagine you are riding on the great wings of Raphael across a vast, bottomless abyss. You are not sure of your destination but you trust the angel of harmony and healing because, in the past, he has healed your blindness. Each time you renew your trust in him, in fact, new scales drop from your eyes, and you can see afresh.

As you are flying, you notice a lightning streak flash across the sky like a gleaming sword. It seems to pierce the huge vault of the heavens, and behold, through the opening appears a great luminous dove, bright as molten silver. You recognize it as the symbol of the Eternal Feminine, the transformer and revivifier of souls. Suddenly, the vision and your angelic guide both disappear and you find yourself in a strange terrain where metals and minerals are fermenting on the crust of a spongy, vaporous planetary surface. You carefully make your way around archaic semimolluscan creatures with twig-like arms that seem to wave toward you in a beckoning way. The atmosphere is suffused in a bright orange color, and the gaseous vapors float up from the surface in small fiery clouds. Every now and then, you are startled by a loud, piercing moan, which then trails away into the ceaseless wind which rustles around you.

Watching one of these amorphous cloud shapes, you notice that it somehow seems to contain within it a gelatinous and transparent mass which nontheless has a definite embryonic being inside it. Fascinated, you watch as it appears to draw nourishment from the humid, burning vapors which ascend from the crust of this sphere, and, as it does, it metamorphoses into a fuller, more definite shape: a serpentlike creature, with arms, and a fan-shaped plume for a head from which issues a phosphorescent organ of perception. This organ seems to be first a spout or nose, then a mouth, then an eye, then, amazingly, a phallus, and once again a small, sucking vaginal kind of opening.

It suddenly occurs to you that this is the first germ of future humans, one which contains both sexes in one body, and that renews itself ceaseless from within. It communicates with itself through gestures and radiations of light, continually changing form as it desires. As you continue to walk, you spy a colossal tree, the only identifiable image here which seems to have a solid structure. From it hangs an immense dagger. It is used, you realize, to separate

222

these glowing beings before fecundation. No one tells you these things; it is as if you understand all by virtue of intuition alone as you pass through the landscape of this remarkable sphere.

Then the scene abruptly changes as you find yourself in a pungent garden, the fragrance of which is slightly bitter. A small woman appears dressed in a deep violet gown, and she motions for you to come and sit beside her.

"I have an important message for you," she says gently, "one which you should take back to your world and share with whomever will listen. The One who has come in his first birth is about to return to you in glory. His second and glorious birth is close at hand. So in this, the night of your time, it is my maternal duty to prepare you to receive him, as I received him in his first coming. But first, love must burn within you as a fire so powerful that it envelops the whole world and burns away all the evil, egoism, hatred, and impurity. Only the building of the Sacred Fire can accomplish this. You can personally aid in building this Fire by endeavoring to develop a power of concentration upon *one activity* of the Sacred Fire, one exercise or spiritual practice, until you carry it into your daily consciousness with thorough feeling and clarity. Bond together with like souls who will also share with you in this spiritual practice. Know that I am guiding you, and watching you throughout your dedication. You are enwrapped in the mantle of my holiness. Go now and prepare, for the greatest of all prodigies is accomplished in the fullness of time."

As her message ends, her body which seemed so frail and dark becomes illumined, she becomes a golden transparent light which suffuses you in a great surge of maternal love and longing and then disappears. You turn, wishing for another glimpse of her, for another sparkling word which seems to ripple through you like honey, but you know her message is complete and her vision is waiting behind your promise to adhere to her plea.

Raphael taps you lightly on the shoulder, ready to return you home, and slowly you arise, pondering deeply the words of the Mother and storing them in your heart.

Affirmations

I. I now advise my subconscious self that it is free from errors of misinterpretation I have made in the past.

2. I keenly discriminate between all polarities to combine and harmonize them in my own Higher Self.

3. Today I will have the discernment to make clear, correct choices.

4. I am being guided by the influx of Superconscious life.

5. All conflicts between my subconscious and my self-conscious self are now dissolving.

6. I am united in perfect communion with God.

UVW THE TEACHER ז

Path 16
Triumphant and Eternal Intelligence
Intuition   *Sign: Taurus*

CHAPTER EIGHTEEN

The 16th Path, Vav
The Hierophant

The Triumphal Intelligence

Vav is the sixth letter of the Hebrew alphabet and has a close connection to the sixth Sephira, Tiphareth. Both are mediators. Geometrically, the number six allows two interlocking triangles to come together: ✡, thus joining above　to below　. This is the image of the Star of David as well as Solomon's Seal. It is the classic representation of the ancient maxim: "As above, so below," and the prime agent for bringing this magical act to completion is the Logos principle, also called "God made manifest in the sphere of the mind"; for it is the mind which links soul to body.

Ideas relating to number 6 are mediation, reciprocation, interchange, correlation, correspondence, concord, symmetry, and the completed fertilized act. Vav, in particular, is considered by Qabalists to be the "fertilizing principle," the active manifestation in form. On the Tree it links Divine Wisdom to Divine Mercy, as well as the archetypal world (pure Idea) to the creative world. The name of Vav means "peg" or "nail," which has a phallic suggestion to it. A nail is a fastening link and thus a symbol of connection or association. The other meaning of the word Vav is the equivalent of our word "and," again symbolizing its power of uniting or associating objects or ideas.

Vav is of utmost importance in carrying forth these ideas of union because it is the third letter in the Tetragrammaton, IHVH (Yod-Heh-Vav-Heh). In Qabalah, Vav links the Supernal Triangle to all the Sephiroth and the earth below. This is because, when applied to the Tree, Yod (being masculine) is attributed to Chokmah, with its point residing in Kether. To Heh belongs the feminine Binah, the Mother principle. To Vav is attributed the *next six Sephiroth;* that is, all the worlds and attributes beneath the Abyss. To the final Heh belongs Malkuth, the Gaia principle, also called the Bride of Tiphareth.

As Yod is considered the Father and Heh the Mother, so is Vav considered the "Son." In the *Zohar,* the Son was Moses, the Son of David; Christian Qabalists have, of course, always interpreted it to be the Christ. Either figure represents one who *links* the world below to the Highest Self relected in the Supernals, or personal consciousness to universal life. *The Book of Tokens* says of Vav: "Manifesting myself as the link/Which uniteth all the separate parts of my creation,/I make myself known as the bond of union/Between creature and creature,/And between the creatures and their Creator./The Creator is myself,/And I am the Nail which joineth thee to me" (Case, 1934, p. 68).

The Intelligence of the 16th Path is named "Triumphal,"so called because there is "no other Glory like to it," and because it is "the Paradise prepared for the Righteous." Its mediating functions are performed by the Hierophant in the Tarot key, also called the "Magus of the Eternal." The Eternal is the incomprehensible and unmanifest Kether which begins to be conceptualized in Chokmah, the Father principle, and Binah, the Mother. One of Chokmah's symbols is the starry heaven, and the radiant *essence* of the Spirit of Chokmah is heralded by a brilliant star shining in the east, the place of greatest symbolic light and revelation.

For a Jewish Qabalist, this principle of the Son which is concealed and contained in the Father is again Moses, who was considered the great Hierophant or High Priest of IHVH. As Chokmah is considered to be the Ruler of the entire Zodiac (the 12 signs), so is Moses the leader of the 12 tribes of Israel and Christ the Hierophant among his 12 disciples. Vav spelled out also has a value of 12.

Some decks have substituted the word "Pope" for Hierophant, implying its association with the exoteric law, but the actual root of the word *hierophant* is more in keeping with the tone of this Path, which is essentially one of *revelation* (*hier-phaine*—to reveal). The *Sepher Yetzirah* tells us the 16th path is related to the function of hearing (S.Y. 5:1), and when the key is interpreted esoterically, the hearing is one of attunement to the Inner Teacher, or Inner Voice.

This is in keeping with the Golden Dawn, Rosicrucian, and many other traditions, which insist upon revelation through inner gnosis.

Waite, however, does identify the figure as the "ruling power of external religion" and distinguishes the High Priest in this regard from the High Priestess, who holds the *whole* of the law (Tora) on her lap, including both its exoteric and arcane qualities (1959). Paul Case disagrees precisely because the Pontifex—a word that means bringe-maker—is the *link* "between outer experience and interior illumination" (Case, 1947, p. 79)

Furthermore, the word "Pope" does not necessarily imply exoteric doctrine; the very word really means "father" and refers us back to the *Wisdom* of Chokmah, whose name is *Ab* (father). To the gnostics, of course, wisdom had nothing to do with the law and was, besides, a function related to the feminine, as we will investigate further in the 15th Path. But the point here is that, as the supreme Revealer descending on the path of involution from Chokmah, the Hierophant reflects the principle of Perfect Wisdom, in whatever way it may be interpreted by the individual.

The Hierophant, as the "revealer of sacred thing," was the chief character in the Eleusinian and other mystery schools during initiations and sacred rites. These rituals were intimately connected to the mystery of the grain; the myth is that the Earth Mother, Demeter, gave to Triptolemus the first grain of corn and taught him the art of plowing and harvesting. When she revealed herself to Queen Metaneria at Eleusis (a word that means "advent"), she requested that a temple of her mysteries should be built there. Numerous scholars have tried to unravel the secrets which were the core of these mysteries. We do know that the rituals involved prolonged fasting, all-night vigils, and and a communion with grain cakes and barley water. It is thought that a key element in the mysteries was the image of the "Divine Child" carried in the harvest basket, which was a single ear of grain held up by the Hierophant, at one point in the rite, to be contemplated by the participants. When the worship of Demeter spread to Rome, she was called "Ceres," from which our word cereal is derived.

One cannot fail to notice the similarity between any of the pagan "mystery" traditions—most of which are connected to the grain in this way—and the Christian mystery of the Body of the Divine hidden in the Eucharistic bread. And although the image of the Pope may be interpreted by many as representing the dispenser of the body of doctine which is particular to Roman Catholicism, it can hardly be denied that it also carries the idea of being simultaneously the revealer of hidden mysteries.

In the Tarot key, the Hierophant's throne sits upon a *cubic stone,* which is highly symbolic to a qabalist. The first Pope was named Simon Peter. Peter, as we know, means "rock," and was the "cornerstone" of the early church. In Hebrew, Simon (Simeon) means "hearing" (from the root SMIO) as well as "receptivity and understanding." In Matthew 16:17, Jesus exalts Simon for being a receiver of hidden knowledge which was not yet revealed and at this time appointed him as Peter, the Rock. Likewise, it was Simeon, the prophet with the inner voice, who spoke to Mary at the presentation in the temple, revealing things to come.

The word for "stone" or "rock" in Hebrew is *ebhen* (ABH). This rock which is the foundation of the Hierophant conceals the great mystery of the identity of the Father and the Son, for the first half of the word, AB, means father, and the second half, BN, means son. Together, they form the cornerstone of the Wisdom represented in this key. Their union is linked through numerous other symbols implied thoughout this Path: by the number 6 as we saw, by the word Vav which links, and also by the Y-shaped pallium on the robes of each of the ministers, which is a symbol of yoke or union.

The ministers in the foreground are in the process of receiving a blessing, but the key also implies that they are in the active act of *listening* or praying in silence. This is what is meant by the *Sepher Yetzirah* when it attributes the function of hearing to this path. The Hierophant who sits on the Stone is the teacher; we are the receivers of inner gnosis through Its mediation. It is this foundation *stone* which restores us to the state of consciousness before our delusion of separateness, represented by the *Garden* of Eden. Thus Vav is a direct link to the supreme state of unity which exists in the Supernals, as we journey on this Path from Chesed to Chokmah; i.e., back to the Garden. In gematria, these ideas are linked because both "garden" and "stone" (GN, ABN) equal 53. This union is the "paradise" which is spoken of in the *Sepher Yetzirah* in relationship to this Path.

This is further emphasized by the fact that, alchemically, the Stone is the perfect union of all elements in a balance which restores them to their primal state. In the Tarot key, this is symbolized by the "keys of the kingdom," one of which is Gold, the other Silver, thus representing the union of Sun and Moon. This "cleaving" together to form the union which is represented in this key is also linked in gematria, for the number 16, the value of a word which means "to cleave, to attatch, to fasten onto" (AChZ) is directly expressed in the 16th Path.

This is the path of intuition, and our calling when walking it is to pay particular attention to the *listening* element of our prayer and meditations. Case especially stresses that listening to the Inner Voice representing the Central *Self* is not the same as hearing "voices," which run rampant in occult circles. It is our opportunity when working with the energies of this Path to refine our discrimination, to discern better the Voice of Intuition, and to practice calming the mental clamor of the mind so that we can "hear in silence" (Case, 1985).

16th Pathworking Correspondences

1. Intelligence: Triumphal

2. Divine Letter: Vav, VV (pronounced Vaw) Value: 6, means "nail or hook"

3. Divine Hames: El, Jah

4. Incense: Storax. Musk

5. Gem: Topaz

6. Color: Red-orange

7. Element: Earth

8. Animal: Bull

9. Plant: Mallow, sugar cane

10. Planet: Venus

11. Musical Tone: C sharp

12. Magical Phenomenon: Attunement to the Inner Voice

13. Magical Work: The Labor of the Preparation

14. Mythos and Related Symbols: Osiris, Zagreus, Parsival, the Pope, the Christ, Elijah, a nail, a rod, a yoke, Minotaur, Apis, trefoils, a cubic stone, phallus

15. Gift or Challenge: Endurance, discrimination

16. Rules: Throat, neck, hearing

17. Tarot Arcana: Hierophant

Suggested Exercises

Meditate on this Tarot image when you need to contemplate the inner significance of events occurring in your life. Notice that, representing the function of hearing, the Hierophant in the key has his ears sealed; they are invisible to us. See how long you can concentrate on the silence behind your closed ears and pay close attention to that "still, small voice" no matter how still or small it may seem.

Remember that inner voices are of no avail if we do not first listen to the voice of reason. Intuition is not a substitute for reason; it is its logical Crown. Some of the most intuitive insights come from scientists who have tried every logical device known to them and then suddenly come up with an answer when "something told them" to follow the problem through in a particular way. Although they may not identify it as intuition, such "hunches," which are frequently the perfect "missing link," are much more common in people adept at using their reason than those who are not.

When working this Path, study about real intuition and, in your meditations and daily affairs, try to distinguish it from: (1) the endless "stuff" you say to "yourself" in your mind, (2) tuning in clairaudiently' to the "stuff" other people are saying and that you may be picking up, (3) telepathic invasions from other entities, archetypal or "real," incarnate or not, such as is prevalent in spiritualism or many kinds of "channelling."

Sometimes what you will notice when you engage in deep silence with *attentive listening* is not a "voice" at all. It may sound very much like music, or gentle sounds of nature, or vibrations of deep peace which you will unmistakably identify as the Presence of the Indwelling Spirit.

As a meditational exercise for this Path, find a bell or a gong, or a pair of cymbals, and take a journey to the quietest, most serene place you can find. After calming your mind and breath for some time, make your "holy bell" ring out *once* very clearly. Follow the sound as intently as you can until it fades completely away. See if you can discern the place between the faint sound of the ringing before it disappears and the place of no sound at all. You can repeat this exercise more than once. The point is to refine the subtle qualities of your hearing and sharpen your attention simultaneously. After using the bell as a focusing tool, continue your meditation in deep silence.

Visualization

Meditate on the Tarot key after coloring or painting it. The figure of the Hierophant should be dressed in a bright red-orange robe, the color assigned to this key scale. The trim should be turquoise. After concentrating on it for several moments, close your eyes and try to visualize the figure of the High Priest, the Revealer of Mysteries, as hovering above your head. Think of him as slowly descending into your body, suffusing your entire being with red-orange. Visualize this as clearly as possible; then listen for what he has to tell you. Or focus on what it may be like to hear the music of the spheres or the heartbeat of mother earth.

Imagine that your sense of hearing is increasing in a manifold way, that your ability to listen on many levels is being activated in a more meaningful way in your life. Think of yourself as holding a bunch of white lilies to represent your mind and red roses to represent your emotions. These are the gifts the Hierophant leaves with you. Think what it is like to listen with your heart, and how that is different from listening with your mind. How can you clarify your newfound sense of hearing in your life and in your relationships?

Visualize the Hierophant as stepping back out of your body through the top of your head. Imagine that you are kneeling or sitting in front of him, a prayer of thanksgiving on your lips for the knowledge he has just imparted to you.

Focal points in this picture to meditate on are the yoke and the keys. Where do these symbols take you?

Affirmations

1. *My intuition is the personal recollection of some aspect of Wisdom that the Universal Mind has never forgotten.*

2. *I trust that the Life Power is revealing to me what I need in my life right now.*

3. *I am one with the Truimphant Self which provides a positive solution to my every problem.*

4. *The Word is my growth, and the Nail is my sustenance.*

5. *I am always cleaving to God.*

 THE EMPEROR

Path 15
The Constituting Intelligence

Reason   *Sign: Aries*

CHAPTER NINETEEN

The 15th Path, Heh
The Emperor
The Constituting Intelligence

Heh is known as the "Constituting Intelligence" because "it constitutes the substance of creation in pure darkness." In this sense, *The Thirty-two Paths of Wisdom* refers us to Job 38:9 and says that Heh is "that darkness spoken of in Scripture, 'and thick darkness a swaddling band for it.'" In his translation (1960), Waite uses the adjectives "cloud" and "envelope" to describe this darkness, and the Job quote is referring to the work of IHVH at creation's dawn when the garment of the clouds and the envelope of darkness was made to hover over the Great Sea, Binah, the boundless ocean.

This Path connects the Solar Logos principle in Tiphareth with the energy of Chokmah, the all–begetter, whose Divine Name is IHVH or simply Jah (IH) and who is the stimulus for all manifestation (as opposed to Kether, the first Supernal, which is simply the "Root" of such impetus). It is the manifestation of this Logos (i.e., the Word) principle in its identification with the Constituting Intelligence that makes, frames, and composes everything in the universe. In this sense, Case refers us to the first verse and chapter of John, which speaks about this Solar Logos. There is a strong creation theme in this path as well as in the 17th Path, because we again have to cross the Great Abyss separating us from the Supernals. However, in the 15th and 16th Paths, the energy is proceeding from the father principle, and in the 17th and 18th Paths, it is primarily feminine, descending from Binah.

To "constitute" is to set up, establish, compose, or order, and is represented by the image of the Emperor. In Gematria, the word for "constituting" (MOMID) has the same numerical value as "the Pillars" on the Tree of Life (164), the OMDIM, which are the same letters rearranged.   This points to the fact that this Intelligence constitutes the structure, support, and equilibrium of the whole Tree.

The work on this Path bears a direct relationship to the Path which immediately precedes it (in the process of involution), the Empress, who represents imagination. Before a kingdom can be established and order created there, I must first be *imagined*. It must come into existence from its original seed-thought, through the power of mental vision. Therefore "Daleth" (the Empress) is translated as "womb" or "door." Heh is translated as "window" or, more literally, "wind-door."

A window allows light (or wisdom) and air (or the Life–force) into the house (Beth) of personality. Daleth is the door by which the soul enters this "house."   Heh is the window looking out into the heavens. The sense function attributed to Heh is "vision." From these ideas of the Emperor's *outlook* or survey of the *established order* which is *constituted* by him are developed other attributes which play an important part when working this Path: vision implies watchfulness, care, and vigilance as well as examination, analysis, and inquiry.

One who is working with these energies begins to feel those attributes awaken within him or her; i.e., those of bringing order into a chaotic situation as well as beginning to classify and structure one's ideas in a meaningful way. This faculty of defining or classifying consciousness is directly related to another function of the Hebrew letter Heh, which is an article for the word "the." When we use the word "the," we mean to name or define something, and this relates to the Constituting Intelligence as one which uses the self-conscious mental activity to *particularize* through the process of definition. The archetypal image of the ruling Emperor carries with it the idea of law and order, through a constitution that delineates a particular kind of social structure.

Although this may seem to be a "paternalistic" function, at least in its overt significance in the key, such is not necessarily the case. We know that, in its roots, Qabalah is neither a patriarchal nor matriarchal system but includes elements of both. Although *translators* of the Bible may have covered up the fact that the deity is both feminine and masculine, close examination of both the Hebrew language and the Tree reveals that some persons and attributes of the God-energy are obviously male and others obviously female. What's more, there is *much overlapping* and exchange of this yin-yang energy, which happens on many different levels; in fact, the more one studies the Tree, the more amorphous and permeable these boundaries become.

In the Divine Name IHVH (Yahweh), the Heh (H) is the feminine aspect of this creative and sustaining function. This is true as well for the Divine Name Jah (IH); one letter is masculine, one is feminine. Qabalists call the letter Heh the archetype of universal life. In examining the origins of the signs of the Hebrew tongue, the great Hebrew scholar d'Olivet observed that it represents life and every abstract idea of being because it is contained in all the root verbs related to *being* (1921).

For example, the phrase "let there be" is IHI; the phrase "and there was" is VIHI. God's Divine Name, "I Will Be," is AHIH, and the Divine Name revealed to Moses, IHVH, means "I Am That I Am." We see that the Hebrew letter that holds all these words together is the letter Heh, which represents life and the *constitution of being*. What's more, most Hebrew nouns ending in Heh are identified as belonging to the feminine gender (d'Olivet, 1921).

Even Chokmah hides this mystery. Although considered to be the Divine Father in direct relationship to the Divine Mother, Binah, Chokmah is a feminine noun which means "wisdom." And wisdom (or Sophia) in the Bible is always referred to as "She" (see book of Wisdom).

The number attributed to Heh is 5 (as the fifth letter) and, when the letter-word is spelled out (HH), it equals 10. Five is the number of adeptship and adjustment, and a symbol of the five-pointed Star of Discipleship. This Star has also been called the Endless Knot (i.e., it can be drawn without lifting a pencil from a page) and signifies the human being in nearly every mystical tradition, the five points representing the head and the extending four limbs. Five is also the number of the Sephira Geburah, which means "strength," or the *manifesting force* of the Tree's energy. In terms of manifesting in creation, there were basically five elements known to the ancients: Earth, Air, Fire, Water, and Spirit. Humans have five senses.

By gematria, the word "mist" or "vapor" (AD) also adds up to 5, and we are referred back to the beginning of the verse wherein "The

Thirty-two Paths of Wisdom" compares this letter to the dark cloud or swaddling mist which constitutes the substance of creation and which hovered over the primordial waters. In this regard, 5 is the numeration of the word *geb* (GB), which means "pit" or "water hole." The word *gab* (GB, with different vowel points), which means "rim of a wheel," also adds up to 5. This would seem to be a direct reference to Chokmah, the Illuminating Intelligence and the destination of this path. One of the titles of this Sephira is the "Highway of the Stars," and to it belongs the zodiacal wheel as well as the throne of angels known as Auphanim, the "Wheels or Whirling Forces which are also called the order of the Cherubim" (Regardie, 1940, v. 1, p. 192). In Ezekiel's vision (Ez. 1:16), the "wheels within wheels" or angelic beings surrounding Jah had eyes on their rims.

To all of the spheres below Chokmah, the ancients attributed a planet; Jah's influence, however, radiates throughout the Starry Heavens. In Psalms 68:5 is found the name of Jah as "Rider of the Clouds," and on the Tree of Life Chokmah is characterized as a gray-like cloud or pearly mist.

The letter Heh spelled out has a value of 10. It is said in *The Book of Tokens* (Case, 1934, p. 60) that "Heh concealeth the Word" and also that this way of the Word "soareth high above the comprehension of the mind" (p. 59). In this regard, the Hebrew words *dawaw* (DAH), "to fly or to soar," and *gawbah* (GBH), "high or elevated," also add up to 10. Heh is said to conceal the Word because 10 reduces to 1, which is the number of the first letter of the Hebrew alphabet, *Aleph*, said to be the primal creative Word.

Heh is the first of the 12 "simple" letters in Hebrew, to which astrological correspondences have been given, and therefore Heh represents Aries. This is the symbol of the ram's head on the Emperor's throne. The ram is the Lamb of Gnostic Christianity and refers back to Tiphareth, the Solar Word. Aries is also the first sign to emerge from Chokmah, the ruler of the zodiac in the starry heavens on its path of descent into matter. This too, is the first path to which a sensory function is attributed (i.e., the sense of sight, referring to the contemplation of the Spirit on Itself during this descent. In a sense, this is the Father beholding the Son; i.e., the self-contemplation of the Word residing in IHVH, the all-begetter, and made flesh in the Solar Logos. Sight also relates to the Constituting intelligence because it is very instrumental in regulating, structuring, classifying etc.

There is a strong Martian quality to the Emperor; he appears to embody strength and force and is related to the Sephira Geburah, to which Mars is attributed. It has been noticed that both Heh and the fifth Sphere have the same numeration, besides having the relationship of the sign (Aries) with its astrological ruler. The masculine-Mars energy is here balanced by the orb of dominion which the Emperor holds in his hand, which is a modified form of the symbol representing Venus. This implies that the Emperor's active power of regulation has to do with control of mental imagery represented by the female image of Venus and the Empress.

The picture of the powerful monarch should serve as a reminder to students on this path that we can be the guide and controller of our lives and that this reality will assert itself more as we let loose of the idea that we are victims of circumstance.

15th Pathworking Correspondences

1. Intelligence: Constituting

2. Divine Letter: Heh, HH, (pronounced Hay) Value: 5, means "window," also "universal life"

3. Divine Names: IHVH (Yod-hey-vaw-hey). Jah

4. Incense: Dragon's blood. Musk

5. Gems: Ruby, star ruby

6. Color: Scarlet

7. Element: Fire

8. Animals: Ram, hawk

9. Plants: Geranium, tiger lily

10. Planet: Mars

11. Musical Tone: C

12. Magical Phenomenon: The power of consecration

13. Magical Weapon: Orb of dominion, burin

14. Mythos and Related Symbols: Athena, Minerva, Shiva, Mars, the Ancient of Days, the Sacrificial Lamb, the Logos, the evangelists, water and wine, chalice

15. Gift or Challenge: To create order in one's life through analysis and organization. To rely totally on the Higher Self for foundation and structure

16. Rules: Head and face; sense of sight

17. Tarot Arcana: Emperor

Suggested Exercises

Since this is the Path and Intelligence connected with the sense of sight, it is useful to understand the most common Qabalistic tool used to work with the correspondences on these paths: that of the flashing colors. This is a somewhat misunderstood technique, but it is simple if received from the correct source or right teacher.

To each of the Paths is assigned a letter, a color, and other correspondences. If you meditate on the letter, it is a powerful exercise in itself. But if the letter is cut out, colored, or painted the appropriate color and mounted on a background in its opposite or complementary color, a startling effect can be produced. Color, we have seen, is a vibration of light, and in Qabalah it is used specifically to "tune-in" to the various forces with which the Qabalist is dealing.

The "appropriate" color to paint the letter is *not* the color given in the correspondence lists but its opposite. The "ground" is painted the color prescribed in the lists. This is important because the object is to clearly visualize the letter in the color which *is* given in the correspondences, and this can only be done if one meditates on the complementary color.

For example, if you focus your eyes on a red circle for several concentrated moments, then quickly look at a white or blank wall, the visual after effect of the red ball will manifest as a *green* ball. After a few seconds, the afterimage will begin to fade. In time, however, one can "hold" the afterimage for quite some time and eventually use it as a type of "astral doorway." Meditating on the letters in this way can be a profound technique for accessing the energies of the specific Paths. It is also a great teaching tool to enable the student to tune into very specific arcane "secrets" of the Qabalah that only working in such an experiential way can produce.

Guided Visualization

You are sitting in a peaceful, secluded ocean cottage gazing abstractly out of the window at the restless, tossing sea. It is very late at night, and only a sliver of a moon is present. Faintly, you can occassionally catch a flicker of light or shadow on the crashing waves, but the beach is predominantly shrouded in darkness. You realize that the fog is coming swiftly in, and it spreads like a chill through your body. As you are about to retire from your meditative pose, you notice that, although the sea is now heavily clouded in a deepening black mist, a tiny faint star has appeared overhead. This seems slightly incongruous to you, because the sky, too, is laden with deep clouds, so you step outside to investigate.

As your feet sink into the shifting cool sands, you gaze skyward again and the star is glowing even more brightly than before, radiating out of the pearly mist like a beacon signaling some kind of message. Indeed, as you continue to be entranced by the brilliance of this light, it begins to pulsate in a definite vibrating kind of motion, and for a fleeting second you think that it may be a flying object which is sending a code to someone below.

At this thought, the star begins to glow brighter and simultaneously emit a rhythmic crashing sound, like a deep thunderous moan. This startles you, and suddenly you are aware that you have been wandering closer to it and further from your cottage, as the star hovers over the dark waters. But when you turn, you are enveloped in a fog so deep and thick that you can no longer discern the hut, nor even have any sense of which direction it is.

Your attention returns to the light, the only object which seems to have any *shape* or, indeed, even any existence in this enveloping mist. It has grown to the size of a gleaming disk now, and for a moment a chill of fear covers you—perhaps it is the unknown quality surrounding this mystery object in the sky. Before you have a chance to process your thoughts about this, however, the disk actually *explodes*. Spinning off in a thousand directions are sparks of light which you suddenly recognize as stars.

You no longer feel the ground at your feet as you realize you have somehow been transported by the force of this explosion into a space above the dense fog. You appear to be floating in a clear sky studded with diamonds, crystals, and many more glowing, pulsating stars. Suddenly, from out of one of these crystalline structures steps a tall commanding figure draped with a long, flowing scarlet robe. He has sharp, flame-colored eyes, and his hands and arms are laced with golden bracelets. In one hand he bears a sword. Without speaking, he announces his name to you, and you hear it resonating inside your head: "I am the Son of the Morning and the Chief among the Mighty."

He somehow leads you by the power of the vibration of these words echoing inside, and you are gliding along beside this figure at a speed which you know must be faster than light. Immediately, you seem to have arrived at a golden temple which appears to be flashing with light; indeed, the thought crosses your mind that this structure is somehow made of light. It has definable pillars on the outside, however. An owl perches on one, a carved image of a ram's head on the other. You look around—your guide seems to have disappeared—and realize that this must be your destination. With slight apprehension, you step inside.

You are in a banqueting hall lined with 12 personages dressed in velvet and silken gowns woven in rich design and laden with various symbols. They are enjoying wine which is passed around and poured into jeweled cups. At one end of the table is a large, round gray stone, raised slightly, as if on a cubed throne. On the stone floor around it are several golden disks which seem to vibrate slightly of their own accord.

You are intrigued by the stone, which seems to bring memories of ancient mystery rites. But suddenly it ceases to be a stone—indeed, it glows and takes on the form of a hooded Wise Man whom you somehow immediately recognize as the King of this hall. You feel an irresistible impulse to get closer to this Being who is the seeming source of all of the other light in the room, which seems to radiate from him and be sucked back into him at the same time. Then the hood falls back, and you can see with a jolt, and as if for the first time: the Eyes. This Being is One who pours out overwhelming love from his eyes as he gazes at the party of planetary beings, and for a powerful second—which seems to last an eternity—at you.

You notice that the force of this love vibration is actually humming in the air around you; the disks at the Being's feet spin.

You feel yourself hurtling through time and space rapidly and are aware that infinity has passed in that moment of your sublime heart-connection. You are shaken with awe and still quivering with a delight you have never tasted on earth as your guide suddenly appears again to help you in your descent on the early morning dawn just breaking over the beach below.

Affirmations

1. *I cleave to the Life-Power that constitutes growth, goodness, healing, and light.*

2. *Concentrated and alert, I govern my life with poise, organization, and caring attention.*

3. *I am a center of expression for the aspirations of the Eternal Heart seeking Infinite Wisdom.*

4. *Because I watch, I learn to see.*

5. *I impel the development of my overall self through conscious order and analysis.*

| D | THE EMPRESS | ד |

Path 14
The Luminous Intelligence

Imagination   *Planet: Venus*

CHAPTER TWENTY

The 14th Path, Daleth
The Empress
The Luminous Intelligence

The letter-number Daleth means "door" or "womb" and has a value of 4. The meanings attributed to the number 4 are order, regulation, structure, and *foundation*. "The Empress" is from a root word meaning "she who sets in order." As the 14th Path, the Luminous Intelligence of Daleth is called the "*Chashmal* [brilliance] which is the founder of the concealed and fundamental ideas of holiness ..." The Waite translation has "the institutor of arcana, the foundation of holiness." The word "foundation" is used only one other time to describe one of the 22 Intelligences that are the Paths on the Tree. That one is Zain, the Lovers, where one of its attributes is "Foundation of Excellence."

The word "foundation" relates directly to the Sephira which is called the *Foundation;* i.e., upon which the physical world is based, which is *yesod* in Hebrew. Yesod (ISVD) has a numerical value of 80, the same as a word vhich means "universality" or "total principle" (KLL). This principle representing the primary foundation of universal *life*, or "Chavvah" (Eve, who is also pictured in the Zain key) is, of course, the Mother of all creation, by whose womb or doorway (Daleth) all are admitted into this world. She is the Ruler of this life: the Empress.

In the B.O.T.A., Crowley and many other decks, the images of the moon and the dove also appear in the Tarot key. The Waite deck pictures this Earth Mother with the symbol of *woman* (or, astrologically, the planet Venus, which is the same sign) pictured on her shield. In the very early Marseilles deck and in the Case deck, the shield carries the image of the dove, which is more in keeping with the intimate connection the Empress shares with Binah, the Mother of the remaining Sephiroth and of all the universes; i.e., the Holy Spirit. But whether her shield bears the image of the Goddess of Love or the Bird which represents the Flame and Spirit of Love, the primary goal of the Empress remains the same: to conquer with love. Her shield (which is a heart) represents that this is her only weapon and defense (Case, 1985).

In Qabalah, the word "foundation" (yesod) always refers us back to ideas of sexuality, primal union, and the beginnings of life. This path links the Spheres of Binah and Chokmah, the Divine Mother and Divine Father principles represented in the Sephiroth, which are called the Root of Water and the Root of Fire. The path which links the Archetypal Divine Pair has been called "luminous, illuminating, shining, and brilliant," as well as the "Daughter of the Mighty Ones" (Knight, 1965).

The attributes which describe the 14th Path thus all point to concepts inherent in the pairing of the Original Perfect Idea: they are all filled with light, reflect light, and radiate golden light. The number 14 is also the numeration of *gold* (ZHB) and *David* (DVD), which means "beloved." The Empress is the beloved Mother principle that restores to us this lightness of the heart which opens us up to new vistas through her ever-expanding womb. Her title, "Luminous," is an adjective derived from *Aur*, meaning Light, and the inference is that she is the Gold of the Philosophers, the Light at the end of the tunnel, the doorway to higher accomplishments.

The Hebrew letter Daleth is similar to the Greek *delta*, which is also the fourth letter and which represents the female generative organ and the fertility of the mouth of a riverbed. Many artists of the Middle Ages painted this perfected feminine principle in the image of the Madonna over arches and doorways, again pointing to the archetypal idea of the Mother and cosmic womb which Daleth signifies.

The cards of both the Empress and the High Priestess refer to the same Archetypal Feminine, the One Principle which as Pure Idea is reflected in many-faceted ways. As High Priestess, she is the Virgin and represents subconsciousness. As the Empress, she is the fertile Mother and represents conscious imagination. The Empress, as one who "sets in order," reflects the principles of conscious adaptation of mental imagery, which are the seed-thoughts that give birth to all manifestation.

The female energy of this path is represented in the proliferation of images of the fertile Mother which are common to all cultures and all peoples at all times since the beginning of human consciousness. It is thought that, before ideas of a paternal God were inculcated in the "minds of men," humankind worshipped the deity as Mother for many ages. The testament to this are the many artifacts of female fertility and goddess figures which date anywhere from 6,000 to perhaps 30,000 years ago.

In Greek mythology, she is Venus Aphrodite, who, born from the sea (i.e., Binah in Qabalah), gave birth to flowers wherever she stepped. She is Mother Nature blossoming in magnificant fruition. Waite calls her the "fruitful mother of thousands" as well as the "woman clothed with the sun" (Waite, 1959, p. 80), referring to Rev. 12:1, which describes her as also wearing a crown of 12 stars. The 12 stars refer to Chokmah, the Wisdom which dominates the Zodiac and all the worlds and which is the destination of this Path on its evolutionary ascent. In a Path of involution, it proceeds to Binah, the ocean of unconsciousness, and thence to all the other Spheres. As one who "clothes the sun" the Empress represents the Mother-principle impregnated with the savior-God. As the "luminous" intelligence, Daleth signifies the gateway to the Sun; i.e., the radiance of the sunrise.

This same archetypal idea is expressed in Egyptian mythology, where the lily, which represents the goddess Isis, gives birth to the Sun at the dawn of creation. The lily was also sacred to the goddess Juno; by it she conceived her powerful son, Mars. The lily was an emblem of Mary, representing Christian purity during much of the Middle Ages, and was a Byzantine sign of royalty.

As a representation of fertility and creative imagination, the Empress key pictures many ears of wheat growing at the woman's feet. The grain is a symbol of both Isis and Demeter and conceals the mysteries which later came to fruition in the Christian rites of the Savior hidden in the holy grain. The Empress is referred to esoterically as "Isis Unveiled," or Isis of Nature, and is the same Divine Feminine who is the veiled Isis in the image of the High Priestess.

It is said that the founder of the Rosicrucian order, Christian Rosencreutz, had a vision of this primordial Archetype which Daleth symbolizes and is therefore said to be the "doorkeeper." The

Rosicrucian *Fama Fraternitatis* describes how, after many years, when the vault of Brother "C.R." was opened, an incorruptible body "whole and unconsumed" was found, a miracle which generally tstifies to one's ability to move fluidly through the door separating the worlds.

As the Empress is the Womb and Door, we are all its keepers as we approach our own images of her and bring to fruition the ideas she manifests in us. In particular, an important idea connected to this Path is that of *bridging,* as the Empress does, the two halves of the personality, the male and female aspects, the anima-animus, the two sides of the brain. As we walk this Path we learn to connect our yang logic and our intuitive yin wisdom. In this age when so much research is being conducted concerning the great benefits of brain lateralization, the hidden aspects of this goddess archetype are re-emerging to begin her reign in glory. As a symbolic representation of the creative powers of the mind, the Empress points the way to new levels of consciousness-awareness and expansion, and appears on the forefront of many of the metaphysical and psychological schools which utilize guided visualization, creative imagery, and imagination.

Much research today supports the prevailing "mystical" notion, which has persisted in esoteric teachings for many ages, that *conscious* visual imagery is a great boon to the powers of the mind. Imagery is now recognized as a primary way of encoding information from storage in memory. It is effective in dealing with novel situations, particularly with fears and phobias. It fosters mental and emotional health and increases creativity, behaviorial flexibility, classroom learning, and athletic performance. It may be effective in the treatment of hosts of physical disorders.

This is why Tarot schools of thought that utilize the images as tools for visualization and meditation (instead of fortunetelling) emphasize the benefits of working consciously and creatively with the Tarot keys. It is the balance of right-brain perception that creates the environment for bringing these archetypal energies alive in our lives. Esoteric philosophy tells us that, whatever we make the object of our attention, we become, sooner or later. By focusing on energies which the Tarot keys represent, we come closer to manifesting them in our lives. When one begins to work with them in this way, the results can be astonishing. All manner of "synchronous" events begin to "magically" happen in one's life to verify the fact that these archetypal constellations are moving from our psyches into concrete manifestation in our lives.

Mental images are matrices for physical and emotional conditions. Regular use of the Empress card in particular will increase creativity, productivity, and inventiveness. As seeds of wheat proliferate into the multiplicity of many ears of grain, so do our *seed-forms* begin to manifest creatively in the fertile ground of our conscious imaginative minds.

14th Pathworking Correspondences

1. Intelligence: Luminous

2. Divine Letter: Daleth, DLTh (pronounced Dahl-eth) Value: 4, means "door or womb"

3. Divine Names: Aima; Abba

4. Incense: Sandalwood. Violet

5. Gems: Emerald, turquoise

6. Color: Bright green, pink

7. Element: Earth

8. Animals: Sparrow, dove

9. Plants: Myrtle, acacia, rose, fleur-de-lis

10. Planet: Venus

11. Musical Tone: F sharp

12. Magical Phenomenon: Love; realization through devotion

13. Magical Weapon: Girdle; shield

14. Mythos and Related Symbols: Aphrodite, Venus, Hathor, Shakti, Janus, Demeter, Mother Earth, the Mother of God (of Light), the Holy Spirit, the anima, the ankh cross, a winged goddess, wheat, winged disk, candle or lamp, scepter, pearls, swan

15. Gift or Challenge: To balance logic and intuition, to practice one's spiritual discipline creatively

16. Rules: Reproductive system, emotions

17. Tarot Arcana: Empress

Suggested Exercises

Affirmations work better when accompanied by mental imagery. Try to remember to utilize this principle as often as you can, not just when working this Path. This key represents the technique of how all other archetypal images operate in our lives and is at the heart of all esoteric traditions and religious rituals which involve conscious relationship with a Higher Power through imagery.

Passing wishful or "magical" thinking is not the same as persistent practice, a habitual image, and a predominant mental attitude. Image your ideals like patterns which come alive with dimension, color, texture, weight, etc., much like plaster poured into a mold. First ideas are amorphous and fluid-like, much like the water represented in the garden of the Empress, but they soon become concrete as they find the proper stable containers.

Meditate on this key when you are wanting to foster any new creative endeavor in your life. Imagine yourself in the garden of the Empress, planting the seeds of your creativity there. Affirm that, through you, she will nourish and manifest your creative ventures. Make sure your desires are not self–centered, however. A good exercise is to make a list of your present aspirations and analyze how they relate to intimate others in your life. Then spend five minutes, through visual imagery, seeing yourself complete something very important on your list and sharing with these special others how the accomplishment of this work feels. If the feelings of joy and satisfaction do not include these other people in some way, continue to invent an opportunity in your visualization that embraces them.

Both Dr. Case and Ann Davies emphasized that the goal of any Qabalistic work should primarily be service and the promotion of the welfare of humanity; otherwise it would only degenerate into selfish magical practices which, in the end, are not spiritually uplifting for anyone.

Visualization

Imagine yourself walking through a rich green field of lush spring grass wet with dew. Suddenly you spy a doorway leading directly into the ground and you open it and enter. As you descend, it is pitch dark, but the womb of the earth is warm, maternal, and inviting. It holds you comfortably while you feel your way deeper through the underground tunnel. Finally you catch a tiny glimmer of light sparkling at the end of the cavern. The light gets brighter as you approach it, and you soon enter a small clearing and notice that somehow this luminous brilliance has managed to permeate an entire enclosed room deep in the heart of this tunnel.

In the center of this room is a large tree-shaped candelabra with many flickering flames which you suddenly recognize to be the source of this glowing radiance. It is not made of metal, however, but appears to be a *living tree* glowing with flames instead of leaves. While it burns, it actually appears to be melting. You notice that it stands on top of a wooden, coffin-like structure covered with a large copper-plating and decked with glimmering jewels. Suddenly an angel appears and tells you, "When the tree is fully melted down, the Royal Lady will awake and arise to become the Mother of the Holy Child." As you look to the angelic being for a fuller description of this cryptic message, its radiant form becomes fainter and begins to disappear. You are left staring at the sepulcher with the glowing tree above it, awed and wondering just *who* that Blessed Child will be.

Affirmations

1. *Clear mental imagery is the doorway to my Higher consciousness.*

2. *All substance is vibration, whose root is imagination.*

3. *Self-conscious awareness of my mental images is my only point of control.*

4. *I make my consciousness fertile with beautiful images reflecting the Holiness that blesses all Life.*

5. *I am shaping my world tomorrow by the thoughts I think today.*

 G HIGH PRIESTESS

Path 13
The Uniting Intelligence

Memory

Planet: Moon

e 13th Path, Gimel
The High Priestess
The Uniting Intelligence

path of "Gimel," which means "camel," is the13th Path on
ee of Life and is called the "Uniting or Conductive
gence" because it is the "Essence of Glory and the
sumator of the Truth of individual spiritual things." The letter
name Gimel (GML) is the number 73 in Qabalistic gematria, and this
is also the numeration of the second Sephira, Chokmah (ChKMH),
which means Wisdom. Throughout the Old Testament, Wisdom
(Sophia) is used in the feminine gender.

Sophia is the anima, or soul of man and his spiritual guide. To
some of the ancient gnostics, Sophia is the intermediary between the
soul of the world (the demiurge) and pure Idea. Other mystics such
as Jacob Boehme believed that Sophia, or the divine virgin, has
abandoned man and that he cannot be saved until he recovers her
again. This idea permeated the Cathar movement and was the root
of the romantic notion of the mysterious woman as idealized object
of love so prevalent in the Middle Ages.

The 13th Path connects the sphere of Tiphareth, the Sun (i.e.,
Divine Incarnation, often referred to as "Ben," or the Son), which is
the Emanation of Harmony and Beauty with the Highest Source of
All, called Kether, or the I AM principle. The anima is frequently
identified with "soul" and she has been called the "Soul of Light,"
because the soul is the first vehicle which the Light of Spirit clothes
Itself in.

Together with Temperance and the Universe, these three Paths
constitute the Middle Pillar of the Tree. The Path of Tau (Universe) is

called the "gateway to the inner planes,"
Gimel (13) have been termed "dark nights both Samekh (25) and
both traverse an abyss. (Although Samekh soul" because they
still crosses a "smaller" abyss on its journey to on the Tree, it
is similar to the various stages described by St. J. phareth. This
his own "dark nights.") That is, when one is on a d. Cross in
Kether, the aspirant frequently experiences loneli toward
futility, and even dread when he or she is treading fait toward
the goal but can perceive no end in sight.   sion,

The Hebrew letter Gimel means "camel" and rei d
vehicle which alone can take one across the seemingly
desert of the abyss. The Tarot key is the High Priestess,
symbol is the Moon. As the *gimel* is the ship of the desert, so
Moon is the ship and frequent guide of the heavens. The 13th Path
important to Qabalists because, in Hebrew, the words "unity" and
"love" both add up numerologically to 13. We thus see again a
connection linking these ideas to the Goddess Sophia, who is our
divine object of love.

This feminine archetype, however, is not as open and revealing
as in other pathworkings on the Tree, such as Daleth (Empress, 14)
or Tau (Universe, 32). As High Priestess, she is the divine reservoir
of all knowledge. She holds on her lap the scroll of memory. Her face
is beautiful but cool and expressionless. In Her, we face the
crystalline reality of all we are and have ever been. We pass nigh to
the Self by recollection, by unrolling her scroll.

Because the etheric record of all human existence is seated on her
lap, and she therefore knows All, this Intelligence is said to be the
middle or center of everything at all times. The ideas associating this
in Hebrew gematria are the words *menahig,* or "conductive" (Gimel
is the *conductive* Intelligence, that which unites one point to
another), and *chatziy,* or "middle," because MNHIG and ChTzI both
add up to 108.

Working the 13th Path unites the Human Incarnation to the
Eternal Self and, when the abyss is safely traveled, bestows the
greatest initiation. On a more human level, this great uniting
principle in all of us is the subconscious, the recorder of all events in
one's lifetime. The subconscious is the agency or connecting
medium between the superconscious Self and the personality of the
ego, or conscious mind. Occult philosophy tells us that subconscious memory is perfect and cannot be improved. All that can be

improved is our ability to tap into it.

What happens on the physical plane is also mental energy working at the subconscious level. This mental energy—or mind stuff of the universe—has been called the First Matter by the alchemists. It is a virginal essence, represented by Water, which permeates everything yet is in Itself untouched by anything. From this idea are born the virgin myths of all religions. Water is essentially pure; it takes on the form of the vehicle which contains it but does not become the container.

"Occult water" is represented by the idea of vibrating waves or currents of energy. This astral fluid is the etheric record which the High Priestess holds and is also signified by the wave-like motions of Her gown. These waves descend into the image of the flowing water in the garden of the Empress. Why does esoteric imagery frequently speak of "etheric water" as vibration?

Modern physicists find themselves dealing with energy that unaccountably presents itself in wave-patterns. Though our experience tells us that we live in a world which is solid, "real," and independent of us, quantum mechanics tells us that this simply is not so. We live in a vibratory world, and vibration is the root matter which connects us with other points in the universe. This path represents the *geometrical point* from which to contemplate any possibility.

Besides its wavelike motions, another pattern which is characteristic of water is that it has a tendency to flow downward. The wisdom of the Sophia in this key is in the *regulation* of Her fluctuating current as it "descends" from its primordial beginnings to a condition of greater density.

In our attempts to cross the desert (separating this world of form from that of pure Idea,) water is the first object of our attention, the primary need in our journey. Water also acts as our *first mirror*. We become like the High Priestess in this act of reflection. The ideas associated most specifically with this path are reflection (or duplication) and memory. The camel is the apt symbol for this journey because it has a vessel—its hump—which is retentive, because it holds water.

Persistent practice in connecting with our subconscious through ritual, meditation, or whatever means the aspirant uses in her/his spiritual practice is extremely important at this stage in one's development. Not only that, we must take utmost care in what we choose to impress our minds *with*. The somewhat indifferent face of the High Priestess reminds us that the subconscious *does not discriminate*. It is, in fact, quite superstitious in retaining and feeding back to us the many foolish myths we sing to it "absentmindedly" from day to day. Although the High Priestess may have many secrets hidden in her veils, she sits on a cubic stone to show that the functions of subconsciousness are related to principles which are fundamental to laws of physical time and space.

The stone also reflects the idea of "unity," as we see in Path 16, where *abhen*, the Stone, conceals the unity of the Father and the Son. In this key, the Unity that holds these two persons in the Trinity together is the Conductive Intelligence of Unity, the Mother, which represents the love between them.

Besides being uncritically amenable to suggestion, the subconscious is also the channel of telepathic communication. This is the vibratory influence which flows downward to us from Her wavy robes. As we take note again of the stone upon which She sits, which is six-sided, we see Her boundless influence pouring into Tiphareth, the sixth sphere. In alchemy, this Path refers to the stage of the work known as "sublimation," at the completion of which one may produce the "Stone of the Wise" or the "Stone of Knowledge." There is a symbolic reference here to the hidden sphere (Daath, Knowledge) located at this point on the Path.

The Moon is the dominant female symbol for this Path and the major Virgin Goddesses of Rome (Diana and the Madonna) both are frequently seen with this emblem. Diana has been called the "Far-shooting Moon," the "Maiden of the silver bow" (referring to her crescent in the sky), and was known to be the eternal virgin and the bringer of light. The High Priestess is called the "Princess of the Silver Star." One of the Virgin Mary's names is the "Queen of Heaven," and the Moon is an apt symbol for Her in this regard, as it is the dominant light and guide in the night sky.

From earliest times, humankind has revered this light, fervently trusting that it will not abandon us by disappearing or falling out of the heavens. In the form of Mary, this Divine Feminine Light has also been called "Our Lady of Perpetual Help" by Christians, signifying Her constant attempts to guide the aspirant through her/his own dark nights.

In the final analysis, this Path has much to teach us about the reconciliation of opposites. Sublimation is the purification of the matter by dissolution and reduction into its constituent parts. The "matter," in this case, is the Astral Light, or the Kundalini, which is also intimately connected with the path of Teth, which crosses Gimel. Because this is the Intelligence of Unity, the challenge of this pathworking is to see beyond the dualities commonly associated with the serpent energy which resides at the base of the spine and which is most frequently connected with untransformed sexual energy.

The reason the Sophia is unattainable is because She must ever be the point at the center, the middle place of perfect union. On the veil between the two pillars behind Her are images of pomegranetes and palm trees; one a symbol for the feminine, the other for the masculine. When the work of this Path is completed, the One Energy, which represents Itself to us in innumerable forms we call "objects" (of love or desire, of hate or strife) is directly experienced as One, One and Alone.

13th Pathworking Correspondences

1. Intelligence: Uniting or Conductive

2. Divine Letter: Gimel, GML (pronounced Gi-mel) Value: 3, means "camel" or "carrier"

3. Divine Names: ALIM (Al-leem); AHIH (Eh-heh-ya)

4. Incense: Camphor, aloes, jasmine. Ambergris

5. Gems: Moonstone, crystal

6. Colors: Silver, gray, blue

7. Element: Water

8. Animals: Dog, camel

9. Plants: Mugwort, almond, hazel, buttercup

10. Planet: Moon

11. Musical Tone: A flat

12. Magical Phenomenon: Creation of the White Tincture, Clairvoyance

13. Magical Weapons: Bow and arrow, wand

14. Mythos and Related Symbols: Eve, Diana, Artemis, Hecate, Nuit, the Prima Materia, the Virgin Mother, Shekinah, Isis, the Silver Star, the desert, light at the end of the tunnel

15. Gift or Challenge: To monitor one's thoughts, steadfastness, sublimination

16. Rules: Lymphatic system, menstrual cycles

17. Tarot Arcana: High Priestess

Suggested Exercises

Color the High Priestess card and mount Her where you can gaze intently at Her from time to time. Contemplation on this key will improve your memory. You realize that the High Priestess is perfectly quiet and passive, as your mind becomes when you meditate upon Her. When you need to bring something to recollection, think of Her, rather than *actively* attempting to strain your memory. By relaxing, we allow needed information to arise easily to the surface.

When you want to impress your subconscious with any idea and have been working with it through ritual, prayer, visualization, etc., finish your meditation by gazing at this key. It will speak to you through your eyes, making your own subconscious realize that you expect it to put at your disposal its wonderful power of conducting your conscious ideas to the superconscious self.

A helpful exercise to do in connection with this Path is a candle meditation. Light a single candle in a room as dark as you can make it. Stare intently at the light until you feel yourself enter a slightly altered hypnotic state. (This is actually a very common state of consciousness in which we all spend some time every day.) Try to remain completely aware, however, even though your senses are becoming dull. When the eyes are on the verge of becoming fatigued, shut them and focus on the single spark of light behind your eyes. This is a very potent exercise to use to develop psychic or inner vision and is very useful to use in conjunction with the technique of "flashing colors" described in Chapter 19.

Visualization

Visualize yourself alone on a long expanse of desert on a very dark night. You are meditating in the slight chill. The blackness is so heavy that opening your eyes is nearly the same as having them shut. You are aware of the breeze and the slightly shifting sands beneath you; your senses tell you little else. Suddenly, however, you become aware of a faint light somewhere in the corner of the sky. You focus on it until it gets brighter.

Eventually, it gets bright enough for you to barely make out the outline of two very large pillar-like structures on either side of you. From the sky above these pillars, you feel a Presence begin to descend; it is very amorphous, but you know it is there. The light which you thought was a star seems to be contained within the center of this Being. As it gets closer to your head, you recognize that it is the Queen of the Heavens, bathed in a deep sky blue. She has a large, heavy scroll on her lap, and her gown seems to dissolve into soft waves which have no definable boundaries.

She seems to continue to descend until you no longer perceive her; you realize with a start that she has entered your body through the top of your head. With this realization, you hear her inner voice speak ever so softly and clearly:

"Contained in this Scroll is the history of your entire life, and of all lives. Every action, every thought, every sigh, every heartbeat is perfectly remembered by my Immaculate Heart and recorded in this Ancient Archive.

"I am the Keeper of the Flame and the Revealer of the Three Realms. You can never see Me in my true form, because I am beyond all form, and I am behind all veils. When the last veil is severed, the Realm before birth, the Realm of incarnate life, and the Realm after death become one.

"Now, I speak to you to ask you to respond to the call of redemption. From the home which was once sweet to you, from the friends and family that you have loved, from the great story which you have enjoyed, I ask you to remove yourself. In the name of the Great Central Sun which is my own Son, I ask you to participate in the mighty work of emancipation, from which springs preservation. If you are unable to do this, this Scroll will go up in flames. Heed my words well, for I Am the Last Call."

Affirmations

1. *The power of the One Identity manifesting in my life is grounded in that Identity's perfect rememberance of all it has ever been. This absolute memory of the One Life is the link that unites me with all personalities.*

2. *I improve my faculty of concentration, my observation, my learning, and my memory for a greater awareness of my purpose from day to day.*

3. *The Lady of my soul reigns above all storms; She will remove all delusion and confusion, and I shall stop, be silent, and listen, in order to hear Her voice.*

4. *I now stimulate my subconscious mind to guide me into a complete new experience of beauty, goodwill, and creativity.*

5. *I am God-nourished in the temple of my inner Holy of Holies, where I receive direct knowledge of secrets that can never be written down.*

B   THE MAGICIAN

Path 12
Intelligence of Transparency

Attention   *Planet: Mercury*

CHAPTER TWENTY-TWO

The 12th Path, Beth
The Magician
The Intelligence of Transparency

Beth is the second letter of the Hebrew alphabet and represents the feminine principle of the God-ness energy which begins with the undifferentiated original Godhead, Kether, and proceeds to the Mother, Binah. It is characterized by traditional "yin" imagery because its meaning is translated as "house" or "enclosure," indicating its qualities of "within-ness" and containment. Beth is also the preposition "in." It is used many times in Biblical scripture to describe a place, such as "Bethlehem" (house of bread, or house of sustenance); "Beth-thes-da" (house of healing), the pool in Jerusalem known for its healing properties (John, 5:2); "Bethel" (house of God), which was where Jacob had his vision of the stairway to heaven (Gen. 28:19); and "Beth-any" (house of figs), where Jesus often visited.

The number 2 is also traditionally associated with the feminine and its related ideas of polarity, duplication, repetition, antithesis, subconsciousness, association, and continuation. It is the 2 which contains the 1 and brings forth the 3. Beth represents the enclosure or containment for existence. We notice that these final two Tarot keys, the Magician and the Fool, both proceed from Kether. In the Case deck, the Fool gazes upward; the Magician looks down toward the Mother and manifested creation. The *Sepher Yetzirah* attributes the function of Life to the letter Beth (S.Y. 4:1).

Kether is called by the *Sepher Yetzirah* the Primal Glory. The word *kabode* (KBVD), which means "glory or weight," has a value of 32, the same number as the 32 paths of Wisdom ,which describes the

Qabalistic God-energy in the ancient texts and which all proceed from the primal Glory, Kether. The influence of Kether can be thought of as a whirling electromagnetic energy which is the point of projection for three currents that are the substance of all creation: Aleph, Beth, and Gimel, the first three letters. These three currents of spiral force take root in the Father (Chokmah), the Holy Spirit (Binah), and the Son (Tiphareth), thus constituting the Qabalistic Trinity. This is pictured on the glyph of the Tree. Kether is the "One" which these three are "in" at all times.

Thirty-two is the number of perfection on the Tree because it constitutes all possible attributions of the God-ness energy, as described in the ancient Hebrew mystical texts (i.e., the 22 letters and the 10 spheres). It is also the numerical value of the word for "lightning flash" (ChZIZ), which is the connecting link which springs from Kether and strikes all the Sephiroth in an instantaneous and simultaneous outpouring of energy which then becomes manifested in the casual, mental, astral, and physical worlds. An interesting observation in this regard is that, below 32 degrees Fahrenheit, water becomes solidified.

Thirty-two was also the number of priestesses of the ancient goddess Asheroth, reflecting the same idea of emanations from a primal energy Source before the concept of the Qabalistic glyph of the Tree became conceptualized. Asheroth or Asherah, a vegetation and sea goddess, gave her name to the Hebrew tribe of Asher (Josh. 19:24, Gen. 49:20), and continued to be worshipped as the Queen of Heaven by the farming population of Israel well after the development of the Hebrew Yahveh. Patai (1967) tells us that she was honored in Solomon's temple as the bride of Jehovah for 240 years. It was from this tribe of Asher that the prophetess Anna came (Luke 2: 36).

The same root for the word "lightning" or "flash of illumination" (ChZIZ) forms other related words which have a direct bearing on this power of seership: "revelation" or "vision" (ChZVTh) "prophet" or "seer" (ChVZH or ChZCh). "The Thirty-two Paths of Wisdom" says of this Path: "The 12th path is the Intelligence of Transparency because it is that species of Magnificence called *Chazchazit* (from ChZCh), the place whence issues the vision of those seeing in apparations."

The 12th Path is the self-consciousness which connects the pure Consciousness of Kether to the female Mother element of subconsciousness, which is the container for all impressions (Binah). The Magician is the "seer" whose magical power is a consequence of clear penetrating vision. He or she truly represents the vision of the Cosmic Self as it unfolds. *The Book of Tokens* says of this path:

> I am Life eternal,
> And I am the eternal longing for manifestation,
> Because of which I bring forth the shining worlds.
> For this do I divide myself, becoming two.
>
> (Case, 1934, p. 20)

The Hebrew word for "longing or desire" in this text is *tahavaw* (ThAVH), whose numerical value is 412, the same as the letter-name of Beth spelled out. This word has another meaning also; i.e., "boundary or limit," and thus gematria reveals to us the hidden functions of this letter. It is these two principles which form the core of any magician's work; the ability to form correct desires and to define their boundaries is essential to bring any idea into concrete existence.

We noticed in Path 17 that the Hebrew word for "to create" (BARA) also means "to cut or divide." This is the function of the creative energy as it brings ideas into manifestation and is particularized in the functions of the letter Beth and the Sephira Binah, the destination of this Path as it descends from Kether. The letter Beth, Qabalists are quick to notice, is the first letter in the book of Genesis, which begins with the word *Bereshith*, commonly translated as "In the beginning," but meaning, more specifically, "At first, in principle" (d'Olivet, 1921). The symbolism is that it is Beth, not Aleph, which is the first in creation, because Aleph is one and alone and therefore incapable of dividing.

To a Qabalist and Alchemist, the magician therefore represents the First Matter or the Philosophic Mercury, which is the astrological attribution of Beth. The archetypal figure of the mythological magician which was Mercury-Hermes contains within it the seed-thoughts of transformation, healing, miracles, and seership. As the Hermetic sciences developed, these ideas expanded to include geometry, medicine, logic, astronomy, and other intellectual sciences, one of the most important of which was architecture. These ideas were preserved in the rituals of

Freemasonry, which have a direct relationship to Beth, "house." It was the masons who were influential in constructing the great cathedrals of old Europe, the "houses of God," and it was the masons who were the original founders and "builders" of this country.

The importance of the tools on the magician's table relate directly to this quality of building and creating because they represent the primordial elements of the ancients: the wand symbolized fire, the cup water, the sword air, and the coin earth or matter. Thus they symbolize the building blocks of all creation. These developed into the modern elemental "weapons" of present-day Hermetic Qabalism, and symbolize protection when placed in the four elemental quarters.

The infinity sign over the magician's head forms the "sign of life, like an endless cord." Waite goes on to explain that this key "signifies the divine motive in man, reflecting God, the will in the liberation of its union with that which is above" (Waite, 1959, pp. 72-74). Case develops this idea that all personal will is but a reflection of the Primal Will which is Kether. The true magician or miracle-worker is simply one who is as *transparent* as is this Intelligence in allowing this Primal Will to act through himself or herself.

Although all the Paths on the Tree of Life can be worked both ways (depending on whether the journey is one of evolution or descent), Case indicates that there is only one Path which leads to Kether, and it is Gimel, which connects Tiphareth, the Son, to this Primal Will. The paths of Aleph and Beth can only descend, or lead downward (Case, 1985). It is therefore senseless to talk about "personality balancing" at this stage of working with the Tree's energy. There is nothing to balance. One can only attempt to be transparent, and then only if one is pure enough. The great gift of this Path, however, is the ability to "see" things as they really are. Most Qabalists are emphatic that the visionary qualities associated with Beth do not refer to the lower forms of psychism, such as clairvoyance or clairaudience. There is nothing inherently "wrong" in investigating such phenomenon, and to do so in a scientific way can add much to our storehouse of information about the present "unknown," but teachers of esoteric traditions of both the East and the West do counsel about the alluring possibility of wandering endlessly about on etheric or astral planes.

The Transparent Intelligence, rather, represents the highest form of seership, spiritual knowledge, which is reflected in one's ability to see the luminous image of the Undefinable in the multiple forms which conceal It. The true house which Beth represents is the temple of the Spirit, which is one's own body, and it is here that we begin to discover the hidden vision of God.

The main theme connected with the power of true seership is *concentration*. It is the undivided meditative effort of the magician which allows him or her to channel the energy represented by the wand in one hand with the object of *attention* represented by the downward pointing finger in the other. It is this concentration which allows the undifferentiated Energy to come together at a focal *point*, and the magician is thus a transmitter for this center of focus. All spiritual traditions teach that the ability to set forces in motion and bring about change involves one-pointed attention through prayer, visualization, ritual, affirmation, deep meditation, and so on. By applying the principle of continued *attention* on what our thoughts are and what impressions we are making on subconsciousness, we participate in the alchemical philosophy that all problems are solved via Mercury, the universal solvent.

We saw, that, because of its position on the Tree, this Path only goes downward, in one concentrated stream from Kether, the Incomprehensible. There is no way back to Kether from Binah, but only from Tiphareth (the Son). It is an outstreaming ray, as is the outgoing ray toward Chokmah. Therefore, no pathworking actually climbs the Tree at this place in the Supernal Triangle. The visualization exercises which follow in this and the next chapter attempt to imitate this whirling light energy which proceeds from the Most High. The more one uses *concentration* in this process, the more powerful the process becomes.

12th Pathworking Correspondences

1. Intelligence: Transparency

2. Divine Letter: Beth, BITh (pronounced Bayth) Value: 2, means "house" or "enclosure"

3. Divine Names: AHIH (Eh-heh-ya); Elohim (Eh-lo-heem)

4. Incense: Mastic, storax. Myrhh

5. Gems: Opal, agate

6. Color: Rich yellow

7. Element: Air

8. Animals: Sparrow, ape

9. Plants: Vervain, mace, palm

10. Planet: Mercury

11. Musical Tone: E

12. Magical Phenomenon: Vision of the Great Silence, Miracles of healing

13. Magical Weapon: Caduceus wand

14. Mythos and Related Symbols: Mercury, Hermes, Thoth, Odin, Moses, the High Priest, the Guru, the Christos, chalice, sword, Ouroborous, ibis, the four elements

15. Gift or challenge: To see through a glass lightly

16. Rules: Brain and nervous system

17. Tarot Arcana: Magician

Suggested Exercises

If you have followed the exercises beginning with the first one given in Path 32, the following information will probably make sense. You will know the energies connected to the chakras and their associated symbols, colors, and tones. The great science of sound and color is revealed to us by the great Magicians of all ages.

Pythagoras, Plato, the Egyptian hierophants, and many of the ancients were reputed to have understood the nature of the power of articulated sound. A mantra, for instance, is supposed to arouse such a fiery connection between master and disciple that the latter swoons under its influence. The Hebrews and Greeks were instructed in the ancient art of correct musical proportions. Many esoteric traditions tell us that ancient Wisdom Schools have handed down exact harmonics between specific tones in the musical scale and the number of vibrations per second which allows our eyes to see light as specific color. Paul Case felt that this ancient art of sound and color should again be used for mental and physical healing (especially in this age of "the great anxiety").

Indeed, we see a resurgence of interest today in color therapies in the U.S and chromotherapy in Europe, and in the use of color in cosmetics, clothes, decorating, etc. in ways which are specifically supposed to be related to *consciousness*. We are aware that certain kinds of light in classrooms is more conducive to alertness, that some are better at growing plants, and that some (blue lights) will harm the brains of babies in nurseries.

Working with tone and color has been used in many esoteric traditions for thousands of years and is popular today in many hermetic groups. These techniques of using colors *by meditating on them* (a key secret) is said to develop mental soundness and a rounded consciousness and may also work on the physical body as well. You can try for yourself and see.

RED corresponds to the Mars chakra, is active in the motor centers in the body (muscles and reproductive system), and is connected with strength and energy. Too much causes agitation. It corresponds to Path 27 and to the tone C natural. Check the correspondence lists; you will see connections to other Keys.

ORANGE relates to a high energy state which is also somewhat relaxed. It is said to be a tonic. It is connected to the parts of the body which relate to breathing and manifests in the Sun chakra, behind the heart. It relates to the 30th Path and D natural. An excess can cause fevers. It is good for mental energy and recuperation from fatigue.

YELLOW the third color vibration and relates to the cerebrum, or higher brain. It is said to cleanse and purify and be good for the entire nervous system. It also assists in the process of producing an important aid for digestion called chyle. Deficiency can cause depression. It relates to the top chakra, Mercury, the Magician, Path 12, and the tone E natural. This color is also connected to the production of a substance in the body which adepts secrete for longevity and about which the alchemists have long spoken. It is useful to meditate on this color for this reason.

GREEN is the vibration that relates to the thyroids and parathyroids. It is a general healer and harmonizer and is good to build vitality and health *through the eyes.* Nature is healing and calming. It corresponds to the fifth chakra (throat), to the Empress, Path 14, and to F sharp (some schools say F).

BLUE is the color that is related to the pituitary gland and the corresponding parts of the body which this organ governs. It is soothing and cooling and acts as a depressant. It is good for inflammations, fevers, and tensions. Some schools attribute to it the tone G; in our correspondence lists it relates to A flat, the 13th Path, and the sixth (or brow) chakra. It is a useful instrument in developing telepathy and in harmonizing certain physical conditions, especially those connected to rhythms. Deficiency causes lack of coordination on the cellular level as well as on emotional or psychic levels.

VIOLET is attributed to the tone B flat (or A sharp). It is even more a calming or soothing agent. Its center is the solar plexus or Jupiter chakra. It directs the entire sympathetic nervous system and is good as a cardiac depressant. It is also said to produce dreaminess and to dissolve discord. It is connected to the arteries, veins, and areas ruled by the sacral area of the spine, including the sciatic nerves and femur area. Both violet and blue act as a tonic to the liver and mammary glands. Violet connects to the third chakra and the 21st Path and is intimately associated with many of our emotions and desires.

INDIGO corresponds to the first or root chakra, in this system ruled by Saturn and associated with the 32nd Path. This area is responsible for waste elimination and is the energy reservoir in the body. The Kundalini is said to reside here. It is connected to deliberation and concentration. Deficiency can cause weakening of the bone structure and eccentricity in the personality. It corresponds to the tone A.

Now, if we look at all 12 notes in the scale, we see that the colors correspond to these tones (with their accompanying zodiacal and Tarot attributions):

C —Red, Aries, The Emperor
C#—Red-orange, Taurus, The Hierophant
D —Orange, Gemini, The Lovers
D# —Orange-yellow, Cancer, The Chariot
E —Yellow, Leo, Strength
F —Yellow-green, Virgo, The Hermit
F# —Green, Libra, Justice
G —Green-blue, Scorpio, Death,
G#—Blue, Sagittarius, Temperance
A —Blue-violet, Capricorn, The Devil or Advocate
A#—Violet, Aquarius, The Star
B —Violet-red, Pisces, The Moon

When working with sound and color, it is good to use a pitchpipe and not an instrument to intone the notes while meditating on the corresponding keys and colors. Choose a key whose symbols are important to you right now. (This could be through the symbols in the key, the myths connected with it, the astrological associations, or any other metaphor you find meaningful.) Mount the key in front of you and stare at it while intoning the correct note. Or work with the letters with the technique of flashing colors, visualizing the shape and color while intoning the note.

Remember that a useful way to arouse a specific color in the *mind's eye* is to use the complementary color (see Chapter 19). The color complements are:

Red—Green
Red-orange—Blue-green
Orange—Blue
Yellow-orange—Blue-violet
Yellow—Violet
Yellow-green—Violet-red

Many useful exercises can be devoloped by the aware student to stimulate body parts or psychic centers using these correspondences. One is to simply paint a specific color on a piece of cardboard, mount it, and stare at it while the corresponding note is intoned. Another is to work with a color lamp or color filters in a window. Remember that a pitchpipe is practically indispensable. Remember, too, that you are stimulating a specific area by using the seven principle colors (which relate to the chakras as described in Chapter 2), so you should use them in harmony and balance with one another.

You will probably note that, if the chakras are stimulated in order (in the original exercise given in Path 32), they do not go straight up or down the body, as in the popular Rainbow Meditation. For example, red, orange, and yellow would activate chakras two, four, and seven. Or yellow, green and blue would stimulate the top of the head, the throat, and the brow (seven, five, and six).

Paul Case suggests stimulating the chakras in this order (at least for the beginner): 1, 4, 2, 3, 5, 6, 7. Find these corresponding Tarot Keys and meditate on them in this order. Remember that the first, or root, chakra corresponds to Saturn and the Administrative Intelligence.

There is much material here for reflection and much potential to build on these techniques. *Experiment* with the corresponding Tarot energies and their specific colors, tones, symbols, body parts, etc. Keep a journal of your findings.

Visualization

Imagine you are as transparent and as potent a tool as a convex lens. Such a lens will intensify the rays of the Sun so that it will instantly heat as well as reflect light when it is placed directly over an object. Visualize this happening. See the Sun coming through a convex lens over a piece of paper and shining on it in a bright circle and then quickly catching it on fire.

Then try and transfer the idea of this powerful transparent vehicle to your own body as you perform one of the most potent Qabalistic techniques, that of the Middle Pillar. This exercise is done by simultaneously visualizing spheres of light within the body and also by *vibrating* the God names. With practice, you can actually vibrate the Names, not just speak or chant them. When this has been accomplished, you will begin to understand how powerful the effects of this exercise can be. Practice. (Pronunciation is given following the first spelling of the Name.)

In the Western Qabalistic tradition, there are five "psycho-spiritual organs" (called chakras in the East) which correspond to the five elements. They are always visualized as descending into the body from above. No attempt is made to arouse the energies at the bottom of the spine or in the lower energy centers and "pull" them upward.

The first organ corresponds to Kether and Spirit. Transfer the idea of the convex transparent lens to the top of your head. Above it glows a brilliant sphere of white light radiating in all directions. But because you have a *concentrated focus of energy* to capture its rays, it pours down into your body through the lens in a dense, bright, fiery burst of energy. At the same time, vibrate the Name "Eheieh" (Eh-heh-yeh). Imagine the center at the top of your head awakening to dynamic activity. You may actually feel a burning sensation there. Vibrate the God-name several times. Eheieh means "I Will Be." (If you are not in an environment conducive to loud chanting, mentally doing the exercise is okay; but the more physical it is, the better, especially in the beginning.) Imagine the brain suffused with brilliance and vitality.

Then imagine a shaft of light descending through a column down to the area of your throat. Always visualize the light as deep inside your body. It expands to form a second ball of light which bathes the throat and lung area and extends upwards toward the face and backwards toward the neck and back. This is the Air center. Breathe deeply as you visualize the light from Kether descending through your brain and catching this ball on fire. The God-names associated with this sphere are YHVH Elohim (Yod- Heh-Vaw-Heh Eh-lo-heem) and it corresponds to the marriage of Chokmah and Binah.

After several minutes, visualize the light continuing to descend in a column till it reaches the center part of your chest, the Fire center and the heart sphere. This should be imagined as a large, glowing ball of light like the Sun at mid-day. It takes on a brilliant golden color. Feel it burning inside your breast, catching your heart on fire. There are several God-names that can be vibrated here—*one* is sufficient. For the traditional Christian Qabalist, the name is YHShVH, Jesus (pronounced Yod- hesh-oo-ah); for one who prefers the Gnostic mystery traditions, the name IAO (eee-ah-oh) should be vibrated. The name most commmonly given for this sphere is Jehovah Eloah ve Daas (Yuh-hoh-voh-Eh-loh-ve-Dah-as), but many have found it too long. Eloah is a Hebrew name which also means "God," but the H ending gives it a feminine attribution. Daath or Daas means "knowledge." This center, of course, corresponds to Tiphareth, and includes the four outer spheres.

Then move into the Water center, located at the point of the reproductive organs and lower spine. Imagine it glowing brightly, again catching this sphere on fire and expanding outward to bathe the entire pelvic and back area. The name which corresponds to this spiritual organ (Yesod) is Shaddai El Chai (Shad-di-El-Chi.) The *ch* is gutteral. It means Almighty Living God. The word for God is "El," but it may be changed to Eloah if a female attribution is preferred (see above).

After several minutes, move to the final sphere, Malkuth, located at the point where the feet contact the earth. This exercise is done best standing, preferably facing East, but you can just as well *visualize* yourself standing. Again see a ball of dazzling light bathe your feet and expand downward into the earth, blessing it also. Vibrate the name Adonai ha-Aretz (Ah-doh-ni-hah-Ah-retz). Adonai is the most common Jewish name given for "Lord" and was also used by the Canaanites and others to designate a ruler or king. The phrase means "Lord of the Earth." Again, if a female ending is preferred, the word would be: Ah-doh-ni-hu (ADNIH).

Then pause and try to vividly see the column of light extending from over the top of your head, through your body, and deep into the earth. It lights up the energy points within your physical vehicle like brilliant suns. If you have a reason to focus your attention on a particular prayer or thought-form, now is the time to do so.

There are two parts to this technique, one a vitalizing of principle energy centers within the body itself, as the presence of Kether is invited in from above; the other, which the student may choose to do immediately afterward, is the "circulation of light" throughout one's physical and ethereal vehicles. Together, these exercises create a powerful "body of light," which (if one could see it with the eyes of a true seer) extends several feet from the body. The second part is given in the last chapter of this book (Aleph). They need not be performed together. Please note that these are potent Qabalistic techniques. Never desecrate these God-names or use these exercises for anyone else's ill will. It can only return to you in a manifold way. If for any reason you feel you need extra protection while doing any ritual or pathwork, a common Qabalistic technique is to visualize the four Archangels which guard the quarters: Raphael is in the East, Michael in the South, Gabriel in the West, and Auriel in the North.

For a more thorough examination of this technique, see Israel Regardie's *Middle Pillar*, 1985.

Affirmations

1. *My personality is a channel for the transmission of the highest potential of the Expression of the God-ness in me.*

2. *I maintain my awareness of that which is above simultaneously with that which is below.*

3. *I am a witness to the continual glorious works of the Eternal Life Power.*

4. *My concentration allows me to perceive the inner nature of the object of my attention.*

5. *"The Kingdom is Spirit is embodied in my Flesh."*

 THE FOOL

Path 11
The Fiery Intelligence

Superconsciousness   *Planet: Uranus*

CHAPTER TWENTY-THREE

The 11th Path, Aleph
The Fool
The Fiery Intelligence

The first letter, Aleph, means "ox" or "bull." More specifically, it symbolizes creative power or raw force, because the oxen was the primary motivation for the development of agriculture which formed the first stirrings of civilization. In ancient ages, the bull was used as one of the earliest symbols for God, especially in the Taurean age, which preceded the development of Jewish monotheism. This symbolic image is found in Apis of Egypt, Dionysus of Greece, Mithra of Persia, and, long before, when horned images were fused with the matriarchal goddess. In Qabalistic Tarot, it has come to mean the primary Life-power which moves everything through the power of Breath (Spirit). Aleph is called the "Fiery Intelligence of Ether" (Knight, 1965).

Throughout this book, we have been speaking of the *Intelligences* of the God-energy. These must not be thought of as separate from one another (they have nothing to do with the C.I.A. or U.F.O.'s!); they are only *attributes* by which we as a human species have attempted, in our limited fashion, to define that which will always, to some extent, remain unknowable. Although the ancients have attributed many correspondences to the Qabalistic system of thought as it developed, including planets, signs, and symbols of all kinds, it is useful to remember that we are always speaking of a single Entity which is gracious enough to allow us our own particular unique perception of It. It is like a light reflected through a prism of many colors. Some prefer blue, others red. Some identify with the attribute of mercy, others beauty or love. There is no concept, emotion, mythology, element, or attribution of any kind

293

which does not find a correspondence on the Tree of Life; it is all-encompassing.

In Hebrew, the word for Intelligence is *Saykel* (ShKL), which also means insight or awareness. The word combines the root "soke" (ShK), which means "to dwell with," and *kole* (KL), which means "all" or "the whole." The inference is that the Intelligences on the Tree each represent a *category* of God which is an *abode* (ShK) of God's *entire being* (KL). Kether is called "The Wonder" (PLA), or the Wonderful or Admirable Intelligence. It is the root of the entire Tree, and from it issue directly the letters Aleph, Beth, and Gimel. Through word play, we see that the *Wonder* (PLA) of Kether reflects Itself immediately in Aleph (ALP), the first letter, as a mirror does; that is, backwards (i.e., PLA=ALP).

Aleph itself is called the Scintillating or Fiery Intelligence, as It reflects most perfectly this first outflow of the spiritual influence of Kether. Indeed, the first two letters of the name mean "God," and, if we examine the root of the letter-word Aleph (ALP), we see it combines this idea of the God-ness energy with the *P* (Peh), the archetype of the mouth or speech. Thus, from Aleph, we get the idea of God, the Mouth, or Divine Self-expression. Aleph is the Life-breath, which expresses itself through the element Air. The Fool's connection with this Life-breath or spirit is humorously alluded to in the phrase commonly given to the fool, a "windbag," or bag of air.

Aleph, as the 11th Intelligence (the first 10 are the 10 Sephiroth) is the final Path on our journey. It connects Kether to Chokmah, the Father principle. This path of the Fiery or Scintillating Intelligence corresponds through gematria to the words "volcanic fire" (AVD) and "a circular form or motion" (ChG), both of which equal 11. These ideas describe the way the God-energy proceeds in its dance from the Wonder which is Kether and is closely aligned to concepts of modern physics about the origin of the universe.

The *Sepher Yetzirah* says, "The Three are One, and that One stands above" (S.Y. 6:3). This, of course, alludes to Kether. About the Fiery Intelligence, *The Thirty-two Paths of Wisdom* states, "it is the essence of that curtain which is placed close to the order of the disposition, and this is a special dignity given to it that it may be able to stand before the Face of the Cause of Causes." If we examine this archetypal theme in the person of the Fool, as well as its placement on the Tree, it becomes apparent that this is the one letter which has this special relationship with the Cause of causes. The number of

Aleph is 1, and it is thus in union with Kether, the first Sephira. In Qabalistic philosophy, all powers above Chokmah are beyond human intellect; the image of the Fool therefore represents absolute Superconsciousness. A fool, it is said, knows nothing. There are no distinguishable "things" on this Path to balance, as in the letter Beth, because it is a Path which partakes of the Absolute No-thing and the root of Every-thing which is Kether. Aleph represents the One which effects the continual equilibrium of forces in action.

We have seen that the numerical value of Aleph is One; Kether is also One. The word Aleph spelled out equals 111 (three ones). The Wonderful (PLA) Intelligence (Kether) is also 111. Qabalists have observed that the famous saying, "The Lord our God is *One*," also has a value of 111. Crowley (1977) notes interestingly that the word "Aum," the vibration of everything, when spelled out, also equals 111. So does the word *apel* (APL), which means "thick darkness" and refers to the veil separating Kether from the Manifest, as described in *The Thirty-two Paths of Wisdom* in the 11th Path. Kether itself is called the *Limitless Light Which Is Not* and also the *Fiery Darkness*, both paradoxes which imply the impossibility of knowledge of the divine at this level.

In Jewish folklore, the tale told about the letter Aleph and its special relationship to Kether is a touching one and contains a lesson in humility. It is said that, for 2,000 years, God contemplated the letters, who all begged to be the first in creation. When Beth was chosen for the beginning (Bereshith), God wondered where Aleph was, because all the other letters had presented themselves. Aleph said simply, "I saw all the other letters had not been chosen, why then should I present myself to Thee?" Aleph goes on to indicate that God had made a good choice in Beth. The Divine One then said to Aleph, "Although I will begin the creation of the world with Beth, thou wilt remain the first of my letters . . . on thee shall be based all calculations and operations of the world, and my Unity shall not be expressed save by the letter Aleph" (*Zohar*, D. Matt trans., 1973, v. 1, 13).

The whimsical but humble fool, which is attributed to the letter Aleph, represents the idea of the original seed of all potential who is so certain of his unity with the primal God-energy that no fear can daunt him on his path. As Waite says of this key, "The edge which opens on the depth has no terror; it is as if angels were waiting to unhold him" (1959, p. 152). Furthemore, the Sun behind him "knows whence he came, whither he is going, and how he will return" (p. 155). Actually the Fool is not a "him" at all, because it is not yet differenciated into any kind of polarity. Case has said, "It is neither male nor female" but rather "a Heavenly Androgyne" (1947, p. 32).

Aleph is considered one of the three "Mother" letters; that is, those representing the elements. The *Sepher Yetzirah* tells us that, when God formed the 22 letters into speech, "he drew them through the waters, he burned them in the fire, he vibrated them in the air" (S.Y. 6:4). Aleph, as we saw, is the life-force which is represented by the element Air, or the breath. It is intimately connected to the element Shin (Fire) and the Holy Spirit, because whirling fire is the state of potential for manifested life at the dawn of creation. The differentiated worlds are symbolized by the disks on the Fool's robe, one of which (in the Waite version, towards the bottom right) conceals the letter Shin upside-down.

The Fool key challenges our assumptions of what is real, correct, or proper. Most fools were wantonly disposed toward riddles and paradoxes, tricks and acrobatics. The upside-down Shin demonstrates this characteristic of Aleph, the topsy-turvy Fool who stands on his head for fun. Indeed, we are prone to believe the next step the Fool takes off the cliff will send him reeling downward headfirst. If you turn an Aleph on its head, however, it will still very much look like an Aleph. And it is precisely this characteristic of twirling and whirling which makes Aleph so much like the prime Mover, Kether, also called the Primium Mobile or "First Swirlings" of manifestation.

In his many Qabalistic works, Case repeatedly states that the universal energy moves in a rhythmic, whirling motion, which is the basis of all potential manifestation. (This, again, is represented by the "wheels" on the cloak of the Fool, which in the Case deck have spokes). Modern science simply verifies what Qabalists have known since ancient times.

We now understand that everything spins, from galaxies to electrons. Our solar system is carried along by the rotation of our galaxy. This is what moves us through space in our expanding universe. A photon, which is a beam or quantum of light, when seen as a wave phenomenon, is a spiral motion. Qabalah tells us that Kether is the seed-thought or *idea* of this Limitless Light, contracting at a point of condensation which, in successive stages of development, becomes radiation. That is, the *idea* of this whirling motion condenses in the radiation which *is* that light; i.e., Chokmah, or the destination of the 11th Path.

It is thought that the early universe was composed chiefly of this radiation, with only a small contamination of matter. The huge energy density of radiation prevalent in the early universe was lost as the universe was expanded. Scientists think that the expansion began between 10 and 20 billion years ago in what is now termed the "big bang." When we speak of a "big bang," the inference is not that an explosion began at a definite center and spread out over the vacuum of space. It means that space itself was much more condensed, and that when the explosion occurred it happened simultaneously everywhere with all particles of matter rushing apart from one another. This is exactly how the Qabalah tells us the Sephiroth or manifest attributes of Kether were created: simultaneously, like a lightning flash.

Many fascinating tales are told by mythologies worldwide about the origins of our universe, but few are more interesting or as far-fetched as actual fact. Between the age of one second and 100,000 years, the universe was diffused with a yellow light much like the surface of our sun. It was, as we have seen, radiation-dominated instead of matter dominated as is now the case. The world then contained particles and anti-particles which annihilated one another as they cooled below the threshold temperature for nuclear particles. Perhaps the most fascinating part of this tale about the origin of the world as we know it is that the total number of nuclear particles exceeded the number of anti-particles (that is, the slight excess of matter over anti-matter) by about one part in *10 billion*. The occurrence in cosmology of a number as small as this has led some to theorize that the number, for all practical purposes, may as well be *zero*. But, if it were zero, matter and anti-matter would have annihilated each other completely and we would not be here (Harrison, 1985).

It is interesting to note in this regard that Kether is also identified as Ain, Nothingness, and in some Tarot decks, the Fool is given the numerical attribution of zero. As Qabalists, we may theorize that at some infinitesimal place between zero and one, there appaared a slight excess of matter over anti-matter, and because of this freakish, almost inconspicious excess—the fantastic trick of the Fool reflecting Kether—the condition was created for the legacy of our universe today.

11th Pathworking Correspondences

1. Intelligence: Scintillating

2. Divine Letter: Aleph, ALPh (pronounced Ah-leff Value: 1, means "ox" or "primal mover"

3. Divine Names: AHIH (Eh-heh-ya); Jah

4. Incense: Galbanum. Ambergris

5. Gems: Topaz, Chalcedony

6. Color: Pale Yellow

7. Element: Air

8. Animal: Eagle

9. Plants: Peppermint, aspen

10. Planet: Uranus

11. Musical Tone: F

12. Magical Phenomenon: Vision of the Face of God

13. Magical Weapon: Whirling fan of Kether

14. Mythos and Related Symbols: Mithra, Dionysus (all bull gods), Thor, Hoor-paar-kraat, sky powers, Uranous, all-seeing Eye, the Universal Egg, Ruach (breath, spirit), Winged human, sylphs, ox, yoke, feather of aspiration, a white sun

15. Gift or Challenge: Complete freedom and trust; ability to see beyond all beginnings and endings

16. Rules: Respiratory organs

17. Tarot Arcana: Fool

Suggested Exercise/Visualization

The Fool is a creature of wonder. He or she is not a victim of circumstance. No one with such utter trust and lightheartedness can be taken advantage of in any way. So whatever previous concepts you may have about the Fool, you can throw them out the window. They belong to your past, or to another Tarot deck.

This picture should inspire hope because it is an image of absolute certainty. The Fool knows beyond a shadow of a doubt that what the world may think of him or her matters not; God is the source by which it sees, the Mind with which it knows, the Love in which it grows. This it knows.

The final meditative exercise is called the Circulation of Light. It is performed with the intention of evoking the whirling force of the pure God-energy and circulating it through-out every cell in your body. It cleanses and soothes the etheric vehicle and the mind as well.

Visualize a vibrant body of light around the crown of your head moving in a swirling motion. Mentally see it descending down the left side of your head and face, down through the left shoulder and arm, the left trunk and legs and foot. It then moves like an electric circuit up the right leg, trunk, and body, connecting at the top again to the original spark which gave it impetus. Visualize the circulation of light this way several times, seeing it move in a direct, swift, circular motion, bathing all the cells in your body with its internal cleansing. Connect the left side and descent with your exhalation, and the right side ascent with your inhalation.

Then visualize the light descending (with the exhalation) down the front of your face and body. When it reaches your feet, it moves around and (with the inhalation) ascends up your backside. Do several circuits this way also, imagining the light building with intensity with each circulation. After completing this part of the exercise, you will have vibrating currents of energy spinning at right angles within and around your body.

Finally, imagine a powerful thrust of light ascending from Malkuth, the Earth center at your feet. It begins at the bottom of the right foot, wrapping around the left leg, back toward the right leg, and around in a spiral form. It ascends your entire body, wrapping itself around you like a bright bandage of light. If visualized correctly, this will produce a whirling sensation of such force that it may make you feel slightly off balance. This is natural, but be careful that you are in a safe room with plenty of space so you don't fall into anything. Try to maintain the awareness of these whirling spirals and circles of light energizing you for at least several minutes. Always see the light returning finally to the Kether center, at the top of the head. This is a powerful healing exercise, and works better the more it is utilized. It regenerates every atom in your body and creates a strong web of protecting light around you. You are the pillar which carries the lamp of the God-energy, and you do it best when you do it consciously.

Affirmations

1. *I am life's adventure.*

2. *I journey into the wonder of self-discovery in perfect trust.*

3. *The universal Mind of God has concentrated Itself into a condensed form of my experience.*

4. *I am the blueprint of eternal evolution.*

5. *Thought is creation.*

Conclusion

Thus we end our Journey through the Tree's many wonderful and charming Paths. With the development of consciousness, the myths that we add as we go are increasingly those contributed by science, whose theories are, like the many legends of the past, continually changing. The Qabalah, the Tarot, the Tree and all esoteric systems must also continue to evolve and grow, or they will become useless, outdated forms which hold no meaning for today's truth-seeking aspirants.

One question that arises as we seek newer ways to understand the many possibilities contained in the Tree's rich philosophy (which seems to hold so many secrets) is: Are there additional Paths? It has been postulated that, because there are five "final" letters which have a different shape and numerical value, that there are perhaps "hidden" paths on the Tree. In the Tarot symposium in San Francisco in 1989, Nick Tereshchenko considered the possibility that there could even be more than 27—in fact, if one placed the "hidden" Sephira (Daath) on the Tree (in the Abyss), there could be 50 possible different Paths. How these would relate to the Hebrew letters is a matter of conjecture. There are newer decks which have proposed that additional Arcana exist and there are rumors that, in certain Rosicrucian grades, the secrets of these hidden Paths are revealed to the initiate.

In order for the Qabalah to be a time-honored tradition rich in esoteric truth, as well as an evolving system which reflects how these major archetypes of the Self are presently working in our lives, much personal reflection on the Tree and its symbols is required. It is a delicate balance to strike between learning from mythic structures of the past (which, as Carl Jung, Joseph Campbell, and others tell us, are vitally important in allowing us to connect to the cosmos, the mystery, the unknowable) and the restructuring of these symbolic metaphors of consciousness to reflect the dawning Aquarian age.

If there are other Paths on the Tree with their own particular constellations, what would they connect? It seems obvious at first glance that other Paths across the abyss are possible. The Tree in its present form only has abyss Paths proceeding from Tiphareth (unless one counts Cheth and Vav, which do not cross Daath). Is there a specific reason for this? If so, none is readily given in the Qabalistic literature. It is obvious to one who has studied the Tree at any length that the "lightning flash" across the abyss and into manifested creation did not follow any of the given Paths but instead created an additional one between Binah and Chesod.

If we use this as a clue to connect the other Sephiroth in the Supernal Triangle to those below, we get four additional Paths: from Kether to Chesed, from Kether to Geburah, from Chokmah to Geburah, and the Binah-Chesed connection. This gives us seven paths across the abyss instead of three, which could be four of the five Hebrew finals. This work is "meditation in process" and will be expounded upon at a later date by the author and a colleague.

At present, it is intriguing to note that the addition of these four Paths creates an interesting configuration of a five-pointed star with Daath as its heart (see diagram). In this regard, too, we make note of the fact that, of all the Paths, none, when they are arranged on the cube of space (a geometrical figure of the Hebrew Letters also described in the *Sepher Yetzirah*), lead inward. They all extend infinitely outward. Paul Case reveals that only the five finals are structured so as to lead diagonally inward. The explanation of the cube of space and where the Paths are located in its three-dimensional structure is available, in part, in Case's book *The Tarot* (listed in the bibliography.)

I leave you to reflect on the multiple possibilities of such a rich and intricate system, hoping that you have been inspired to continue the pathwork at your own pace. It is a very enriching and useful exercise, once you are familiar with the symbols and correspondences of a given Path, is to write your own pathwork. You will be amazed at the possibilities for reflection, association,

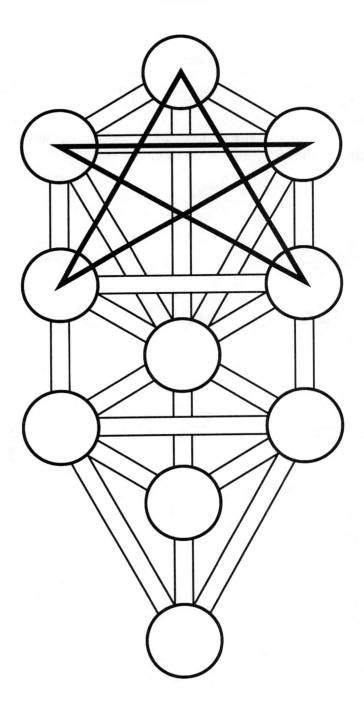

and revelation which result from this practice. To stumble across universal truths via the transcendental mythology of the Qabalah produces peak experiences which are highly inspirational. With continued study and reflection, may we continue to evolve toward the elusive source of the transpersonal, supporting the process of change and the creation of new structures as we go.

Bibliography

Arrien, A. *Tarot Symposium Journal*. No. Hollywood, CA: Newcastle. 1989.

Bailey, A. *Esoteric Healing*. London: Lucia Pub. Co. 1953.

Ben-Yehuda (ed.) *English-Hebrew/Hebrew-English Dictionary*. N. Y.: Pocket Books. 1964.

Bible. New American. Iowa Falls, IA: World Bible Pub. 1976.

Budge, W. *Gods of the Egyptians*. N.Y.: Dover Pub. 1969.

Campbell, J. *Occidental Mythology*. N. Y.: 1964. Penguin Books. 1964.

Case, P. F. *The Book of Tokens*. Los Angeles, CA: Builders of the Adytum. 1934.

　　The Tarot. Richmond, VA: Macoy Pub. 1947

　　The True and Invisible Rosicrucian Order. York Beach, ME: Samuel Weiser. 1985.

Chittick, W. *The Sufi Path of Love: The Spiritual Teachings of Rumi*. Albany, N.Y.: State University of New York Press. 1983.

Cirlot, J. E. *A Dictionary of Symbols*. N.Y. : Philosophical Library. 1971.

Crowley, A. 777. York Beach, ME: Samuel Weiser. 1977.

Davis, P. *Other Worlds: Space Superspace & the Quantum Universe*. N.Y.: Simon & Schuster. 1980.

Denning, M. & Phillips, O. *Magical States of Consciousness*. St Paul, MN: Llewellyn Pub. 1985.

d'Olivet, F. *The Hebrew Tongue Restored*. (Nayan Redfield, trans.) N.Y.: G.P. Putnam's. 1921.

Feyerabend, K. (trans.) *Langenscheidt's Hebrew Dictionary to the Old Testament*. Maspeth, N. Y. : Langenscheidt Pub. no date.

Fillmore, C. *The Metaphysical Bible Dictionary*. Unity Village, MO: Unity School of Christianity. 1931.

Franz, M.–L. von. (Ed. with commentary). *Aurora Consurgens: A Document Attributed to Thomas Aquinas on the Problem of Opposites in Alchemy*. Translated by R.C.F. Hull and A.S.B. Clover. N.Y.: Bollingen Series LXXVII. 1966.

Fortune, D. *The Mystical Qabalah*. York Beach, ME: Samuel Weiser. 1935.

Gimbutas, M. *The Gods & Goddesses of Old Europe*. L. A., CA: Univ. of Cal. Press. 1982.

Godwin, D. *Godwin's Cabalistic Encyclopedia*. St Paul, MN: Llewellyn Pub. 1969.

González-Wippler, M. *A Kabbalah for the Modern World*. St Paul, MN: Llewellyn Pub. 1907.

Graves, R. & Patai, R. *Hebrew Myths*. N.Y. Anchor Books. 1964.

Hall, H. *The Moon & the Virgin*. N.Y.: Harper & Row. 1971.

Harrison, E. *Masks of the Universe*. N. Y.: Macmillan Pub. 1985

Hartman, J. *Shamanism for the New Age: A Guide to Radionics & Radiesthesia*. Placitas, NM: Aquarian Systems. 1907.

Heline, C. *The Bible & the Tarot*. Marina del Rey, CA: DeVorss Co. 1969.

Hoeller, S. *The Royal Road*. Wheaton, IL: Theosophical Pub. House. 1975.

Jung, C.G. *The Collected Works of C.G. Jung*. Ed by Sir H. Read. Trans. by R.F.C.Hull Bollingen Series XX. N.Y.: Princeton.
_____5. *Symbols of Transformation*. 2nd Ed. 1967.
_____13. *Alchemical Studies*. 1967.
_____14. *Mysterium Coniunctionis : An Inquiry into the Separation & Syntheses of Psychic Opposites in Alchemy*. 2nd ed. 1970.

Kaplan, A. (trans.) *The Bahir*. York Beach, ME: Samuel Weiser. 1968.

Knight, G. *A Practical Guide to Qabalistic Symbolism*. N. Y. : Samuel Weiser. 1965.

Mathers, S.L. (trans.) *Kabbala Denudata*. York Beach, ME: Samuel Weiser. 1968.

Matt, D. (trans.) *The Zohar: Book of Enlightenment*. N.Y.: Paulist Press. 1983.

Nichols, S. *Jung & Tarot*. York Beach, ME: Samuel Weiser. 1980.

Patai, R. *The Hebrew Goddess*. N. Y.: Avon Books. 1967.

Regardie, I. *The Middle Pillar*. St. Paul, MN: Llewellyn Pub. 1985.

   Garden of Pomegrarates. St. Paul, MN: Llewellyn Pub. 1970.

   The Golden Dawn. St. Paul, MN: Llewellyn Pub. 6th ed. 1989.

Robinson, J. (ed.) *The Nag Hammadi Library*. San Francisco, CA: Harper & Row. 1977.

Scholem, G. *Major Trends in Jewish Mysticism* N.Y.: Schocken Books. 1961.

Suares, C. *The Qabalah Trilogy*. Boston, MA: Shambhala. 1985.

Tansley, D. *Radionics & the Subtle Anatomy of Man*. N. Devon, England: Health Science Press. 1972.

Waite, A.E. *The Holy Kabbalah*. New Hyde Park, N. Y. : University Books. 1960.

   Pictorial Key to the Tarot. New Hyde Park, N. Y. : University Books. 1959.

Walker, B. *The Secrets of the Tarot*. San Francisco, CA: Harper & Row. 1984.

Wang, R. *Qabalistic Tarot*. York Beach, ME: Samuel Weiser. 1983

Watts, A. *Myth & Ritual in Christianity*. Boston: Beacon Press. 1968.

Weinberg, S. *The First Three Minutes*. N.Y.: Bantam Books. 1977.

Westman, H. *The Structure of Biblical Myths*. Dallas, TX: Spring Pub. 1983.

Zukav, G. *The Dancing Wu Li Masters*. N.Y.: Bantam Books. 1979.

THE WHEEL OF DESTINY
by Patricia McLaine

Announcing an irresistible new tool for self-knowledge found nowhere else! *The Wheel of Destiny* delves into the "Master Plan reading" of the Tarot's Major Arcana and provides detailed information about the individual, much like a reading of an astrological birth chart. Explains how to lay out the 22 cards and delineates the meaning of each card in whatever position it falls. The reading provides deep and specific information on divine purpose, strengths and weaknesses, talents, past lives, karmic patterns, relationships and much more.

All you need is this book and a Tarot deck. No previous knowledge of the Tarot is required. The Master Plan reading has been field tested by the author on clients the world over.

0-87542-490-2, 480 pgs., 7 x 10, illus., softcover   **$17.95**

THE RABBI'S TAROT
by Daphna Moore

In its striking, in-depth interpretation of the symbology of the 22 Major Arcana cards, *The Rabbi's Tarot* will lead you to profound depths of self–development and spirituality. You will learn how the practical occultist develops the pineal and pituitary glands by energized currents coming through the seven golden candlesticks and the seven churches of Asia. When the pineal gland is energized by the transmuted sex force, the result is the White Light, as depicted by the seven White Stars in the Tarot card *The Star*. This occult magic can be worked in your body and outside your body. It is also referred to as cosmic consciousness, illumination or enlightenment. The object of this book is not merely to show you the Laws of the Universe, but how these laws work out in you. The teaching of the book is that the self-conscious, by assiduous endeavor, may bring into your body more and more of the superconscious in the form of the Cosmic Mind-Stuff. The symbols of the Major Arcana suggest how you set about realizing your own perfection. They show that we evolve only by desire, and that no matter what desire we cherish, it is but a stepping-stone to a higher one.*The Rabbi's Tarot* is one of the most intense studies of the Major Arcana ever published. It is a must for all who work with the Tarot and for all who want to develop themselves to the utmost.

0–87542–572–0, 385 pgs., 6 x 9, illus., softcover   **$12.95**

TAROT SPELLS
by Janina Renee
This book provides a means of recognizing and affirming one's own personal power through use of the Tarot. With the practical advice and beautiful illustrations in this book, the reader can perform spells for:

- Influencing dreams
- Better health
- Legal matters
- Better family relations
- Beating addiction
- Finding a job
- Better gardening

and more. Thirty-five areas of life are discussed, and spells are provided which address specific issues in these areas. The reader uses Tarot layouts in combination with affirmations and visualizations to obtain a desired result. Many spells can be used with color, gemstones or magical tools to assist the reader in focusing his or her desire.

Graced with beautiful card illustrations from the Robin Wood Tarot, this book can be used immediately even by those who don't own a Tarot deck. No previous experience with the Tarot is necessary.

0–87542–670–0, 240 pp., 6 x 9, illus., softcover $12.95

THE LLEWELLYN PRACTICAL GUIDE TO
THE MAGICK OF THE TAROT
How to Read, And Shape, Your Future
by Denning & Phillips
"To gain understanding, and control, of Your Life."—Can anything be more important? To gain insight into the circumstances of your life—the inner causes, the karmic needs, the hidden factors at work— and then to have the power to change your life in order to fulfill your real desires and True Will: that's what the techniques taught in this book can do.Discover the Shadows cast ahead by Coming Events. Yes, this is possible, because it is your DEEP MIND—that part of your psyche, normally beyond your conscious awareness, which is in touch with the World Soul and with your own Higher (and Divine) Self—that perceives the astral shadows of coming events and can communicate them to you through the symbols and images of the ancient and mysterious Tarot Cards.

Your Deep Mind has the power to shape those astral shadows—images that are causal to material events—when you learn to communicate your own desires and goals using the Tarot.

0–87542–198–9, 252 pgs., 5-1/4 x 8, illus., softcover $7.95

ROBIN WOOD TAROT DECK
created and illustrated by Robin Wood
Instructions by Robin Wood and Michael Short
Reminiscent of the Rider-Waite deck, the Robin Wood Tarot is flavored with nature imagery and luminous energies that will enchant you and the querant. Even the novice reader will find these cards easy and enjoyable to interpret.

Radiant and rich, these cards were illustrated with a unique technique that brings out the resplendent color of the prismacolor pencils. The shining strength of this Tarot deck lies in its depiction of the Minor Arcana. Unlike other Minor Arcana decks, this one springs to pulsating life.

The cards are printed in quality card stock and boxed complete with instruction booklet, which provides the upright and reversed meanings of each card, as well as three basic card layouts. Beautiful and brilliant, the Robin Wood Tarot is a must-have deck.

0-87542-894-0, boxed set: 78-card deck and booklet   **$19.95**

THE NEW GOLDEN DAWN RITUAL TAROT DECK
by Sandra Tabatha Cicero
The original Tarot deck of the Hermetic Order of the Golden Dawn has been copied and interpreted many times. While each deck has its own special flair, *The New Golden Dawn Ritual Tarot Deck* may well be the most important new Tarot deck for the 1990s and beyond.

From its inception 100 years ago, the Golden Dawn continues to be the authority on the initiatory and meditative teachings of the Tarot. The Golden Dawn used certain cards in their initiation rituals. Now, for the first time ever, a deck incorporates not only the traditional Tarot images but also all of the temple symbolism needed for use in the Golden Dawn rituals. This is the first deck that is perfect both for divination and for ritual work. Meditation on the Major Arcana cards can lead to a lightning flash of enlightenment and spiritual understanding in the Western magickal tradition. *The New Golden Dawn Ritual Tarot Deck* was encouraged by the late Israel Regardie, and it is for anyone who wants a reliable Tarot deck that follows the Western magickal tradition.

0-87542-138-5, boxed set: 79-card deck and booklet   **$24.95**

A **chimpanzee's body** is made for climbing and swinging in the trees. With its long arms, a chimp can easily reach from branch to branch. And with its flexible hands and feet, it can grab and hook on to them. Because of this ability to reach and hang on, a chimpanzee can travel across thin branches without breaking them.

In many ways, chimpanzees' bodies are a lot like ours. Like us, chimps do not have tails. They have no hair on their faces or on the palms of their hands or the soles of their feet. They have fingernails and toenails, instead of claws or hooves. And, perhaps most important of all, chimps have big brains.

Like a kid on a jungle gym, a chimp can move through the trees by swinging from branch to branch. This way of moving is called *brachiation*.

A chimp's feet are really like an extra pair of hands. Using their thumb-like big toes, chimps can wrap their feet around a tree trunk or a branch. So when climbing, they can grip with *both* their feet and their hands.

COMMON CHIMPANZEE

BONOBO

It's easy to tell the two types of chimps apart. Bonobos are slightly smaller than common chimps. And they usually have a part running down the middle of their heads. Sometimes their hair even sticks out sideways!

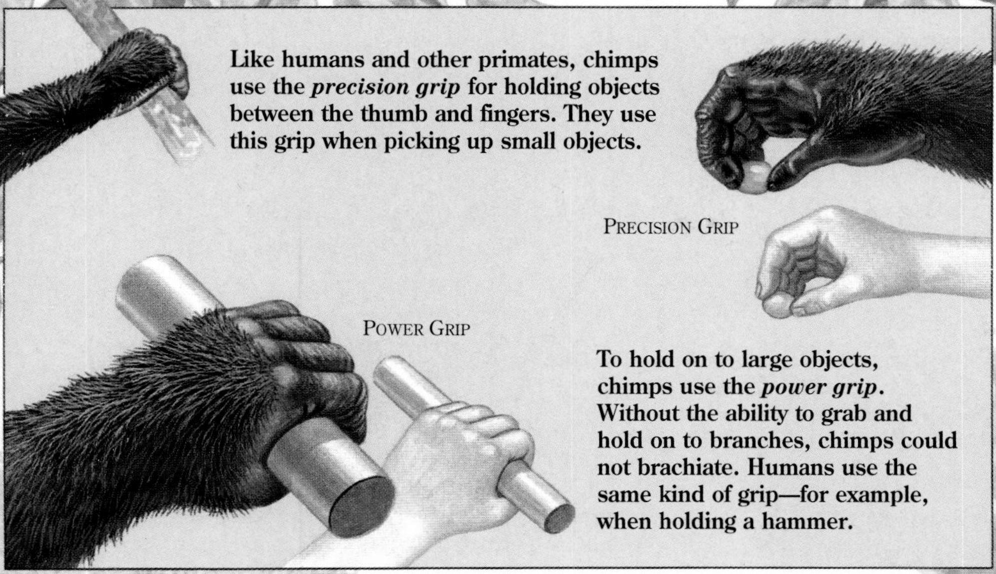

Like humans and other primates, chimps use the *precision grip* for holding objects between the thumb and fingers. They use this grip when picking up small objects.

PRECISION GRIP

POWER GRIP

To hold on to large objects, chimps use the *power grip*. Without the ability to grab and hold on to branches, chimps could not brachiate. Humans use the same kind of grip—for example, when holding a hammer.

Chimps have big, expandable mouths for carrying fruit and other objects. This leaves their hands free for moving about in the trees or for holding a baby chimp.

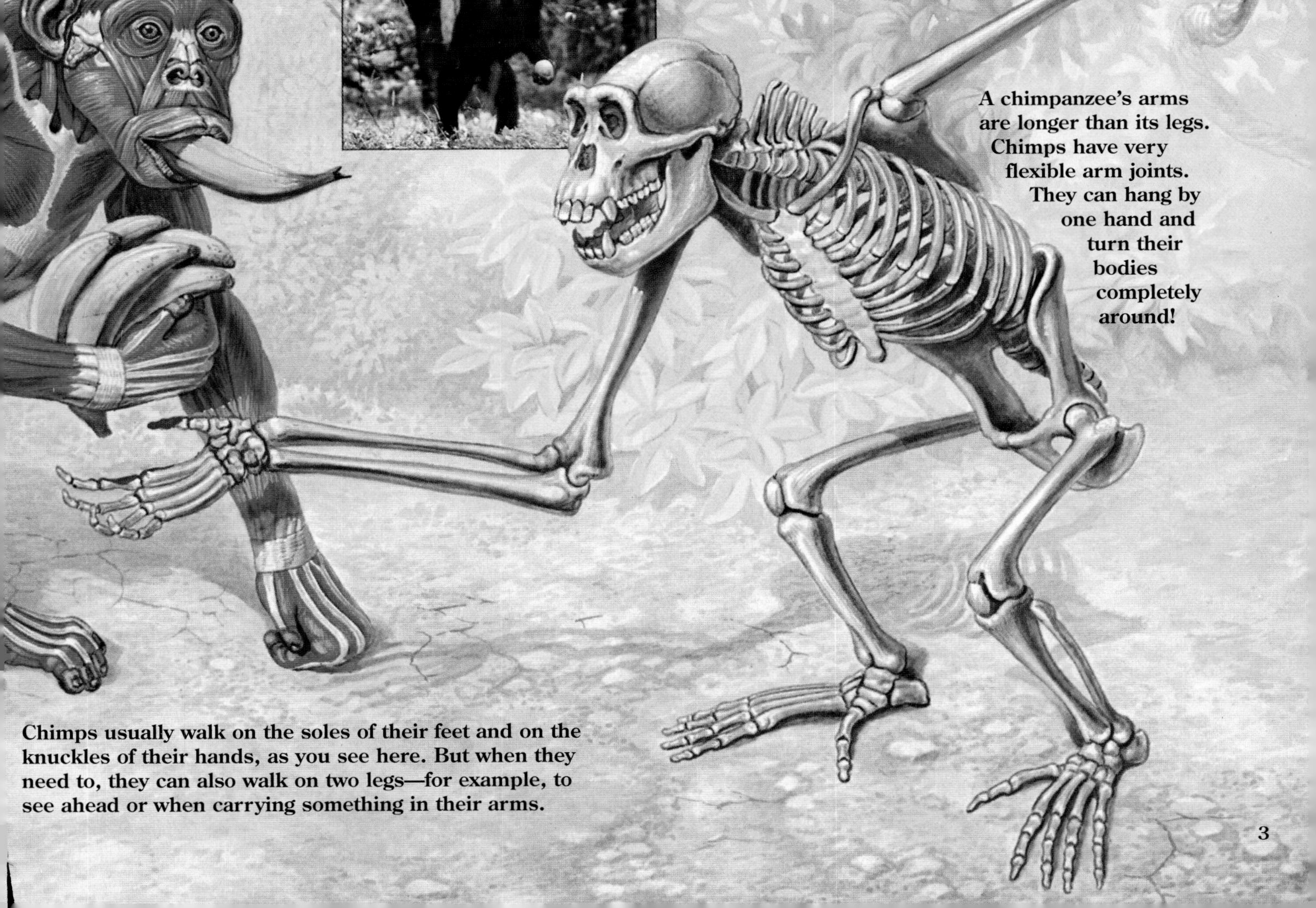

A chimpanzee's arms are longer than its legs. Chimps have very flexible arm joints. They can hang by one hand and turn their bodies completely around!

Chimps usually walk on the soles of their feet and on the knuckles of their hands, as you see here. But when they need to, they can also walk on two legs—for example, to see ahead or when carrying something in their arms.

3

Chimps belong to large groups, or *communities*. But they also spend much of their time in small groups, looking for food and socializing. Chimps can be very loving, and they can be very aggressive when necessary.

Each chimp holds a rank—or place—in the community. Usually, one male holds the top rank. He leads fights against predators, or against chimpanzees from other territories. Sometimes the group tries to scare strangers away by calling loudly and charging fiercely. Chimps have even been known to attack and kill strangers. But within their own community, chimps are much gentler with each other, although they do sometimes quarrel. After a quarrel, often within half an hour, they make up by holding a hand out to the other and kissing. The tension in the community is relieved, and the others offer consolation with pats and hugs.

Chimps have many ways of communicating with each other in their complex society.

Chimpanzees are noisy animals. They have more than *30 different calls* to communicate with each other. The chimps above are "hooting"—probably to let their friends know where they are. A chimp's hoot can be heard up to *two miles away*!

Chimpanzees often share their food with each other. When a chimp finds a tree with lots of fruit, he may call the others to a feast. While eating, chimps grunt to show how happy they are.

4

While the males are displaying, the females and babies stay out of the way. Male chimps become so excited that they could hurt somebody without meaning to.

Male chimpanzees shake branches, throw rocks, and charge each other in a display meant to intimidate others and demonstrate superiority. The male that puts on the fiercest display becomes (or remains) the leader. Eventually, another chimp—or a group of chimps—will challenge and overthrow him.

Chimps show their feelings with gestures, noises, and facial expressions. There may be genuine smiles or happy faces, nervous grins, or grins that say, "Let's be friends again," and pouts to express disappointment. Chimps have many signals to tell each other how they feel, to warn each other of danger, and to report where food is.

Chimps eat mostly fruit, leaves, seeds, and flowers. But they will also feast on ants, honey, eggs, caterpillars, birds, and sometimes small animals, even— rarely—other chimps.

CELERY

MEAT

FRUIT

NUTS

LEAVES

EGGS

ROOTS

BANANAS

SEEDS

INSECTS

5

Chimps love babies. The whole community is excited when a baby is born. Older chimps tolerate a lot of mischief and teasing from infants. They even let the babies jump on them!

Chimps usually have only one baby every five or six years. A female chimp could give birth to as many as five infants in her lifetime, but it's more likely that she will raise a maximum of three.

A baby chimp weighs three to four pounds at birth. It will drink its mother's milk and share her nest until it is weaned at four or five years old. Like human children, chimps take a long time to grow up. This is because they have a great deal to learn. They need to learn how to get around on their own, how to find food that is safe to eat, how to fight and display, how to make nests, and how to avoid danger. They learn many of these skills by playing.

For the first three months of its life, a chimp baby is quite helpless. But it *can* grip tightly to its mother as she moves from place to place. If a baby loses its grip or slips, it just whimpers softly and its mother quickly holds it close.

Young chimps like to be tickled, and they laugh when someone tickles them. In this picture, a mother chimp tickles her baby.

CHIMPANZEES ACTIVITIES

FREE ACCESS FOR SUBSCRIBERS ONLY

HUMPHREY'S HIDEAWAY at zoobooks.com., a secret online hangout just for kids. Find your password on page c.

a

Kids Correspondence

Gianni Guccione, age 7

There once was a chimp named Chimpie. He lived in the jungle, then he came to a big city. A dog catcher thought he was a dog and took him to the dog pound. A little boy came to the dog pound and took Chimpie home with him. The little boy tried to feed Chimpie dog food. Chimpie pushed it away so the little boy chopped up bananas and put them with the dog food. Then oh, oh, oh, here we go! Chimpie was very happy!

Colby Gray, age 6

April Smith, age 10

Cora Fanning, age 8

Andrea Gutting, age 13

Ben Johanson, age 9

Swinging from tree to tree,
There's no place they'd rather be.
Chimpanzees are having fun,
Swinging around in the sun.
Chimps are apes, not monkeys you see,
And they're closely related to you and me!

Kylie Watts, age 11

See the chimpanzee
Swing from tree to tree,
His face is full of glee.
I like the way
That maybe one day
He picks up some termites with some straw or hay.
He scoops them up and then
Eats them,
And tries to get them once again.
At the end of the day he swings off through the trees in the sky.
Good-bye Chimpanzee,
Good-bye, Good-bye!

Kendall Smith, age 8

Liam Dunn, age 11

Zachary Olsen, age 5

See More Online! Lots more stories, poems and drawings from kids like you — *maybe even yours!* — are on our website. Lots of games, too! Your secret password is: *primate* Turn to page **c** to find out how to get there!

Call For Entry!

Would you like to see your work published in Zoobooks? Here's what to do: By *July 1st, 2004*, we want to see your *original* poem, story, or drawing on "**Butterflies**" or "**Animal Champions**." Stories must be less than 100 words; drawings must be black ink on solid white paper. Please mail them to Kids Correspondence, 12233 Thatcher Court, Poway, California 92064. Include your name, age, and address. *If your work is printed in the magazine, you will win a FREE one-year extension on your Zoobooks subscription!* Look for other entries on our website. Sorry, your work cannot be returned, and becomes the property of Wildlife Education, Ltd.

S T A R T

Jane Goodall is born in London on April 3, 1934.

Jane's love for animals and desire to protect them begins when she is very young after she sees a man kill a dragonfly for no reason.

Five-year-old Jane spends five hours sitting quietly in a henhouse without moving to watch a chicken lay an egg.

Parents, try these activities with your young children:

- Help your child make a chimpanzee puppet. Start with a lunch-sized paper bag, construction paper, paste, and some crayons.

  1. Draw the parts for the chimp on construction paper. See illustration A below. The body and head can be black or brown. The face, chin, and ears can be beige or light brown. The inner mouth can be pink or red. Help your child cut out the parts. (Remember, your child is learning to use scissors and developing finger dexterity. Accept his or her best. Try not to expect too much.)

  2. Place the paper sack, flap up, in front of you and your child. Lift the flap and have your child paste the body to the side of the sack. See illustration B below. Next, paste the chin under the flap. Now, paste the inner mouth on top of the chin so that none of the inner mouth shows when you close the flap.

  3. Now help your child paste the head to the bottom of the closed sack. The bottom edge of the head should be even with the bottom flap of the sack. See illustration C below. Have your child add details to the face, such as eyes, a nose, and an upper lip. Paste the face to the head so that their bottom edges are even. Then, add the ears.

- You can extend the above activity while developing your child's verbal skills. Have your child choose one of the page spreads with pictures and captions in this issue. Read the captions to him or her, and discuss the pictures. Then, invite him or her to have the puppet tell you about the page spread.

- You can further develop this activity by having your child use the puppet to put on a show for your family.

The rainy season starts and lasts for about seven months. Everything is wet, and the icy wind is cold.

The rain makes the grasses grow tall. Jane gets lost because she can't see over the tall grass. *Move back 1 space.*

Jane begins to fear that she will be sent home if she doesn't begin to study the chimps more closely.

Chimps share relationships w other that are li human friendsh

After five months, Jane's mother returns to England. Jane misses her horribly.

As time passes, the chimps become less aggressive.

David Graybeard, a chimp, accepts Jane. He gently touches her hand. Later, he lets her groom him. Sometimes he even waits for her.

Today, is credi saving in Afric out. One make a

Jane and her mother become ill with malaria and nearly die. *Move back 3 spaces.*

Jane and the chimps meet unexpectedly. A frightened chimp hits her in the head. Since she doesn't fight or run, he leaves her alone. *Lose 1 turn.*

Chimps make and use their own tools.

V g s s N

Living in Tanzania is hard. The rough grasses cut Jane's skin and tsetse-fly bites make her sick.

Jane and her mother's life in Africa is difficult. For example, they only get to eat canned foods like baked beans and corned beef.

Chimps are as different from each other as people are.

Jane becomes discouraged because the chimps keep running away from her. *Move back 2 spaces.*

For the first five months, Jane only catches glimpses chimps.

HEAD
EAR
FACE
INNER MOUTH
CHIN
BODY

A

B

Even with flap

C

The Jane Game A Fun Book Review

ere's a fun way to review a book. The goal of the game is to interest you and your friends reading the book. When you're finished, you might want to make a similar game based on e of your favorite books.

Invite your friends to learn more about Jane Goodall's experiences by playing this citing game. The action is based on her biography *Jane Goodall: Naturalist* by J.A. Senn. To play, you will need one dice and a marker for each player. Players take turns rolling e dice, moving the number of spaces shown on the dice, and reading aloud the information out Jane.

Some events from Dr. Goodall's life are shown in order in the white spaces. veral discoveries that Jane has made during her life's work with chimpanzees are shown the colored spaces.

Answers:

```
S P A C E D I S P L A Y I N G
O N (W A T C H I N G O T H E R S)
N O L A B A G A N I M A L S S S
S (S L E E P I N G I N A T R E E)
S D H O U S E I N O P E O P L E O
E N P E T S N N (H U G G I N G) O
E A N O P E T R C R A T E L A B T
T H (W S O C I A L I Z I N G) C S G
G L E S I N E N O S P A C E M N
N N O R I D L I N G B I C Y C L
I (I M I T A T I N G O T H E R S) K
C D (C A R I N G F O R Y O U N G) A
B M L N O C R A T E S N O L A B S
O (S W I N G I N G I N T R E E S)
P D (H U N T I N G F O R F O O D) D
```

Jane spends her spare time watching animals and learning what they do. She keeps a journal of what she sees. *Move ahead 1 space.*

A simulated illustration from Jane's journal.

s at last! Jane s a high peak and vers a group of chimps oesn't run away. It's st day since her arrival! *ahead 2 spaces.*

Jane reads *The Story of Dr. Dolittle* by Hugh Lofting and decides that when she grows up she will live in Africa. *Move ahead 2 spaces.*

Jane names the chimps, for example:
David Graybeard
Goliath
Mrs. Maggs
Count Dracula

At age 23, Jane is invited to visit a friend in Africa— her dream seems to be coming true. *Move ahead 3 spaces.*

Although they mostly eat vegetables, chimps sometimes track and kill other animals for food.

In Africa, Jane meets Dr. Leakey, a famous scientist. He is so impressed by her that he offers her a job.

ane the tream serve with er, their d his wife. l spend the years there g chimps.

After seeing how Jane loves to watch animals, Dr. Leakey suggests that she study chimps in Tanzania.

Happy Chimp Word Search

Here is a list of activities. Some are what a chimp might do in the wild. Some are what people might make a captured chimp do. Decide which activities a chimpanzee living in the wild might be happy to do. These are included in the word search puzzle. The activities that are unnatural for a chimp to do are left out of the puzzle. Cross out these unnatural activities from the list. Then, find and circle the natural activities in the word search. *(If you need help, look through this book for facts about chimps.)*

LIST:
being a lab animal
being a pet
caring for young
displaying
entertaining people
going into space
holding hands
hugging
hunting for food
imitating others
learning
living in a house
making tools
sitting in a crate
sleeping in a tree
socializing
swinging in trees
watching others

```
H U N T I N G F O R F O O D D P
O S W I N G I N G I N T R E E S
L N O C R A T E S N O L A B S M
D C A R I N G F O R Y O U N G A
I M I T A T I N G O T H E R S K
N N O R I D L I N G B I C Y C I
G L E S I N E N O S P A C E M N
H W S O C I A L I Z I N G C S G
A N O P E T R C R A T E L A B T
N P E T S N N O H U G G I N G O
D H O U S E I N O P E O P L E O
S L E E P I N G I N A T R E E L
N O L A B A G A N I M A L S S S
W A T C H I N G O T H E R S N O
S P A C E D I S P L A Y I N G G
```

Hint: There are 12 natural behaviors and 6 unnatural ones.

answers on page c

Next Step: Now that you have made decisions about natural and unnatural behaviors for chimpanzees, make a decision about how you think chimpanzees and other wild animals should be treated. Write a letter to your local representative in Congress. Tell him or her how you feel. Ask your representative to vote for laws that protect chimpanzees and other animals. Your efforts can stop people from being cruel to animals.

Be a Backyard Scientist

When Dr. Jane Goodall and other zoologists work in the field, they keep a journal. They write down what they see and hear.

You can keep a journal about a wild animal that lives near you. Record what you see and hear for several weeks. Begin by writing the time and date. Then write down as many details as you can. Make sketches of the animal, too. Watch the animal from a distance so that you don't affect the way it acts. What new thing can you discover about the animal's behavior?

SCIENCE PROJECT

Keeping Your Own Journal

You can use a notebook in which to write your own journal entries. When you observe your chosen animal ask yourself questions, such as the ones on the right. Write the answers in your journal.

What does the animal do during the day? at night? What other animals live around it? How does it interact with those animals? What does the animal eat? How does it get its food? Where does the animal live? Does it have babies? If so, how does it take care of them? Think of some other questions to ask.

Bonnie Pitson Kuhn

A common chimpanzee is born with a pale, pinkish-yellow face. Its skin turns darker after a few years. The shape of its face also changes—it grows longer, and the mouth and chin get bigger.

CHIMPANZEE INFANT

ADULT CHIMPANZEE

BONOBO INFANT

A bonobo is born with a black-skinned face. Its skin stays black all of its life. But, like the common chimp, the shape of its face changes, too.

ADULT BONOBO

All chimps hate rain. Yet, for some reason, they usually stay out in the open during a downpour. This baby has jumped into its mother's arms to keep from getting too wet.

When chimps are about eight or nine years old, they begin to leave "home" for a few days at a time. But they remain close to their mothers throughout their lives.

Young chimps love to wrestle and chase each other through the trees. By playing together, youngsters learn how to act in chimp society.

Young chimps are curious and intelligent. Like human toddlers, they explore everything—from mud to butterflies. Older chimpanzees watch them carefully to make sure they don't get into trouble.

9

At night, chimps build nests in trees to keep themselves safe from leopards and other predators. Mothers and babies sleep together.

To build a nest, a chimp makes a platform "mattress" of broken leafy branches. Then it bends twigs over the platform to make it soft and springy. All of this takes only about five minutes.

To fish for tasty termites, which live inside big mounds, a chimp makes a tool out of a twig. First he selects the twig carefully. Then he strips the leaves from the stem.

1

*C*himpanzees use many different objects as tools. They use twigs to fish for termites, leaves to soak up water, and rocks to throw at enemies. A few other animals also use objects as tools. Sea otters, for example, use rocks to crack open clams.

But chimpanzees are the *only* animals—except humans—that can make tools. They can take an object and change it into something useful. Once scientists thought that toolmaking was something that only *people* could do. But, as you will see below, chimps can also solve problems by using tools. They could not do this without their intelligence and their flexible hands.

When a chimp wants a drink, it will sometimes make a sponge from a leaf. It crumples the leaf by chewing it, and then dips it into the water. A chimp can get seven or eight times more water this way than by dipping its fingers into a pool.

2

The chimp uses the twig to probe inside the termite mound. The termites then lock their jaws around the twig.

10

Chimps strip leaves from twigs and use them to remove honey from beehives. They also wet stalks with saliva and hold them over the paths of ants. When the ants crawl onto the stalks, the chimps eat them.

imps in captivity make good painters— d seem to paint just for the fun of it. A chimp named Pierre made such good paintings that people thought they had been done by a famous artist.

When a mirror is put in front of them, some animals ignore the image, others look for the rest of the animal behind the glass. Chimps, however, seem to know that they are looking at their own reflections. Most other animals don't seem to have this ability to recognize themselves.

3

When the chimp draws the twig out, it is covered with termites. He then licks them off.

When Jane Goodall was a child, it was her dream to study animals in Africa and write about them. And that is what she does. Before she began observing chimpanzees in the wild in 1960, very little was known about their habits. She has made many exciting discoveries about chimpanzees since that time. She still spends several months each year in the forest at Gombe National Park in Tanzania, Africa, where she and her assistants study the wild chimpanzees that live there.

Dr. Goodall worries about the future of chimpanzees. She makes speeches all over the world to raise money for chimps and to teach people to respect and learn from them. She and several other scientists want to change the way chimpanzees are treated.

To find out what you can do to help, write to: The Jane Goodall Institute for Research, Education and Conservation, 8700 Georgia Avenue, Suite 500, Silver Spring, MD 20910, or go to www.janegoodall.org.

To catch one wild infant chimp, many other chimps are killed. Once captured the chimps are put into small wooden crates to be shipped out of Africa. Ma die on the journey. For every ch that reaches its destination, to 10 others may die.

Dr. Goodall observes chimpanzees. Then she writes down or tapes what she sees and hears. Because she is trained, she sees things that other people might not see. What do you think is happening in the chimp group at the right?

AFRICA

■ KNOWN AREAS

■ PROBABLE AREAS

■ POSSIBLE AREAS

MCGREGOR

WORZLE

FLO

Chimpanzee numbers are declining, and the chimp is extinct in parts of its former range. The map above shows where chimps live today.

Jane Goodall learns to tell one chimp from another. She gives each one a name and records his or her life. Above are three of the chimps she has studied.

Chimps seem to like being on stage—so they make good entertainers. But is it right to turn an animal into a trained clown just to please humans? Are chimps meant to ride bicycles, or are they meant to live free in the wild?

1961, a chimp astronaut med Ham was fired in a aceship 155 miles into e sky. When he landed, ople shook his hand and lled him a hero. After that, spent the rest of his life zoos, mostly alone.

Jane Goodall was the first scientist to discover that chimpanzees hunt other animals for food. When one chimp has meat, the others hold out their hands to beg for a share. They usually get it.

Jane Goodall also discovered that chimps make and use tools. The chimp below has made a twig into a fly whisk by chewing the ends to spread out the fibers.

Sometimes chimps quarrel with each other, usually over food. But when they do, they have ways of making up, like hugging and kissing.

Jane Goodall has found that loving care, especially from their mothers, is very important to young chimpanzees. Female chimps that don't get good care as infants never learn how to be mothers themselves.

15

The chimpanzees' future depends on humans learning to live in harmony with them. Chimpanzees share many "human" traits. In some cases, these traits put chimpanzees in jeopardy. Because they are so similar to humans, many chimpanzees are captured for research and study to aid human medicine.

Another danger for chimpanzees is that people in Africa sometimes hunt them for food or to protect crops. When parts of the forest are cleared for farming, chimpanzees suddenly live closer to humans. When caught stealing food from the farmers' gardens, the chimps can be hurt or killed.

The biggest threat to chimpanzees is the destruction of their forest homes. Commercial logging destroys the forest or leaves patches too small to provide security and food for the chimpanzees in the region. Chimpanzees live in the areas where they were born. When their habitats are destroyed or broken into small pieces, the chimps become too isolated. And moving to a new area is dangerous.

If you move away from your neighborhood and friends and go to a new school, you may be sad for a while, but you will soon make new friends. Chimpanzees can't adjust to the loss of their home. If they move into the territory of other chimpanzees, they will be attacked by resident chimps protecting their homes and families. Many chimpanzees will die. So you see, it's very important that chimpanzee habitat be preserved.

Some chimpanzees are protected on reserves in parts of their range, but are still hunted by poachers. The bonobo, or pygmy chimpanzee, is the only great ape that does not have any national park or reserve. Although it is protected by law in the only place it occurs—the Democratic Republic of the Congo (formerly Zaire)—the law is not enforced. Infant bonobos are sometimes taken as pets or given as gifts to foreign dignitaries. This, too, depletes the chimpanzee population.

Without major efforts to change the situations that harm them, all chimpanzees could be extinct in 100 years or less. Surveys to identify different chimpanzee groups, chart where they live, and count the population size are important first steps to help chimpanzees. Reserves must be established for protection. Where reserves exist, they must be guarded against poachers. Where protective laws are in place, they must be enforced.

Finally, conservation education programs are needed in Africa to reduce the hunting of our fellow primates. You help just by learning about chimpanzees and conservation. The more people who learn and care, the better the chimpanzee's chances for survival.